What People Are Saying About
Chicken Soup for the Bride's Soul . . .

"This thoughtful and deeply moving selection of stories reminds us that love is the cornerstone of marriage, family and life itself. I smiled, laughed and cried my way through the book."

Rosanna McCollough
editor in chief, *www.WeddingChannel.com*

"After a hectic day of wedding planning, reading *Chicken Soup for the Bride's Soul* is the perfect way to unwind and be inspired by incredibly emotional stories of love's triumph before, during and after the wedding ceremony. These wonderful stories should not be missed by any one who has any part of the wedding planning process, including Mom, Dad, attendants, and especially the bride- and groom-to-be."

Debbie Hansen
director, *Bridal Show Producers International*
www.bspishows.com

"*Chicken Soup for the Bride's Soul* grounds us. It is a moving and gratifying book, full of real-life stories that give us a kind and warm reminder of what love and marriage are all about. This is a perfect book to be shared with anyone involved in a wedding—its message will also touch those with relationships that need reconnecting."

Sherra Meyers
editor, *Southern Bride Magazine*

"Being huge fans of the *Chicken Soup for the Soul* series, we were genuinely excited to hear about *Chicken Soup for the Bride's Soul*. To have a loving and fulfilling marriage takes much more than just planning a wedding. This resource of heartwarming and inspirational stories will definitely help couples in the first stages of a long and happy life together!"

Erik and Beth Kent
copublishers, *NJWedding.com*

"Of all the things brides need—a little laughter and encouragement are what they truly cannot do without. This wonderful book will take you there with stories that will have you holding your sides and wiping away a few stray tears. Let *Chicken Soup for the Bride's Soul* help you make this the start of a lifetime together. . . ."

Paula Rinehart
author, *Strong Women, Soft Hearts* and
Sex and the Soul of a Woman

"Well-written and moving, the stories in *Chicken Soup for the Bride's Soul* will help readers reflect on what's *really* important in their lives—light-hearted attitudes and a lifetime of loving commitment."

William S. Doddridge
CEO, The Jewelry Exchange
www.jewelryexchange.com

"After reading *Chicken Soup for the Bride's Soul,* the first thought that came to my mind was: *Thanks for the memories.* This book is a warm reminder of how precious life and the relationships we have are, and how they never should be taken for granted. Get together with someone special, light some candles, read *Bride's Soul* to each other and just enjoy each other's company."

Steve Dines, "BridalMan"
www.bridalman.com

"What an ideal gift for a future bride to turn to while planning her *big day! Chicken Soup for the Bride's Soul* is the perfect remedy for a chaotic time in a woman's life. These true tales will inspire an emotional bride, remind her to enjoy time with loved ones and cherish her day with the love of her life."

Matteo Bossio
vice president of planning, *iweddings.com*

"The *Chicken Soup* series has done it again—this time for all things wedding! From the proposal to the honeymoon, these heart-warming, funny and enlightening stories will inspire and entertain all readers involved in virtually any aspect of a wedding. You'll get a kick out of these fantastic stories."

Cynthia C. Muchnick
author, *The Ultimate Wedding Idea Book* and
The Frugal Bride

CHICKEN SOUP FOR THE BRIDE'S SOUL

Chicken Soup for the Bride's Soul
Stories of Love, Laughter and Commitment to Last a Lifetime
Jack Canfield, Mark Victor Hansen, Maria Nickless, Gina Romanello

Published by Backlist, LLC,
a unit of Chicken Soup for the Soul Publishing, LLC. www.chickensoup.com

Front cover design by Larissa Hise Henoch
Originally published in 2004 by Health Communications, Inc.

Back cover and spine redesign by Pneuma Books, LLC

Distributed to the booktrade by Simon & Schuster. SAN: 200-2442

Publisher's Cataloging-in-Publication Data
(Prepared by The Donohue Group)

Chicken soup for the bride's soul : stories of love, laughter and commitment to last a lifetime / [compiled by] Jack Canfield ... [et al.].

  p. : ill. ; cm.

  Originally published: Deerfield Beach, FL : Health Communications, c2004.
  ISBN: 978-1-62361-013-5

  1. Brides--Anecdotes. 2. Marriage--Anecdotes. 3. Anecdotes. I. Canfield, Jack, 1944-

GT2796.5 .C46 2012
306.81   2012944068

PRINTED IN THE UNITED STATES OF AMERICA
on acid free paper
21 20 19 18 17 16 15 14 13 12   01 02 03 04 05 06 07 08 09 10

CHICKEN SOUP FOR THE BRIDE'S SOUL

Stories of Love, Laughter and Commitment to Last a Lifetime

Jack Canfield
Mark Victor Hansen
Maria Nickless
Gina Romanello

Backlist, LLC, a unit of
Chicken Soup for the Soul Publishing, LLC
Cos Cob, CT
www.chickensoup.com

Presented to: _____

By: _____

Date: _____

Contents

3. THE PERFECT DRESS

4. THE BIG DAY

5. WHO GIVETH?

6. FOR BETTER OR FOR WORSE

7. TREASURED MOMENTS

10. TIMELESS WISDOM

Foreword

Dear Future Bride,

You're one of the lucky ones. Lucky to have found your best friend; lucky to be in love, lucky to know deep in your heart that you're ready to share your life with him; and lucky to be holding this timeless treasure in your hands— your personal "Bride's Diary." Refer to it in your time of stress. Read the stories for inspiration. That's what the book is for.

There is a common regret among marrying couples that after twelve months of planning and attention to details, they forget to savor their hard-planned celebration. Don't let this happen to you! Remember to have *fun* and enjoy the planning process. Don't become so bogged down with details and etiquette that you forget to enjoy yourselves. Try to remember that mistakes will happen—plan on it: forgetting the bouquet, the family dog eating the wedding cake, a train passing by and drowning out your vows. Know that these mistakes will be some of your most treasured memories—the favorite stories told around the family dinner table for years to come. These are the memories that you will hold closest to your heart.

Keep your sense of humor, as well as your sense of perspective, firmly intact. In fact, the skills you acquire

and use in the planning of your wedding will lay important foundations for your marriage—the ability to listen,
compromise, respect each other's needs and boundaries,
and stay passionate and committed to the task at hand.
Whatever else you vow, promise to create an opportunity
for the two of you to savor this day.

I hope you enjoy *Chicken Soup for the Bride's Soul.* Turn to
it for the wonderful illustrations of the sorts of tender
moments you can look forward to in your lives. Use it as a
loving reminder that our imperfections are part of our
charm; and a reminder that the sentiments of love, family
and friendship shared on your big day are the truly important wedding accessories.

Beverly Clark,
author, Planning a Wedding to Remember
creator, The Beverly Clark Collection
www.beverlyclark.com

Introduction

From the time young girls start dreaming of their wedding day, the vision is quite clear—wearing that perfect princess-like gown, walking down the aisle toward their Prince Charming and giving themselves completely when they speak those famous words, *"I do."* From the proposal to the wedding day, happiness and joy ring in the air—a magical opportunity to demonstrate unconditional love and commitment to the man of their dreams.

As the bride-to-be, planning your wedding can be bittersweet. What is ultimately the happiest time in your life can also be the most stressful. Much like an emotional roller coaster ride, the anticipation of starting a new life runs headlong into the chaos of wedding details, family feuds and financial stress.

Chicken Soup for the Bride's Soul celebrates you—*the bride*—from the moment you meet your beloved to the day you marry him. But more importantly, the stories in this dynamic collection bring to light the true meaning of love and commitment. This book will warm your heart and melt away your stress and fears as you prepare for a lifelong commitment with your future husband. The captivating, inspiring and humorous true tales will not only comfort you during this eventful time, but show you that beyond the wedding details lies a powerful message about marriage.

Whether you're getting married, have been married for thirty years or just love a great love story, this book will lift your spirits with stories about unique proposals, the perfect dress, wedding day memories, first years and the meaning of marriage. You'll be touched by the story of long-lost loves reunited after twenty-five years; of the unconditional love between a groom and his dying fiancée; and of the undying love between a bride and her deceased father. But what's a wedding without laughter? With humorous tales from a groom's little sister who plays a mischievous joke to a woman who mistakes her boyfriend's proposal for something else, over and over again these stories will make you laugh and cry while filling your heart with delight.

But you don't have to be a bride to enjoy this book. *Bride's Soul* is for anyone who believes in the power of love and commitment. Authored by other brides-to-be, husbands, mothers, fathers of the bride, ministers and family members, this book, chapter by chapter, will take you on a journey beginning with the courtship of a man and woman, and culminating in the wisdom offered by those who have loved their spouses year after year after year.

While compiling this book, our vision of its impact on the reader changed. In the beginning, we thought *Bride's Soul* would be a fun book for a bride planning her wedding. As we became entrenched in the lives of the thousands of people who graciously shared their love stories, our hearts seemed to grow—thus the vision grew. We are blessed to have the opportunity to share with you what this book has done for us.

It is our hope that this book brings you comfort and joy—that the stories will allow you to pause for a moment and reflect on your life and the experiences that brought you to this time. We hope the stories of friends and family will evoke a celebration of family during your time of transition; that proposal stories will take you back to that unforgettable moment when he asked you to be his forever; that stories of gleaning wisdom will exemplify ways to keep your love alive. But most importantly, we hope that once you read this book, you will realize that perfection is of no consequence—that logistical mishaps are trivial and unimportant—and that when it's all said and done, what's most important is your commitment to one another.

As you enjoy *Chicken Soup for the Bride's Soul,* we hope that you marvel in the true meaning of this precious time by enjoying the laughter and touching moments of your wedding day and of your life together.

1

THE MEANING OF MARRIAGE

Sometimes it's like being on opposites sides of a chasm and lovingly building a bridge toward each other.

> *Becca Kaufman and Paula Ramsey*
> *Creators of* WeddingQuestions.com

Twenty-Six Years—
An Unfolding Romance

Throughout our years together, we had built up a history and a closeness so subtle we didn't even know it was there.

Erma Bombeck

"Now, who is it that's getting married?" my husband whispered to me as we settled into our pew after being led down the church aisle by a solemn-faced young usher.

We'd had this discussion at least three times. Once when I discovered the calligraphied envelope buried under a pile of discarded grocery flyers after he'd reached the mailbox first. Another when he knocked the invitation off its magnet on the refrigerator door—where I had mounted it in plain view. And a few days earlier when I reminded him we couldn't go to the opening of an action flick because we were going to the wedding of a teaching colleague of mine.

Despite all this, I wasn't concerned he'd forgotten the names embossed on the invitation. After twenty-six years of marriage, I've learned that the mere mention of the word "wedding" seems to trigger a memory lapse in my husband.

So, as we took our seats, I calmly whispered back, "The computer teacher and the Bible teacher's son."

"Sounds like the title of one of those romance novels you read on the treadmill at the gym," he muttered and settled down, probably to count the number of women sitting by themselves who had left their lucky husbands behind.

The ringing chords of the organ accompanied a lilting soprano and filled the flower-scented air. It reminded me of my own wedding day and the joy-tinged nervousness that made my stomach dance with butterflies as I stood hidden from guests, awaiting my cue. I wondered if the bride was calming her own fluttering emotions.

I knew the groom was. He was a quiet man who didn't seek the limelight and for whom, according to his mother, the anticipation of standing to face 400 guests was daunting.

When, tuxedoed and handsome, he led his entourage to take their places at the altar steps, I looked for signs of distress. Fidgety hands. Sweating brow. Restless feet. Instead, I saw the sweet smile of a happy man as he anticipated the sweeping entry of the woman he loved. And I didn't need the strains of the "Trumpet Voluntary" to know the bride was poised to enter. The groom's face reflected her presence.

As we rose in honor, I felt a twinge of envy. It had been a long time since my husband had looked at me with that kind of glow. *Maybe twenty-six years of marriage does that,* I thought. Maybe the day we said our vows, the day he looked at me in my bridal white and his eyes said, "I love you and you are beautiful" was the climax of our own romantic saga, the best it was ever going to get. And maybe our confidence in the first blush of love became a memory buried under years of hard work to keep our marriage going.

The last strains of music faded and the bride's glowing face, shadowed by layers of pearl-encrusted tulle, turned from her father to her groom. That's when a little tear threatened to slip down my cheek. In the candlelit softness, they *did* look like a perfect couple from one of those romantic novels I liked to sneak into the gym.

A tiny part of me mourned the loss of my storybook-romance illusions as the groom reached for his bride's hand. I wanted to be them again—partners facing a clean slate, oblivious to all but their love. I wanted to steal a piece of the mystical magic of new love and rediscover its feelings of hope, promise and possibilities—the same fresh feelings my husband and I shared on our own wedding day.

Suddenly, as if he knew my thoughts, my husband turned to me and whispered, "I like the way you look in that red dress, Kris." His eyes filled with a warmth that still melts my heart, and his thumb stroked my palm like it did twenty-six years ago when we stood in a rose-perfumed garden and he said, "I do."

Inching into the shelter of his encircling arm, I remembered the long-ago wedding promises we made and have honored over many good and some not-so-good years. I thought of our mutual respect, of the love that drew us together, of the sure foundation of trust and commitment we continued to build on.

All too soon, the groom kissed his bride and, beaming, they walked hand-in-hand down a petal-strewn aisle . . . into a star-studded night.

As the bride left to face her future, I wished her happiness. But I no longer wanted to be her. I was glad I was right where I was. With the man I love. Hand-in-hand, we followed the newlyweds into the luminous night—and a beckoning future of romance.

Kris Hamm Ross

"What I'm really looking for is someone
who can clean up after me."

Reprinted by permission of Bob Schochet.

My Love Is Like a Red, Red Marker

*For two people in a marriage to live together day
after day is unquestionably the one miracle the
Vatican has overlooked.*

Bill Cosby

I am, admittedly, a hopeless romantic. Not surprisingly,
then, when my husband and I celebrated our anniversary
recently, I bought him one dozen red permanent markers.
These are, after all, the traditional gift for the man who
spends many of his waking hours drawing shapes on the
toes of his white tube socks.

Why does he do this? Because, he explains, for every
white tube sock there is only one perfect partner. To preserve these sacred unions, my spouse assigns each pair its
own symbol—a triangle, a square, a stick-figure wife
throwing up her arms in despair.

For a man who on more than one occasion has mended
his clothing with a staple gun, such conscientious sock
matching seems strange. Just the same, I admit I find my
husband's little eccentricities endearing and often make
note of them in a growing file labeled "Mounting Evidence."

One recent entry reads: "Today husband is very happy. Seems the supermarket is having a buy-one/get-one-free rump-roast extravaganza. Spouse believes a freezer should always contain enough meat to host an intimate barbecue for all branches of the U.S. military."

I could understand hoarding power tools. Or fishing equipment. But discounted cuts of meat? My husband wasn't deprived of food as a child. He doesn't overbuy generally. And, to my knowledge, frozen hunks of beef do not increase in value over time.

His other fixations are no more easily understood. Take this recent notation:

"Today husband is mad at me. In what can only be described as a wild crime spree, I removed sixty-six cents from his change dish, in order to purchase two postage stamps."

To my husband, loose change is not actual, usable money, but some sort of endangered species he is determined to preserve. Every night he lovingly removes all coins from his pockets, and then gently places them in the dish. When the dish is full, he separates the change and stores it in large containers at an undisclosed location in our garage. As I understand it, the plan is to buy even larger containers at some point.

The Mounting Evidence file continues to grow with each tender entry. But yesterday, it closed with this startling observation: "Today husband claimed I'm sexy. Hmmm. Make sure to carefully match his socks, overstock the freezer and self-fund all future stamp purchases."

Carrie St. Michel

A Second Chance

When I first open my eyes upon the morning meadows and look out upon the beautiful world, I thank God I am alive.

Ralph Waldo Emerson

I lay in my hospital bed, eyes filled with tears as I stared longingly at the crisp October sky. This was my long-awaited wedding day. But I wouldn't be strolling down the aisle in my white satin gown as planned.

I dated Yates for six years, during high school and part of college. We were the proverbial high-school sweethearts— he was my first love and I his. Young and naive, we discovered we each had unique, individual dreams that required pursuits down different paths. So, we parted ways.

For a decade, Yates and I lived separate lives, with different geographies and different experiences. Several failed relationships and many mistakes along the way, we each discovered an unexplainable void within ourselves. After almost ten years of no contact, Yates reached me through my mother. We reunited and immediately realized what we had been missing in our lives was each other.

Within three months we were engaged.

On that beautiful October day, my husband-to-be sat next to me on the hospital bed, caressing my hand with sympathetic understanding. We both knew our journey together would not commence that day.

An unfortunate twist of fate two days prior left me with a collapsed lung, several broken ribs, a fractured pelvis and a fractured clavicle. Hours of phone calls ensued, canceling vendors and airline reservations, informing family and friends. Anger welled as I relived—over and over— the memory of the truck that ran the stop sign a block from my home. It T-boned my car, catapulting me into the passenger seat, leaving me virtually paralyzed, physically and emotionally.

We entertained the idea of holding the nuptials in the hospital chapel, a suggestion from my childhood pastor who had driven 300 miles to officiate. But I so wanted to share my joyous day with family and friends, many who lived miles away.

Why me? I thought. *What did I do to deserve having my special day ripped from me?*

Suddenly the details of reception centerpieces and invitation designs, which had seemed so monumental during the planning stages, were now so trivial. Why had I spent hours and hours poring over what color ribbons to use on those darn bubbles?

Now, what was important was having my life, my fiancé by my side and a future of memories to make. I had a new perspective on the importance of marriage. We were already living the "for worse" before even exchanging vows. I knew this was a test of love—and we would pass it.

Despite the doctors' predictions, within a month I was walking without a walker. I had renewed energy and purpose: I was determined to walk down the aisle and marry the man who had bathed, fed and comforted me through weeks of physical and emotional agony.

Three months after my accident, I sat in the bride's room of St. Mary's Chapel embracing the thrill of my wedding day. Yates and I would finally become one.

A torrential downpour shrouded the chapel, accompanied by soft, rumbling thunder. I smiled to myself and thought, *God is shedding His tears of joy and expressing His voice of approval of our marriage.*

The emotional and physical scars I still endured were constant reminders of my mortality. I was fortunate. My experience provided a self-discovery I might otherwise never have known: I realized a perfect wedding day does not a perfect marriage make. But the strength of love between two people can make every day perfect.

Ariana Adams

Roses Not Required

*Love one another and you will be happy. It's as
simple and as difficult as that.*

Michael Leunig

My husband and I still chuckle over the memory of a
summer afternoon when our two sons were small. After
noticing they were busy playing LEGO, we seized the
opportunity to escape to our bedroom and lock the door.

Suddenly, we heard talking right outside our bedroom.
The boys must have needed us for something. With bed
sheets in a flurry, we immediately ceased all activity and
listened quietly, but intently.

I'm sure a small hand was raised, ready to knock on our
door when our nine-year-old intervened with the now
infamous words to his little brother, "Don't even think
about it. They're having a private time." Complete silence
descended, and then a hushed discussion gradually faded
down the hall. Recapturing the ambience was impossible;
we were laughing too hard.

My husband and I will be celebrating our twentieth
wedding anniversary, and I still can't wait for him to come

home at the end of each day. There's a sweet warmth of completeness that surges through me. The boys feel it too. "Dad's home!" they often announce when they hear his truck pull in the driveway.

Little did I realize as a young naive bride so many years ago that the threads of our beginnings would weave together the sumptuous tapestry of a beautiful marriage.

The way my husband looks for me when we're separated at a gathering, the feel of his hands on my shoulders as he massages away the aches, the sight of his wedding ring on his finger, my morning cup of coffee made just the way I like it are all simple yet priceless things.

Against all logic, the magic has deepened. There's adoration in his eyes, intimacy in his voice and a knowledge in his touch that fills me with the desire to reciprocate. Loss, grief, times of growth and change, disagreements and uncertainties have reinforced our marriage with strong resiliency. I can think of no greater gift to our children.

With busy schedules, a night out together is rare and cherished now more than when we were dating. Holding hands in the dark at a Tuesday night movie and sharing a purse full of smuggled-in chocolate bars and chips fills me with a fluttery delight.

This is the source from which real romance springs. I don't subscribe to the stuff of soap operas or steamy novels. I don't accept there's such a thing as "falling out of love." I believe in the beauty of sacrifice, the wonder of loyalty and the joy of trust. I believe in promises. I believe in forever. These are the stars my husband and I see in each other's eyes. *Roses not required.*

Rachel Wallace-Oberle

A Change of Heart

The heart that loves is always young.

Greek Proverb

Grandma got Grandpa out of bed and helped him to the kitchen for breakfast. After his meal, she led him to his armchair in the living room where he would rest while she cleaned the dishes. Every so often, she would check to see if he needed anything.

This was their daily routine after Grandpa's latest stroke.

Although once a very active man, his severely damaged left arm, difficulty walking and slurred speech now kept him housebound. For nearly a year he hadn't even been to church or to visit family.

Grandpa filled his hours with television. He watched the news and game shows while Grandma went about her day. They made a pact—he was not to leave his chair or his bed without her assistance.

"If you fell and I threw my back out trying to help you, who would take care of us?" Grandma would ask him. She was adamant about their taking care of themselves and living independently. The Brooklyn brownstone had been their first home and held wonderful memories. They weren't ready to leave it behind anytime soon.

Immigrants from Ireland, they met and married in America. Grandma was friendly, outgoing and unselfish; Grandpa was reserved, a man devoted to his family. But he wasn't big on giving gifts. While he wouldn't think twice about giving my grandma the shirt off his back, he subscribed to the belief that if you treated your wife well throughout the year, presents weren't necessary; so he rarely purchased gifts for her.

This had been a sore point in the early days of their marriage. But as years passed, Grandma realized what a good man he was. And, after all, anything she wanted she was free to buy herself.

It was a cold, gray February morning, a typical winter day in New York. As always, Grandma walked Grandpa to his chair.

"I'm going to take a shower now." She handed him the television remote. "If you need anything, I'll be back in a little while."

After her shower, she glanced towards the back of Grandpa's recliner but noticed that his cane was not leaning in its usual spot. Sensing something odd, she walked toward the recliner. He was gone. The closet door stood open and his hat and overcoat were missing. Fear ran down her spine.

Grandma threw a coat over her bathrobe and ran outside. He couldn't have gotten far; he could barely walk on his own.

Desperately, she scanned the block in both directions. Small mounds of snow and ice coated the sidewalks. Walking safely would be difficult for people who were steady on their feet, much less someone in Grandpa's condition.

Where could he be? Why would he leave the house all by himself?

Wringing her hands, she hardly felt the frigid air as she watched traffic rush by. She recalled overhearing him tell one of their grandchildren recently that he felt he was a "burden." Until this last year, he had been strong and healthy; now he couldn't even perform the simplest of tasks.

As she stood alone on the street corner, guilt flooded her.

Just then, Grandpa walked around the bend of the corner. Head bowed, eyes focused on the sidewalk, he took small, cautious steps. His overcoat barely draped the shoulder of his bad arm; his cane and a package filled his good arm.

Desperate to reach him, Grandma raced down the block. Relieved to see that he was okay, she started to scold.

"I only left you alone for a short while. What did you need so badly that couldn't wait? I was so worried about you! What on earth was so important?"

Confused and curious, she reached into the brown bag. Before Grandpa had a chance to explain, she pulled out a heart-shaped box.

"It's Valentine's Day," Grandpa explained. "I thought you might like a box of chocolates."

A gift? All this worry for . . . candy?

"I haven't bought you a gift in a long, long time." His stroke-impaired words warmed the winter wind.

Tears flooded Grandma's eyes as she hugged his arm to her chest and led Grandpa back home. She shook her head slowly.

It just goes to show, she thought, *it's never too late for romance.*

Denise Jacoby

Dancing in the Aisles

Love is the true means by which the world is enjoyed.

Thomas Traherne

Money was a precious commodity and time together even more scarce in the early years of our nearly two-decade marriage.

My husband, Michael, and I juggled opposite work schedules and shared household duties, savoring one another's company in the still hours of the night when the world became our private playground.

While most people were settling in for the night, we were eagerly venturing from our modest three-room apartment to gather treasured memories of hilarious tennis matches in the dark, long and contemplative walks under the glow of streetlights, lazy swims under twinkling stars, or friendly rounds of miniature golf at a nearby twenty-four hour course. Our wonderful, spontaneous excursions took the sting out of the endless hours we spent apart.

Although we discovered many creative and inexpensive ways to enjoy our limited time together, there was one place we returned to again and again. By far, our most cherished date was dancing in the aisles of the supermarket. On many evenings, long after midnight and in the calm of an all-night grocery store, we would sway gracefully to the melodies flowing from the overhead Muzak that filled the empty aisles.

Oblivious to other nocturnal shoppers and store personnel, we sashayed down one lane and up another in a tender and playful embrace, filling our shopping cart with necessities and our hearts with romance.

In those innocent days of twirling among cabbages and oranges, boxes of Jell-O and cartons of milk, we unwittingly defined our relationship and set the tone for our future together.

Amid pot roasts and canned vegetables, we learned to mingle the mundane with the eternal, accepting our challenges and successes while staying focused on each other and the love that brought us together in the first place. Surrounded by bags of chips and sponge mops, we became best friends, ready to respond to life's triumphs and tragedies.

Adversity inevitably finds its way to every home, and ours was no exception. In our modest eighteen years of marriage, we suffered the discouragement of infertility, the worry of illness and the loneliness of rejection. We endured the fearful frustration of unemployment, the weariness of unexpected debt, the agony of miscarriage and stillbirths.

While every couple must find its own way to face the difficult times and still protect the romance, for us the answer is a simple one: We've never stopped dancing in the aisles. Almost every time we go to the store, in good times or bad, in sickness or health, in depression or joy, madly in love or feeling wounded by the other, we dance together.

We have learned to feel safe with one another. To trust

and go with the flow—of dance and of life. To make everything an adventure. To find joy whatever the circumstances.

We have learned to count our blessings and prepare for our future. To marvel at the miracle of birth and the joy of parenting. To understand the power of prayer and righteous living. To share hopes and dreams.

We appreciate these major life experiences because we never forget how to have fun and laugh a little along the way. Midnight waltzes have given way to sometimes chaotic Saturday family shopping trips; his hair is now more gray than chestnut-colored, and my girlish figure is well padded. Money remains a precious commodity, and time together is scarcer than ever.

Hand-in-hand we continue to dance the dance of daily life with the same beauty and enthusiasm as those days of sweet innocence. Maybe even more so. You see, we have come to understand the wisdom that longtime dance partners already know.

The longer you dance together, the better it is.

Amanda Krug

The Porsche Factor

I held my ring under the light and watched it sparkle. Newly-married life was as bright as my new diamond . . . except for one nagging shadow of doubt. The Porsche factor, I called it secretly. Yes, my new husband actually owned one of those sleek, red cars that belonged in a James Bond movie.

The Porsche was a constant reminder of the different worlds we came from. His family belonged to a country club, donated generously to charities and took exotic vacations. My family struggled to make ends meet. We shopped at thrift stores, cut coupons and took public transportation.

Rich people seem to care so much about stuff, I thought. After the honeymoon was really over, would my husband love me more than his stuff? If only there was some way to be sure.

On his first morning back to work, he handed me his keys. "I'll take the bus," he said. "You drive the car."

I fingered the worn leather key ring. "Are you sure?" I asked. I'd never driven the Porsche, although he'd been offering it ever since my ancient car died a month before the wedding.

"Sure," he said, "but . . . be careful."

I felt a twinge of irritation even though I knew he couldn't keep himself from adding the warning. I said a prayer as I started the engine. After all, this was no ordinary car.

My father-in-law had driven it home for the first time almost fifteen years ago. Under his care, the car gleamed like a jewel and purred like a well-fed tiger. The boy who grew up to be my husband spent hours beside his dad, handing over a needed tool, studying the correct way to wax and learning the well-crafted intricacies of a Porsche engine. Sometimes he'd even sneak out to the garage in the middle of the night and climb carefully into the driver's seat. Without actually touching anything, he'd pretend he was driving fast along the curves of an empty road.

One day, his dad took him aside. "Son, if you save the money by the time you turn sixteen, your mother and I will sell you this car."

The amount he named was far less than what the Porsche was worth, but it was a big amount for a boy to earn and save. My husband found a job cleaning the garage in an apartment complex, emptying garbage cans, sweeping and mopping. He worked after school and on weekends and saved every penny he earned. On his sixteenth birthday, he proudly handed his dad a check and took the Porsche out for a drive.

There was a mystical male bond between my husband, his dad and that car. Even now, when we drove the shiny Porsche into the driveway of my in-laws' house, his dad came out to check on it.

"Good job, son. The car looks great."

With all that history in mind, I drove slowly at first, like I was handling a piece of heirloom china. I pulled to a stop at the first hint of a yellow light and clung to the right lane on the freeway. As the car picked up speed, my confidence grew. I rolled down the window, turned up the radio and nosed into the fast lane.

After doing some shopping, I couldn't wait to drive home. I walked eagerly to where I'd parked the car in the crowded lot—and stopped. The Porsche had moved a good three feet forward in the parking space.

Somebody must have hit it from behind.

I stood for a moment, trying to gather my courage to inspect the damage. The back end wasn't bad; the bumper seemed to have absorbed most of the shock. But when I saw the crumpled fender and the dent on the hood, my heart sank. A sign that read "ten-minute parking only" leaned over it like a warrior gloating over a fallen enemy.

Oh no! I thought. I'd left the gearshift in "neutral" instead of "park," and the car had lurched forward when it had been hit.

I drove home slowly, fighting my tears. For the first time since our wedding, I didn't want to see my husband. He found me hiding under the covers.

"What's wrong, honey? Are you sick?"

"The car," I said, my voice muffled. "Something bad happened. I left it in neutral and somebody crashed into it while it was parked and they didn't leave a note."

I waited while he went down to the parking garage to inspect the damage. When he returned, the sadness in his eyes made me hide my face in the pillow.

"It's okay, honey," he said. "Don't worry about it."

But we both knew that this was no ordinary car. To make things worse, we were scheduled to drive that very night to his parents' house.

"Do you want me to tell them you're not feeling well?" he asked.

"No," I answered grimly. For better or worse I'd promised just a couple of weeks earlier. And this was definitely the worst day so far.

As we drove to my in-laws' house, I felt a rush of hatred for the Porsche. Why was this material object such a treasure, anyway? It was a pile of metal welded together with some wiring inside, destined for rust and decay.

When we pulled into the driveway, I shrank in my seat. My in-laws were coming out of the front door, both of them beaming as usual.

My father-in-law began walking around the Porsche with an appraising glance. When he reached the front of the car, I caught my breath.

"Oh no!" he shouted. "What happened?"

Feeling like a criminal about to be sentenced, I waited for my husband's answer.

"We had a little accident," he said.

As the two of them began to discuss repairs, I wondered if I'd heard wrong. Had he really said, "we"? I was responsible for the first damage ever done to this family treasure. Surely he'd explain to his dad that there was no we about it at all. Before I could speak up, my mother-in-law pulled me into the house.

"I'm going to tell them the truth," I told him, when the two of us had a moment alone later. "It's not right for you to take the blame."

"Who cares who did it?" he answered. "It's just a car."

I felt like shouting for joy, but I hugged him instead. I was still determined to tell his parents the truth, but that didn't matter now. The secret shadow of my last doubt was gone. Without the Porsche factor, our life together sparkled even more brilliantly than the diamond on my finger.

Mitali Perkins

2
PROPOSALS

My most brilliant achievement was my ability to be able to persuade my wife to marry me.

Winston Churchill

"To tell you the truth, Maureen, on our first date I was hoping things would progress a little less quickly."

Treasure Hunt

*She whom I love is hard to catch and conquer,
Hard, but O the glory of the winning were she
won!*

George Meredith

Andrea slammed the phone into its cradle and shrieked, "I can't believe him!"

Her mom entered the room. "Jeff?"

"Yeah. He just did everything he could to pick a fight!" Shaking her head, she added, "I haven't seen him in three days and it doesn't even bother him. He says he's busy at work and can't break away. I don't know how much longer I can take this."

"Don't get impatient," Emma smiled slightly and patted her frustrated daughter's shoulder. "The best things in life are worth waiting for. Trust me."

"I don't know, Ma. Maybe he's the one that should be doing the waiting." She stormed out of the room.

Emma's smile widened.

Not an hour later, the doorbell rang. Andrea rushed to answer it. *It just has to be Jeff,* she thought. *He'd never hang up angry.*

Emma stood back, wiped her hands on a flowered apron and reclaimed her mischievous smile.

Andrea tipped the young messenger and rushed the package into the house. Under the watchful eye of her curious mother, she tore through the brown wrapping. It was the most beautiful dress she'd ever laid eyes on. As she lifted the white lace into the air, a piece of stationery floated to the floor. It read:

> *Baby Cakes,*
>
> *Sometimes I say things I don't mean. Sometimes I'm stubborn and defensive. Sometimes I want to go to you, but fear rejection. Andrea, I love you, and because I love you I'll try harder to be understanding and have more patience. Forgive me. I saw this dress and thought how beautiful you'd look in it. Please wear it tonight and meet me at Capriccio's at 6:00. Can't wait to see you!*
>
> *Love,*
>
> *Jeff*

As she wiped her eyes, Andrea caught her mother's grin. "I'll be there, "she smirked. "But this time *he's* gonna wait!"

Her mother just laughed.

It was almost 6:30 when Andrea screeched into Capriccio's lot. She intended to be a few minutes late, allowing extra time to get ready. She wanted his wait to be worth it when he saw her. The valet attendant took one look and swallowed hard. She noticed and smiled. The extra time had paid off.

Greeted by the maitre d', she expected him to escort her to Jeff's table. Instead, the older gentleman smiled and handed her a dozen long-stemmed roses.

"Mr. Stanton called and said he was running late. He said that the card would explain."

Blowing a wisp of hair from her eyes, Andrea reached into the baby's breath and retrieved the card.

> *Babe,*
>
> *I would say I'm sorry, but those would just be words that you have heard many times before. This time, I'll say I love you, a truth that lives within my heart.*
> *Meet me at the Eagle for drinks at 7:00.*
>
> *Jeff*

Andrea looked at the maitre d' who continued to grin. "Did he say anything else on the phone?"

"Not exactly," the kind man muttered. "Just that he can't wait to see you."

"It certainly doesn't seem that way," she lamented.

As she reached the parking lot, she was surprised to find that her car hadn't been moved. The valet attendant opened the door, smiled sweetly and said, "Best of luck!"

"Same to you," she replied, confused by his curious comment.

Within ten minutes she was at the Eagle waiting in the lounge. She would give him 10 minutes to show; otherwise she'd go home to contemplate their future.

The bartender sauntered over. "What'll you have, Miss?"

"Margarita, no salt and a cup of ice on the side."

"Cup of ice on the side?" the man questioned with a silly grin dancing across his face.

"Yeah," she confirmed, her irritated tone approaching anger. If she didn't know any better, she'd swear she was the butt of some cruel joke. She checked her watch again. He had seven more minutes. Looking down at the beautiful white dress she wore, she shook her head. *What a waste,* she thought, fighting back the tears.

Within seconds, the bartender returned with a bottle of champagne and the same smile he'd left with.

"I ordered a margarita," she roared, then realizing her rude outburst, quietly added, "I'm sorry; it's just that my boyfriend was supposed to . . ."

"Meet you here at 7:00? I know. He called and asked that I pour you a glass of champagne and give you this card." With a wink, the bartender was gone. Andrea reluctantly opened it.

> *Sweetie,*
>
> *Please bear with me! There are going to be times when other things might seem more important than you, but you have to trust that they're not.*
>
> *The rest is up to faith. I'll be at the Dockside at 7:30. I'm hoping more than anything that you meet me. Please be there with the champagne.*
>
> *Jeff*

Andrea stood and noticed that every patron in the bar was gawking. She was right; it was a conspiracy. Her first thought was to go home and put an end to Jeff's foolish game.

Then it hit her. There was no way Jeff would have had the time to drop off both cards. Realizing it was all a carefully planned scheme; she smiled back at the crowd. Her excitement grew and, within minutes, she was in her car speeding to the Dockside.

As expected, Jeff was nowhere to be found. Instead, a white stretch limousine idled in front of a dilapidated shack. The chauffeur held a sign that read *Andrea Evans.*

With her dozen red roses, bottle of champagne and tears in her eyes, she climbed into the car. The driver offered a familiar smile and handed her a tiny card.

> *I knew you wouldn't give up on me. Enjoy the ride. I'm waiting! I love you!*
>
> *Jeff*

Andrea enjoyed the ride and when the car stopped, she stole a peek out the window. She was at the beach and Jeff was waiting somewhere in the dunes.

The driver parked the car, opened the door and assisted her out. "Have a beautiful time," he said. "I'll be here when you get done!"

Andrea felt like hugging him for his smile—the same one she had seen on the faces of strangers all day. Something big was up and the quest was not yet complete. Not forgetting her roses and champagne, she kicked off her shoes, grabbed them and started for the ocean.

A path of small seashells glimmered under a full moon. It was obvious each shell had been carefully placed, looping through the shifting dunes until they reached several large conch shells. Arranged in the shape of an arrow, they were the last clue on Jeff's peculiar map. She took a deep breath before stepping over the last dune.

The sight nearly brought her to her knees. Jeff was seated at a small round table in the middle of the beach. Dressed in a black tux, he stood when he saw her. She hurried toward him.

On the table, a hurricane lamp illuminated two place settings, an empty vase and empty ice bucket waited to be filled, and soft music drifted through the breeze.

As she reached him, she expected Jeff to embrace her, but he didn't. Instead, he dropped to his knees, grabbed her hand and blurted, "Be my wife, Andrea. Spend the rest of your life with me."

Instinctively, Andrea dropped to meet him in the sand. "Yes!" she answered through her sniffles. "I thought you'd never ask!"

Jeff laughed and pulled her to him. "I love you," he whispered.

"And I love you," she countered. Gesturing toward the table, she added, "I love all of this! But why?"

"Because I needed to know that you wouldn't give up on me when you thought I may have given up on you. I needed to know you love me as much as I love you."

"Do you know now?"

"I do," he whispered.

"Good," she giggled. "Because this is the last time I chase you!"

Steve Manchester

The Last Quarter

*Think not because you are wed
That all your courtship's at an end.*
Antonio Hurtado de Mendoza

When I decided my girlfriend Maria was the woman I wanted to marry, I told her I wanted to date her exclusively. A good friend of ours suggested we start "courting."

Since neither Maria nor I knew the difference between courting and dating, our ever-helpful friend quickly pointed out they were similar, but with significant differences. "Appropriate physical boundaries" needed to be respected; and a dedicated commitment would enable us to grow individually and as a couple.

Finally, according to my friend, courtship meant every time Maria and I saw each other, I was to give her a quarter. Yes, that's right—a quarter. *Is this some mysterious, ancient ritual,* I wondered? "Never mind," said my friend. "Just do it."

So I took the "quarter" challenge, and decided to make a game of it. It became second nature to check my pockets for the appropriate pieces of silver. A dime wouldn't do. I hid quarters under her plate in a restaurant or left them with notes on her steering wheel, or gently slipped them into her hand as we walked to the movies.

I loved to see the excitement and joy in her face every time I gave her a quarter. She saved each one and collected them in a green corduroy drawstring bag. When we were apart, Maria would hold the bag and think of all the fun we shared.

Finally, the right time came for me to ask the Big Question. Almost finished with our premarital classes at the church, I'd never been more positive about a decision in my life. But doubt crept into my mind—did Maria feel the same way?

More than anything, I wanted the proposal to be special and to incorporate our "quarter theme." Carefully, I formulated my plan.

First, I chose a nice restaurant across from the performing arts center and bought tickets to a jazz show I knew she wanted to see. Then, I put words onto paper about how much Maria meant to me:

> *The Last Quarter*
>
> *In the first quarter a comfort level was formed,*
> *In the second quarter a friendship was spawned,*
> *In the third quarter silver tokens of affection did abound,*
> *And in this final quarter—my true love I have found.*
>
> *This is the last "quarter" I will give you to celebrate our "courting" stage. For today I ask you to be my wife, and in exchange for the silver tokens that daily show my love, I humbly ask you to accept a silver ring, and thus daily share my life. I love you, Maria.*
>
> *Ward*

I framed the poem and letter and placed a quarter inside, too. I arranged with the manager of the restaurant to have the frame placed on a secluded table with the menus set directly over it. My plan? When Maria lifted the menus she would find the poem and, at that point, I would drop to my knees and propose.

On the way to the restaurant, I felt confident. At least until Maria grabbed hold of my hand in the car.

"Your hand is clammy. Are you nervous about something?"

I made some lame joke in response while thinking, *This woman knows me pretty well.* I took that as another sign I'd made a good decision.

About five minutes after we sat down, Maria lifted her menu and saw the framed poem beneath it. She picked it up and exclaimed, "Hey, they've got a quarter theme, too!"

I didn't say a word. Maria was still reading. A look of confusion crossed her face. I guessed she reached my name at the bottom. That was my cue.

I knelt down beside her and asked her those four little words: "Will you marry me?"

Well, would she? There was a tantalizing moment before everything sank in. Finally, Maria said the one word I most wanted to hear.

"Yes."

The waiter brought the champagne on cue. As we laughed and held each other, I handed Maria my cell phone, programmed with her mother's number, so she could tell her mom the good news.

Within a short while, Maria and I married. All the quarters I gave her remained in the same bag, sitting next to the framed poem.

Our marriage was wonderfully happy, but I found I missed our quaint little custom. So I planned another surprise. Over a year later, we moved into our new home and had a special dinner on Valentine's Day. When Maria opened a box of chocolates she found—wrapped in tissue in place of a chocolate—a quarter.

She looked at me, mystified. "Why am I getting a quarter?"

"I miss 'quarting' you." I rolled the quarter up her arm. "I want to *quart* you and *court* you for the rest of my life!"

Since then, I've been giving Maria a quarter every day. Sometimes I put them in the most unexpected places.

Maria puts all the "new" quarters in a ceramic jar on her nightstand. She stores them in *quart*-size mason jars in her hope chest and promises to keep them forever. I've no idea how many are in her collection, but I do know that many quarters make infinite riches—of love.

Ward Nickless

The Changing Tide

Grow old along with me, the best is yet to be.

Robert Browning

I could feel the cool sand rising between my toes as we neared the water, my hand in my boyfriend Mark's. In the distance, fishing boats returned with the day's catch while shrimp boats were headed out for the night. Living near the Louisiana coast, Mark and I looked forward to our occasional strolls along the shore after a candlelit dinner. It was always romantic and especially so this beautiful night.

As we walked and talked quietly along the water's edge, I noticed a line in the sand at our feet, curving in and out and looping here and there. At first I didn't think anything of it, but then it dawned on me that the line was forming letters.

"Hey! There's a message in the sand!" I pointed it out to Mark. I looked forward and back, trying to make out the words. When I looked to Mark for help, I saw excitement on his face.

Suddenly I knew. My mouth dropped open, and I felt like I was on a roller coaster ride. I looked up and down the beach and saw it clearly now. "Will you marry me?" was written in the sand, waiting to be washed away by the rising tide.

Mark beamed and motioned me toward the question mark further down the beach. I ran to it and found a large spiral-shaped seashell lying where the dot would have been. I picked it up. Something rattled inside.

When I rotated the shell, a diamond ring fell into my hand. I turned to Mark and found him on one knee at the edge of the surf, the question burning in his eyes. My acceptance was obvious as I ran to leap into his arms and embrace him with a kiss. Within minutes the tide swept away the words of Mark's unique proposal.

Nothing, I thought breathlessly, *could ever be as romantic.*

But I was wrong. Over time, I've discovered romance in the most unique places.

Watching Mark change diapers and rock the baby to sleep, catching him washing a sink full of dishes, even seeing him fold clothes can take my breath away. Or our time together when the baby sleeps and we put on pajamas and soft socks and head for the couch. During commercials, we toss popcorn into each other's mouths and rub toes. He tells me he loves me, I tell him the same, and we Eskimo kiss.

Sure, sometimes the only candles we see now are the ones on our daughter's birthday cake. And our strolls along the beach are replaced with treks through the grocery store aisles. But I've learned that romance can always be found where love is—even between two socks. And that kind of romance no tide can ever wash away.

Michelle Marullo

Until Death . . .

Brian and I were in a serious relationship. But as a divorced mom, dating, for me, was more often than not a family affair. There seemed to be many more grade-school basketball games, dance recitals and family movie nights than romantic dinners for two. When Brian and I finally planned a "real" date one weekend, we put a lot of thought into it.

Knowing my love of everything Irish, Brian suggested we attend a play called *Flanagan's Wake*. That sounded great to me, so Brian ordered tickets. Saturday arrived and, with kisses to my daughters and a thank-you to the sitter, we were off to the show.

Flanagan's Wake was an interactive play with audience participation as part of the action. Everyone was given nametags. The men used their real names, followed by the name "Patrick." The women were all called "Mary," followed by our first names. We, or should I say "Brian Patrick" and "Mary Barbara," sat chatting as the actors entered the intimate venue from the back of the theater.

"Boo-hoo," sobbed the grieving widow of the poor, deceased Flanagan as she walked toward us. Stopping next to my aisle seat, she took my arm and sniffled through her thick brogue, "No one can coomfort like a girl-friend, Mary Barbara. Coom and sit wit me, will ya?"

Wouldn't you know, I thought, *I'm the first one they pick on.*

Nevertheless, I cooperated and followed the widow Fiona, the Irish priest and several other cast members to the small stage. As the play progressed, I tried to look con-soling at the appropriate moments, but I felt so self-conscious I could barely think how to act appropriately. Sitting at Fiona's side as the "wake" proceeded, I wished I were back in the audience with Brian. Here we were, finally on a real date, sitting thirty feet from each other.

My thoughts were interrupted by the widow.

"Mary Barbara, haf ya ever looved someone like I looved Flanagan?"

Somehow I thought I should play along with the cast but, surely, no one had ever loved anyone the way Fiona had loved Flanagan.

"No," I said, shaking my head.

"Well," she continued, "doo ya haf a special soomeone to loove?"

Nervous beyond belief, I again shook my head. "No."

I could tell by her expression that I was not following her cues the way she wanted, but I felt too uncomfortable to reveal my feelings for Brian in front of the whole audience.

"Tell me, Mary Barbara, did ya coome here to mourn Flanagan ahl by yerself?"

"Yes," I answered, the lie slipping from my lips. A com-bination of shyness and stage fright kept me from telling the truth.

"Well, then," the priest jumped in. "Who's that over there? I saw ya wit him earlier. Is that your broother, then? Bring her broother oop here!"

They're picking on Brian, too, I laughed to myself. Now *he* would have to talk in front of the audience along with me.

An embarrassed-looking Brian walked forward and stood in front of the small stage on which I sat. Looking at him with a skeptical expression, the priest spoke again.

"Yer not her broother, are ya?"

"No." Brian shook his head.

"Well, then," said the priest. "Do ya have anything to say fer yerself?"

Brian turned to me with an ornery grin. Suddenly, I *knew* what was going to happen. I jumped to my feet just as he knelt on one knee. He gently tugged me back to my seat while I laughed and cried simultaneously.

"Barb," he held both my hands and my gaze. "I truly believe God has written your name on my heart. I love you with everything that's in me. So, I'm here to . . . ask you if you'll marry me."

"Of course I will," I whispered, tears in my eyes. "I love you, Brian."

We joyfully embraced and—amid the clapping, cheers and congratulations of the smiling audience—floated back to our seats. I can barely remember the rest of the play. I sat with my head and heart in the clouds, touched that my bashful Brian had orchestrated such a public proposal.

You know, I've always liked the Irish tradition of honoring a life well-lived with a joyous celebration. But, I don't believe anyone's ever felt more joy at a wake than I did!

Barbara Loftus Boswell

Storybook Proposal

I like not only to be loved, but to be told I am loved.

George Eliot

Emily and I met in our first semester of college and dated for almost six years. Regardless of how crafty and intuitive my ideas, I was never able to surprise her with anything. Emily was investigative and I was naive—not a good combination for a surprise. Leave it to me to accidentally leave behind a receipt or just happen to be checking voicemail on a speakerphone when the restaurant or florist would call to confirm.

Time after time, I tried to surprise her. Time after time, I failed.

When I began to think about a long-overdue proposal, I wanted nothing more than to surprise her. So I embarked upon a personal journey to find a unique and special way to pop the question.

After much thought—and some interesting suggestions from friends and coworkers—I decided to incorporate two of Emily's loves: reading (her graduate-school pursuit) and pigs (her favorite animal since childhood) into a story-book proposal. My dream was to create and publish a children's book in which two little pigs, Emmy and Matty, would parallel the story of Emily and me.

I was working in public relations for a school district. I asked an art teacher if she knew any students skilled in cartoon illustration. Without hesitation she put me in touch with Jeremy, a tenth-grader who excitedly showed me his portfolio. I hired him on the spot. Page by page, I sent the manuscript to Jeremy for custom drawings. And I began to write.

I wrote about two little pigs that meet in a college computer lab, just like Emily and I. My story detailed Emmy and Matty's journey through the years. On page eight, the two little pigs find themselves in front of a sunset.

"One fall evening, Matty had an important question for Emmy," the page read. The proposal page followed.

Upon completion of the illustrations, text and layout of the story, my creation was ready to be printed. It came back in the form of a real book, hardbound. I had done it. I successfully produced the entire book in complete secrecy. After all these years, I would surprise Emily.

On a random Thursday, I told Emily I had found a couple of cute children's books on sale for her collection. Naturally she wanted to take a look, so the first one I gave her was *The Story of the Two Little Pigs*.

As she read the first couple of pages, she started to catch on that I had written a book for her, but had no I idea it would change both of our lives forever.

As she approached the proposal page, I asked her to stand up. I bent down on one knee as I watched her eyes follow the words on the paper that simply said, "Emily Suzanne . . . Will You Marry Me?" She was speechless as she looked up and saw me with a ring in my hand.

Stunned, she closed the book and gave me a big hug. "Yes, yes and yes! Of course. I love you!"

We hugged for a couple of minutes and I wiped the tears from her eyes. I urged her to turn to the last page of her storybook proposal—an illustration of pigs dressed in wedding gown and tuxedo.

It read, in appropriate storybook fashion: "Emmy and Matty lived happily ever after."

Matthew Cummings

copyright kathy shaskan 2002

Love Is in the Air

I love you. I want to be together all the time. When I think about us, I am thinking about forever.

Willis Newton
in the movie *The Newton Boys*

John and I were on our way to St. Louis, Missouri, for a quick trip of job interviews and apartment hunting. His job promotion required him to move, and, even though we weren't engaged yet, he asked me to move with him.

We had discussed getting married and already looked at rings. John even asked my parents for their blessing (a little old-fashioned, but it scored points with the soon-to-be in-laws). Everything was set, though we weren't officially engaged.

As we boarded our plane, I found our seats and put my bag into the overhead bin. Behind schedule, we sat waiting for departure and noticed one of the pilots leave the plane. When he returned we were ready for takeoff.

About twenty minutes into the flight the captain made the usual announcements: altitude, weather, arrival time, my name.

What? Did I just hear my name? My heart started pounding. *Did I do something wrong? Did my bags not make the flight? What was going on?* Even with all of these thoughts racing through my mind, I somehow heard every word:

"Attention please. Attention Lynette Baker. Lynette, John Helms would like to know if you would spend the rest of your life with him. If you accept, please press the 'call' button and the attendants will be with you shortly."

My heart continued its thumping and my eyes filled with tears. When John opened a small ring box and smiled, I whispered, "Yes."

He placed the ring on my hand and we embraced as the other passengers cheered. But wait . . . I was supposed to push the call button. I couldn't reach it with my seatbelt still fastened, so my new fiancé gladly pressed it for me. All three attendants responded, one carrying a bottle of champagne.

As we landed and approached our gate, the captain again included us in his announcements.

"Congratulations to the newly engaged couple. On behalf of the entire crew, let me wish you the best."

As we exited the plane, John thanked the flight attendants for helping with his plan. It was then that we learned that the pilot had left the plane earlier to get our bottle of champagne!

Lynette Baker Helms

Hidden Treasures

My love is deep; the more I give to thee,
The more I have, both are infinite.

William Shakespeare
Romeo and Juliet

Ike was closed-lipped about our Valentine's weekend getaway. I was to be ready to leave from the Air Force base where we both worked by 6:00 P.M. He gave no other clues.

A few hours after our departure, we arrived at the beautiful cabin he had rented near a Northern Georgia mountain town. Valentine's Day morning, we had breakfast, exchanged gifts and cards, and then headed into Helen for some sightseeing.

After a full day, Ike informed me he had brought some work he needed to do. Knowing him to be a workaholic, I was neither surprised nor disappointed. He went to the bedroom while I curled up on the couch to watch a Doris Day movie.

Sometime later and half asleep, I felt Ike gently shaking my shoulder to rouse me.

"I forgot to give you a few presents," he said, sitting down next to me. I sat up, groggy but curious.

Ike handed me several small boxes and told a story about each present as I opened them one by one.

I unwrapped delicate pearls from Hawaii and listened as he painted a picture of turquoise water and white sand paradise. Next was a pair of exotic gold earrings from Saudi Arabia and I listened as he described the stark deserts of the Middle East. I opened box after box of jewelry and enjoyed Ike's descriptions of the distant places where he'd found them.

Then he pulled out several sheets of paper—the "work" he had been doing. A list of everything he liked about me. A beautiful love letter. A letter that reduced me to a blubbery, weepy mess.

"Michelle, each one of these gifts I've given you were all purchased on different occasions, in many different locations during my ten years in the Air Force." Ike paused. "They were all purchased with my future wife in mind."

As I tried to process it all, he slipped down on one knee, took my hands in his and asked me to marry him. I drew him into a passionate embrace with my equally passionate answer.

Today, a beautiful jewelry armoire cradles those wonderful, worldly gifts. But my most cherished treasure is the man who so lovingly thought and planned and shopped for his future wife. My jewel of a husband.

Michelle Isenhour

A Trail of Love

Because April had been planning "the happiest day of her life" since she was twelve, I felt pressured to plan a romantically resplendent marriage proposal to precede our wedding.

I began by making a list of the things needed to create a memorable atmosphere in which to pop the big question. It included the certainty from God that April was "The One," our parents' approval, a diamond engagement ring, some flowers, the perfect location and some creativity.

With the list completed, I set out on my mission. Since April and I loved hiking, I picked and prepared a worthy location in the hills.

The day before, I hiked the trails loaded down with a backpack of flowers and a wooden sign that read: "On this spot, July 4, 1997, Shad Stewart Purcell and April Dawn Smothers were engaged to be married." After a time, I located a cove of trees with a beautiful scenic overlook. There I planted the flowers and hung my sign.

I carried several large stones to the spot, setting them in the shape of a heart. Not totally satisfied, I added more to the center in the shape of a cross, symbolizing our love as complete with Christ at the center of the relationship.

The next day, April and I drove to the hills. We hiked and splashed in the streams along the trail, as I checked my front pocket every ten yards to make sure the ring was still there.

As we approached the cove of trees, I told April how much she meant to me and how thankful I was to God for giving us the wonderful gift of love to share with each other. When she noticed the flowers and the stones, she looked at me and made the sweet *awww* sound girls make. I knew then the day was ours and I had done something truly romantic.

But suddenly April tugged on my arm, stopped and looked around. "Wait, Shad." Her voice hushed. "Look around. I think someone died here!"

Well, *that* was a response I hadn't put on my list. With no Plan B in place and feeling panicked, I pointed out the sign. "Uh, April, let's walk a little closer and see what it says."

She read the sign aloud and turned to look at me.

"Are you kidding?"

"Of course not," I said, dropping to my knees with the ring in my hand. "I love you. Will you marry me?"

"I will! I will! I will!"

Six years later, and happily married, we still laugh about our so-called tombstone. The irony of what initially appeared to be the end of a life was just the beginning of one for us. Soon after our engagement, we hiked back to that special spot to find that only a small piece of our sign remained.

The piece of wood is now a priceless souvenir, not only in our home, but also in our hearts.

Shad Purcell

Taking Care of Business

Daisy, Daisy, give me your answer, do!
I'm half crazy, all for the love of you!
It won't be a stylish marriage,
I can't afford a carriage,
But you'll look sweet upon the seat
Of a bicycle made for two!

Harry Dacre

Luckily, Randy never minded being a pack mule for our outings, holding all the stuff I brought along.

The first three grueling miles of our hike in Armstrong Grove went straight up a rocky trail. But the breathtaking coastal view at the top would make it worthwhile. While an ever-willing Randy hauled our over-stuffed backpack onto his shoulders, I drank in the scent of pine trees and fresh air.

We didn't talk much on the way up; instead there was a lot of heavy breathing. Much of the ground was covered in leaves, which made some parts slippery and precarious. After some time, we successfully made our way to a grassy glade for our picnic lunch. While Randy set down the backpack and pulled out our blanket, I got out the bottle of wine, plastic cups, crackers and cheese.

It was almost one o'clock now and I was starving. But when I asked Randy to open the wine, he looked away.

"Uh . . . honey . . . I have a little business to take care of." He nodded toward the trees behind us.

"Oh, yeah, sure. Go ahead." I grinned and gave him a knowing look.

A cool breeze feathered my hair and I sighed with contentment. I opened the wine and filled the cups. I arranged cheese and crackers. I admired the view and the perfect day. I was tempted to start eating but I wanted to wait for Randy to return. So I waited. And waited. And *waited.*

The "business" Randy needed to take care of was taking longer than usual.

My goodness, he didn't even take any tissue or a napkin with him. I grimaced at the awkwardness of the situation and continued to wait. *Should I look for him? Or, maybe I should holler and ask if he . . . needed anything? Yes, that might be better.*

Just as I started to call his name, Randy reappeared unapologetically wearing a self-satisfied expression.

"My goodness, honey, I was starting to get worried about you." I patted the blanket. "Come on. Sit. I'm starving."

Ignoring the spread of food, Randy knelt in front of me. "You mean everything to me." He smiled into my eyes. "I love you so much and don't want to live without you." He held my hand in his. "Will you marry me, grow old with me, share your life with me?"

My heart leapt as I gasped at the suddenness and blurted out, "Yes! Oh Randy! I love you. Yes, *yes.* . . ."

Randy reached into his pocket. Tenderly, gingerly, he slid a dainty ring onto my finger. And it was then that I realized what "business" had taken so long in the woods.

My "engagement ring" was a delicate strand of dried

grass tied into a circle.

The poor, patient man had tried over and over to form fragile native grass into this eternal symbol. Touched, I hugged him tightly as he whispered that we would get a "real" ring after our hike.

We had our lunch and toasted each other. I giggled and laughed, loving the world, the man who wanted to marry me and the romanticism of the moment. I wanted the day to last forever.

When it was time to head down the trail, I sang and danced. Randy shook his head and laughed at my antics, still hauling the backpack. But now he carried even more.

He carried my heart.

Leigh P. Rogers

Popping the Question

It was so much fun, we proposed to each other all day long.

Melissa Errico

It was a typical Tucson winter day, cool and sunny. I met my boyfriend for lunch at a sandwich shop near the college I was attending. We had limited time so we ate quickly. Jeff had to get back to work; his afternoon would be busy. Before parting, Jeff asked if I wanted to go to Happy Hour that evening. I agreed and we kissed goodbye.

That afternoon biology class was dismissed early. I jumped into my car to drive home, change clothes, and freshen up before our date. As I headed up the ramp to the freeway, my cell phone rang.

"I'm off early. Had to go to the post office and bank," Jeff explained. He was in his car only minutes ahead of me.

"Isn't this great? We have plans and we both got out early!"

"Where are you?" Jeff asked.

"Still a couple of miles behind you." I gave him my cross streets.

Jeff suddenly interjected, "I'm sorry I haven't been very romantic lately."

"No, I guess you haven't," I agreed. "But we've been busy, it's okay."

"Valentine's Day is coming up. I promise to do something romantic, at least get you a card."

"That's a start."

"Where are you now?" he asked, more impatiently. I looked at the street signs and read them off to him. "Well, hurry up. I want to get to Happy Hour."

We had plenty of time. Why the hurry? He was acting so strange.

"I can meet you at the restaurant if you prefer," I suggested. "Or, if we meet at the house we can ride together and catch up on our day." He agreed, and we hung up again.

My cell phone rang again.

"Beth, I just got home. What happened to the garage door? Did you break it this morning?" The garage door was our main entry to the house.

"It was fine when I left. Maybe your automatic opener isn't working?" Minutes later I pulled beside Jeff's car in our driveway. I repeatedly pressed the button on my garage opener. Nothing. With a shrug, I walked up to the front door and turned the knob.

As I stepped into the living room my jaw dropped and my eyes grew big. A camera flashed.

I was swimming in a sea of balloons. Balloons on the floor. Balloons on the ceiling. Dozens and dozens . . . hundreds of colorful balloons. Jazz music played in the background.

After my eyes adjusted, I saw Jeff sitting on the couch, camera in hand. He said, "You agreed I wasn't very romantic, so I decided to whip something up."

Still in shock, I trudged through the balloons to hug him. I felt like I was in slow motion.

Jeff nodded toward the coffee table. "You have something to open." There sat a bucket with a champagne bottle on ice, two crystal champagne flutes, two candles and a blue ribbon . . . tied around a little blue box.

I picked up the box and slowly pulled the ribbon. Inside was a ring box. I lifted the lid and found . . . a gold stickpin? I looked at Jeff with raised eyebrows.

He folded his arms across his chest, settled back and grinned. "It looks like you have some popping to do."

"What?" I looked around the room. "Oh!"

Not wasting a moment, I grabbed the pin and began sticking balloons. Laughing all the while, I searched for "the" balloon. But there were so many, I finally started shaking them and throwing them to the side.

"Don't forget there are balloons on the ceiling," Jeff reminded me. I looked up.

After an eternity, I shook a red balloon. Something rattled! When I poked it with my gold stickpin, shiny heart-shaped confetti cascaded around me. A blue ring bag fell to the carpet.

Trembling, I tipped it open until a ring fell into my hand. Jeff gently took it and urged me to sit on the couch.

"You know me. I have to do this the traditional way." As he lowered himself to one knee, his brown eyes gazed into mine. He asked me to be his wife and slipped the princess-cut diamond on my finger.

After my eager "Yes!" and many kisses later, Jeff said, "Oh . . . and . . . by the way . . . we are *not* going to Happy Hour."

Elizabeth L. Blair

A Friend, Indeed!

Friendship often ends in love, but love in friend-ship—never.

Charles Caleb Colton

"Mom . . . it's over!" I wailed into the telephone. After being wined and dined for two years, I'd been dropped like a hot potato. My first heartbreak.

In the following days, tears gave way to a blank sadness and the bitter taste of betrayal. By Wednesday evening, I was lying on the living room floor curled in a ball, trying to ease an inner pain that would not cease. Then I heard a voice in the distance.

"Julia . . . come on . . . get up! Get dressed! We're going out."

I looked up with glazed eyes, dazedly recognizing my old friend Alex, whom (guiltily, I realized) I had not made much time for during the past couple of years.

"No," I muttered with self-pity. "I'm not going anywhere."

I felt myself elevated by strong, sturdy arms and gently placed on my feet. "Get dressed, Jules," he repeated. "I'll wait right here until you're ready."

Thus began the healing process. Through Alex, I

reunited with friends I had somehow drifted away from through the years. He appeared at my doorstep each evening with a new agenda for the night, gently prying me from my misery as our mutual respect and quiet love for each other grew in friendship.

After a particularly difficult day, he took me to a lively café. Drowning my sorrows in a frothy latte, I blurted, "Alex, will I *ever* meet the right guy?"

His deep brown eyes danced with laughter. "Jules, one thing I can promise you: Someday, I'll be dancing at your wedding."

I gazed at my trusty, dependable friend. Taking in his broad stance, olive complexion and endearingly familiar smile, I tried to picture Alex waltzing with his date at my wedding. But I couldn't. Something didn't seem quite right. I resolved that this could only mean one thing: I might be destined to never get married. With a sigh, I turned my attention back to the latte.

As the years passed, I decided to concentrate on my career as an artist rather than on my downfalls with men. Alex was there to share my disappointments and successes, no matter how large or small. He helped me recover from the likes of Brad, Lou and John—although failed relationships no longer shocked my system.

I occasionally shot him an earful of advice on the ladies and suffered only mild pangs of jealousy toward the women in his life. But it wasn't until Dan that I truly opened my eyes.

Dan. He was thrilling, exciting, handsome—and famous, too. What more could a girl want? Our dates consisted of exclusive shows and private parties, a fantasy come to life. So why did I find myself comparing him to Alex?

In fact, I realized most of the men I'd dated couldn't hold a candle to Alex's kindness. None had his sense of humor or rich, hearty laugh. None had his overwhelming compassion and genuine optimism. None had the qualities I had taken so for granted in Alex.

So, when Dan left me behind to go on tour, I didn't feel disposed of like the crumpled, used tissue I thought I'd be. I had Alex and that was what mattered.

One summer night, to celebrate our "thirteen years of friendship," Alex invited me to dinner at a quiet Italian restaurant in the city. Afterwards, we cruised around town with the car's top down. I laughed happily at the sheer joy of the evening, loving the freedom of wind tumbling my hair and the comfort of Alex beside me.

On a whim, he parked the car near the harbor.

"I know it's getting late," he said. "But it's too beautiful for the night to end."

"It is gorgeous out tonight," I agreed, taking his hand as I climbed from the car. We strolled along serenely, oblivious to the world, until Alex stopped suddenly.

"What is it?"

"Look," he pointed. "We're right beneath the CN Tower."

The massive grand structure—landmarking Toronto's skyline—was directly in front of us. I had lived with the majestic view of this building all my life, but I had never seen her towering frame silhouetted against a blazing moon. Judging by the look in Alex's glowing face, he hadn't either.

Then, all at once, I realized it wasn't the tower but *me* he was looking at.

"Alex," I began shyly, not knowing how to respond to this new feeling. "Do you find it . . . odd . . . that I didn't notice the tallest freestanding structure in the world? Especially since we're standing right beneath it?"

"No, actually . . . not odd at all," he drew me closer. "Because when I'm with you, the world seems to disappear."

The moment his lips touched mine, breathless yearning and passion laced the deepest love I could ever imagine and poured from his heart to mine. It only took one kiss to change my life. One kiss to see what had been right before my eyes, right beside me all along.

"Julia," he whispered. "I am so in love with you!"

"I love you, too, Alex. So much. And I think maybe I always have."

"Well," he smiled. "I need to clarify one thing, though."

"What's that?"

"Remember the promise I made a few years ago . . . to dance at your wedding?"

"Uh-huh."

"I lied." He broke into a big grin. "I should have told you I plan to dance at *our* wedding."

Sylvia Suriano

Never Say Never

Do not be too timid and squeamish about your reactions. All life is an experiment. The more experiments you make, the better.

Ralph Waldo Emerson

"How would you like to accompany me to England for a week of sightseeing?" I stared at the e-mail in disbelief. It was from Mel, the widower I had been dating for six months.

I immediately replied, "Thank you for your generous offer, but I must respectfully decline. As much as I enjoy your company, I would not be comfortable traveling with a man I wasn't married to. Besides, I don't have a passport."

My dear husband of fifty-one years had died three years earlier. I learned to ease my grief by reading, writing, attending church functions and visiting my children and grandchildren. But as time passed, I missed belonging to a partnership.

Then friends invited me to a party where I met Mel. He was attractive, intelligent and had an engaging personality.

To my surprise, he called two weeks later and invited me to join him for dinner.

I discovered being part of a couple again opened new vistas. Soon we were receiving invitations to parties and meeting each other's friends. After being in a desert of loneliness, I enjoyed the social oasis of dinners, concerts and theater.

We talked freely about our deceased spouses and how lucky we were to have found true love with them. Because we didn't think it was possible to find that level of love more than once in a lifetime, we both admitted our decisions to never marry again and decided to enjoy the companionship we found in each other.

Consequently, I was shocked at the invitation to travel together and questioned Mel's motives. Certain my response would sever our relationship, I was surprised when he phoned.

"I got your reply. Let's forget I asked about the trip."

Relieved, I mumbled, "Thanks for understanding."

"We are still going out tomorrow night, aren't we?"

"Sure." After all, he didn't seem to feel awkward about the situation, so why should I?

The following evening he held the car door open with one hand and handed me a legal looking paper with the other. "Just happened to be in the post office today and picked this up for you."

It was an application for a passport. *What? Why, that sly man!* Without comment, I tucked it into my purse and changed the subject. Nothing more was said, and we enjoyed the evening.

Amused he had bothered to get me an application, I filled out the papers, had my photo taken and doled out the $75.00 fee without telling him.

While attending a party with friends, we were invited to join their dance club. I was excited, but Mel resisted. "I played trumpet in a swing band during my youth so I never danced very much."

"If you're a musician, you've got rhythm," I reminded him. "If you've got rhythm, you can dance."

Although reluctant at first, Mel relented and agreed to take ballroom dance lessons—where he held me in his arms for the first time. With him holding me, I felt my heart melt . . . and immediately rued our platonic relationship. But I couldn't tell him lest he remind me about our "never marry again" agreement.

Then he began bringing candy and flowers, and I knew I was being courted. Although he was careful not to mention marriage, I sensed we were falling in love. Still, neither of us said a thing until the day he invited me to dinner at his house.

Fine china, crystal and sterling silver on a white linen tablecloth greeted me. Red roses graced the table. Before we sat down to eat, I confessed I had applied for and received my passport. When I showed it to him, his eyes sparkled and he flashed a mischievous grin.

He served a delicious rack of lamb with all the trimmings and we had a lively conversation as we ate. During dessert he said, "Sally, if I asked you to marry me, what would you say?"

"You haven't asked me yet." My startled response was quick. Awkward. Even a little coy.

"I think I just did."

Unprepared, I stammered, "Oh. *Oh.* P-p-probably."

He looked dejected, but didn't pursue the subject. I was so surprised I didn't know what to say. We cleared away dinner and cleaned up his kitchen, then he took me home.

Most of that night I lay awake pondering his proposal. I had been married to an extraordinary man once. But Mel was wonderful, too. Was it possible to marry two extraordinary men in one lifetime?

The next morning, he called. "Last night I asked you to marry me and you said probably. How about a more definite answer," he urged. "Like yes?"

"But . . . what about our agreement?"

"Let's just forget it."

"Forget what?" I smiled into the phone, tingling with excitement.

"Let's fly to England for our honeymoon and *never* say *never* again."

Sally Kelly-Engeman

3

THE PERFECT DRESS

What is a princess on this day without the garnish where beauty lay?

Gina Romanello

After having to wear hideous bridesmaid's outfits at the weddings of her two closest friends, Donna welcomed the opportunity to carry out her revenge.

She Did It Her Way

The best and most beautiful things in the world cannot be seen or even touched. They must be felt with the heart.

Helen Keller

"Mom, we're getting married . . . sometime in June." This from my hippie daughter calling on a pay phone in Maine. (No phone or electricity at her house—or perhaps cabin is a better word.)

"We don't want a fancy wedding or dressy clothes or a lot of guests. We just want to be married in your backyard. I'll let you know the date."

Long ago, her father and I made up our minds to listen to her and do things the way she wanted as much as we could. And of course, I was thrilled she was getting married. I was always secretly worried that marriage was too "old-fashioned" for her. She was a child of the '60s, eager to right the wrongs of the world, to live life on the edge and to never be part of the "establishment."

Well, backyard weddings can be lovely, I thought. *It's not our beautiful church with a majestic organ, flowing white dress or bridesmaids. But, still. . . .* I took an upbeat approach, which was really the only sensible thing to do under the circumstances.

Later with dates arranged, a guest list of sorts (our family and best friends and "a bunch of friends . . . we'll let you know how many") and the food decided on ("only veggie stuff and some champagne"), she agreed I could ask the minister of our church to perform the ceremony "for legal purposes."

All negotiations were going well until I mentioned the wedding gown. "No special dress, Mom. Sorry. Your first daughter, your good daughter [said with a wry smile, a favorite family joke] did the white dress and veil thing. Not me. I have lots of clothes that would do for a wedding."

I thought of all her dresses (short, wild, braless) and realized that she mostly wore jeans or cut-offs. Nothing I had seen her wear in years even whispered "wedding" to me.

So in the following days, ignoring my own good advice to let her do it her way, I wandered around different stores and looked at dresses that might do for my bride-to-be daughter. Then I saw it: simple, unbleached muslin with a shirred waist, scooped neckline with just a bit of Irish lace and little capped sleeves. It was long, but not floor-length. It was graceful, but not formal. It was lovely and simple, and it was my daughter.

Envisioning her wearing it, I bought the dress and took it home.

Later that day I placed the box on her bed with a little note stating: "I just happened upon this while shopping (okay, a small white lie). This looks like you. Would you try it on for me?"

When she came in that evening, she went to her room and all was quiet. A bit worried I had hurt her feelings with my purchase, I went upstairs to her room where she sat on the bed holding the dress on her lap while tears rained down her cheeks—and she was smiling.

"I never knew you thought of me like this, Mom. The dress is so lovely and soft and simple. I love it. And I'll love wearing it for the wedding. Thanks for knowing me so well."

Two weeks later, on a sun-filled afternoon, friends gathered in our backyard. Our daughter walked down the steps—to the strum of a guitar—smiling proudly in her surprise dress. She looked wonderful, like I knew she would.

It was a perfect wedding . . . almost.

Had I known her fiancé would be wearing yellow paisley bell-bottoms, I might have shopped for him as well!

Julie Firman

Priceless

How beautiful a day can be when kindness touches it.

George Elliston

We had shopped for hours, my mom and I, and we were having a ball. We knew in our hearts that we would find just the right dress. Five months remained until the wedding; we had plenty of time and we had lots of patience. And then we found it—at J.C. Penney's Bridal Shop.

I stood on a dark-blue carpeted platform, surrounded by mirrors. The clerk brought gown after gown for me to try. I felt like a queen, admired by my mom perched in a cozy, overstuffed chair. As soon as she zipped the back of the third dress, we both knew we had found *the* one.

I never felt closer to my mom than when she fluffed out the train and said, "This is it. It's you."

The moment burrowed its way into my heart and my memory.

Which is why I was so touched by the lovely young lady now trying on my wedding gown.

I was having a yard sale to pick up a little extra cash. I

had many things to sell when the young woman and her mom pulled up in their rusty maroon Oldsmobile. But my wedding dress wasn't one of them; I planned on saving it for my daughter.

They walked hesitantly up the driveway. The daughter stayed near her mom as they walked around the deck and lawn looking over the piles on the tables. They picked up an item or two but didn't appear interested in buying anything.

Just when I thought they would leave, the mom turned to me. "You wouldn't happen to have an old prom dress, about size 16, would you? We have been looking every-where." She paused. "My daughter is getting married in a few weeks and we want something nice for her to wear."

I didn't answer right away, so they started back down the driveway.

"Wait! Wait just a minute." Without stopping to think, I hurried inside to the extra closet, pulled out the large gray bag and rushed to catch them before they drove away.

"I don't have a prom dress. But, would you like to try on my wedding gown?"

The young lady smiled at her mom and then at me.

"Yes, please," she answered timidly and got out of the car.

Although I invited them inside the house, they insisted the garage would be fine. I was embarrassed at its condi-tion, but they didn't seem to mind at all. Giving them some privacy, I steeled myself. It felt . . . right. Still, I wondered if I would have regrets.

My worry evaporated when I peeked at the bride-to-be in my garage. She stood on a battered red milk crate, star-ing down at the dress, beaming as her misty-eyed mom smoothed the lace sleeves of the antique-white dress. Both seemed oblivious to the lawn tractor, auto parts and oil cans surrounding them.

Any lingering regrets faded when I heard her mom say, "This is it. It's you, honey."

I stepped back, afraid to intrude on their personal moment—a moment as special as mine so many years before.

It was a few minutes before they came out of the garage.

"How much do you want for the dress?" asked the daughter.

I hadn't even thought of that. I had no idea what to charge. "How much do you have?"

Reaching into her pocket, she pulled out a wad of crumpled, damp dollar bills and counted it out. "I have seventeen dollars, that's it, and I bet it's not enough." Regretfully, she started to put the bulky gray bag on a table.

"Sold!" I blurted, surprising us both.

I cried as they drove away.

Oh, not tears of mourning for my wedding gown. I cried at an important revelation. I realized that—although my pocketbook didn't hold much—my heart was full of priceless memories. My shopping experience with my mom and my wedding day will be in my heart forever. The dress hadn't made those days special; love had.

Nora E. Kessel

Given the Green Light

Sometimes the heart sees what is invisible to the eye.

H. Jackson Brown Jr.

It was June 14, 1951, my last official day of nursing school at St. John's Hospital in Tulsa, Oklahoma. I hurried to finish my late shift on Three North—my wedding was only two hours away.

Everything was necessarily jammed together in my life because the Korean War had started and Uncle Sam called my fiancé to serve. Our plans—in fact, our entire lives— were suddenly turned upside down. Besides worrying whether my darling would return from war, I was faced with immediate and chaotic superficial changes.

Our wedding plans were moved up six months and slashed to the bone. With both of us fresh out of school, there was no time to accrue money. So the big ceremony shrank down to the minister, my fiancé's mother, my housemother and us.

Even the $120 white satin wedding dress at Mrs. Ramsey's wedding shop was out. Instead, I would buy a white street dress for $30. I called Mrs. Ramsey.

"What a tough break," she said. "But I've got a sugges-tion. If your heart isn't set on that white street dress, I could credit what you've put down to the lovely brides-maid's dress your friend is holding for you to wear in her September wedding."

The bridesmaid dress would cost only $30 dollars that way. Plus, I'd be set for my friend's wedding, too. It made sense then. And the bridesmaid's dress was beautiful.

But, now, as I laid out the green dress, I felt a twinge of sadness at not wearing white—the traditional symbol of purity I deserved and wanted to wear. Logically I told myself the color of my wedding dress wasn't important.

Besides, I thought ruefully, *few will be at the wedding anyway to see me in it, so why feel sad?*

As I showered and dressed, my head argued that the green was all right, but my heart was unconvinced. Glancing in the mirror, all I could see was a bridesmaid, not a bride. Sighing, I took a last look at the white Easter pumps I'd polished and started downstairs to the refriger-ator for the nosegay of rosebuds to carry on my nursing Bible. Just then the phone rang.

"Child, I know it's asking a big favor," Sister Tabitha said in her heavy accent. "But word has spread through the ward about your wedding today. The patients want me to ask if you might visit in your gown before you go to the church."

I glanced at the clock. I'd really be cutting it close. *And in this green bridesmaid's dress? Ugh!* On the other hand, many of Three North's patients were terminal and I really loved them.

"Of course, Sister," I heard myself say. "I'll be right there."

I grabbed my purse and white Bible. Then I ran down-stairs and got the yellow rosebuds. Once in the parking lot between the nurses' residence and the hospital, I dodged puddles from an earlier afternoon shower. Gathering the yards of ankle-length green taffeta to my knees, I ran across the lot amid honking and cheering from passing motorists.

Short, plump Sister Tabitha met me when the elevator door opened. "Oh, you look so lovely! The patients need to see you," she said. "So close to death, they need to feel a vital part of life that a wedding is. Now, don't worry child, I'll call a cab for you. Just tell me what time they should pick you up and I'll be sure you're downstairs then."

She trotted beside me in her white starched habit as I went from room to room.

Trying not to worry about time, I went to each patient and chatted for a few seconds. I was amazed at how their eyes, dulled from the pain of terminal cancer, suddenly brightened when I swished through the door in taffeta and netting.

No one cared that the dress was green.

No one noticed it was intended for a bridesmaid.

Over and over they called me "such a beautiful bride" and asked me questions about my fiancé. As I told them about the wonderful man I was marrying, I felt my own eyes shine. Before I left, I hugged each fragile patient and kissed each feverish cheek.

And I walked away from Three North in my lovely— green—wedding gown.

Jeanne Hill

Holding It All Together

Because I was an accomplished seamstress, I decided to design and sew my own wedding gown.

Perusing pattern catalogs and fabric selections, I opted for a sleeveless dress of white crepe with a long-sleeved, full-length coat of lace. Meticulously, I figured out every last detail before cutting into the fabric. I did the sewing in spare moments between college classes, studying, working part-time and spending hours with my beloved fiancé.

In the 1970s, it was customary to sit for a bridal portrait in wedding finery several weeks before the wedding. This photograph would be sent to the local newspaper to appear in the society pages on the Sunday morning following the wedding.

But when the date for my appointment arrived, the lace coat of my wedding dress was still under construction, with only the bodice complete. The understanding photographer carefully framed only head-and-shoulder shots— to avoid including the ragged edges along the bottom of the lace bodice. No one looking at the portrait would ever know I wore only three-quarters of a wedding gown.

In the following weeks, the coat came together. But I

couldn't decide how to attach the lace train to the back of the dress. Wanting to get the full effect while trying it on, I pinned the back section of the skirt and bodice together. Pleased with my efforts, I continued the finishing touches on the gown.

The remaining pre-wedding days passed in a flurry of last-minute details, appointments, rehearsal and packing. Then the big day dawned, and preparations consumed the morning and early afternoon. When the church sanctuary and reception hall were ready for guests, I went to a church classroom to dress.

I was astonished to discover my dress still pinned together in back. I couldn't believe it! I had forgotten to finish the most important dress I would ever wear. Feeling panicked, I stopped for a second and thought about it. Then I managed to laugh, realizing the wedding guests would be oblivious to the fact that I was held together with pins. No one was the wiser when I walked down the aisle in my unfinished creation.

After the wedding, I packed my dress away. Twenty-eight years later, as I prepared to transform it into family heirlooms for my daughters' weddings, I examined the dress more carefully. There in the back were those familiar pins . . . I had still never finished my dress.

I was stirred by the thought that even though my wedding dress had been held temporarily with pins, the marriage had been secure and lasting. The dress was just an accessory and only had to hold together for several hours. But the most significant element of the day—the commitment I shared with my bridegroom—had endured almost three decades of better and worse, richer and poorer, sickness and health.

Clearly, no pins were required.

Adele Noetzelman

Tagged for Delivery

Somewhere, Samantha knew, there must be a young woman crying her eyes out. One of the boxes taken off the moving truck contained a wedding gown Samantha had never before laid eyes on. Great care had been taken to preserve it, judging from the sturdy white storage box and tissue paper. Sam's name and address were on the box, but someone from the moving company had made a terrible mistake.

It was a vintage dress—Sam estimated the 1930's era— about size 3, with an overlay jacket and intricate beadwork. Was it an heirloom? Passed down to the bride by her grandmother? Samantha worried someone had lost a cherished family treasure.

She made phone calls to the moving company requesting information to help her find the owner, but they refused to cooperate. Discouraged, she gave up the search.

Over the years, Sam was offered money for the antique dress but always refused. Something about the gown defied explanation. To her romantic mind, she only knew that sometime a young woman was destined to wear this dress, marry a handsome prince and live happily ever after.

Time flew, but for Sam and her family, life was anything but a fairy tale. Her husband lost his job and they decided to relocate. To save money, they planned to move themselves this time, but the rental trailer was small and could hold only necessities.

I offered to hold a moving sale for Sam and began by bringing her tables and clothes racks from my home. As we sorted and tagged items, I came across the wedding dress and listened while Sam explained its mysterious past.

"I wish I could have found the rightful owner," Sam sighed. "Now it looks like a stranger or a dealer will get it."

Reluctantly, I placed a $70 price tag on the gown, and Sam hung it next to the other clothes. When we finished marking all the items, Samantha suddenly remembered she had a large patio set in the back yard. My family needed patio furniture, so I put $90 into the cash box and bought it sight unseen.

The next morning sales were brisk. As the day wore on, however, we lowered prices in an effort to move the merchandise more quickly . . . and regretfully reduced the dress to $45. At the end of the day, the wedding gown still hung on the rack. Except for a man who'd said he'd mention it to his daughter, no one seemed interested.

Perhaps tomorrow we'll have better luck, I thought. We moved everything back into the garage, closing and locking the doors behind us.

While loading the patio set into my van, we discovered the umbrella and stand were weathered and rotted.

"Samantha," I suggested, "instead of refunding me half of the money I spent for the patio furniture, would you consider giving me the wedding dress instead, and calling it even? I have a sister I'd like to give the dress to."

"What would she do with it?"

"She has antiques throughout her house. She'd display the gown."

Samantha smiled. It wasn't the fairy-tale ending she envisioned, but somehow it seemed right. "You have a deal," she said.

While Sam was at work the next morning, I carefully removed the dress from the rack and put it in the house before the crowds arrived. About an hour before the end of the sale, the man from the previous day suddenly appeared with his daughter.

"I'm sorry," I explained. "The dress is no longer for sale."

The young woman's face fell even as I noted that, just like the heirloom gown, she was tiny and petite. I looked into her eyes, and knew I couldn't disappoint her.

"Come with me." I led her into the house.

The dress fit her perfectly; she would be a stunning bride. Her father must have thought so too. He handed me a $100 bill and told me to keep the change.

"No," I protested. "I can't do that. It's right your daughter should own the dress. It almost could've been made with her in mind."

"I want you to take this," he insisted. "Please." He looked me squarely in the eye. "It is really amazing that we found this dress. She searched months for one like it, even looking in shops along the east coast, without any luck until today."

Now her search had ended.

I took $45 for myself, and left the rest in the till.

That night, I told Samantha about the bride, how stunning she looked and what her father had said. Misty-eyed and always the romantic, Sam drank in every word. The well-preserved dress had traveled many miles, but now its journey was over and she finally had the fairy-tale ending she always wanted.

At last the homeless vintage gown had reached its destination.

Pat Phillips

The Blessed Dress

Believe in fate, but lean forward where fate can see you.

Quentin Crisp

I got an engagement ring for Christmas. My boyfriend and I had been dating for almost a year and both felt the time was right to join our lives together in holy matrimony.

The month of January was spent planning our perfect Alabama June wedding. My mother, two sisters and I went to Huntsville, the closest town with a selection of bridal shops, to buy the gown that would play the leading role on my special occasion.

We had a wonderful time just being together and sharing silly jokes, but the day soon turned serious by afternoon: still no sign of the dress of my dreams. Both sisters were ready to give up and try another day in another town, but I coerced them into one more boutique.

I had a good feeling as we entered the quaint little shop filled with the scent of fresh flowers. The elderly clerk showed us several beautiful gowns in my size and price range, but none were right. As I opened the door to leave, the desperate shop owner announced she had one more dress in the back that was expensive and not even my size, but perhaps I might want to look at it anyway. When she brought it out, I squealed in delight.

This was it!

I rushed to the dressing room and slipped it on. Even though it was at least two sizes too large and more costly than I had anticipated, I talked Mom into buying it. The shop was so small it didn't offer alterations, but my excitement assured me I would be able to get it resized in my hometown.

Excitement wasn't enough. On Monday morning, my world crumbled when the local sewing shop informed me the dress simply could not be altered because of numerous hand-sewn pearls and sequins on the bodice. I called the boutique for suggestions but only got their answering machine.

A friend gave me the number of a lady across town who worked at home doing alterations. I was desperate and willing to try anything, so I decided to give her a call.

When I arrived at her modest white house on the outskirts of town, she carefully inspected my dress and asked me to try it on. She put a handful of pins into the shoulders and sides of my gown and told me to pick it up in two days. She was the answer to my prayers.

When the time came to pick it up, however, I grew skeptical. How could I have been so foolish as to just leave a $1,200 wedding dress in the hands of someone I barely knew? What if she made a mess out of it? I had no idea if she could even sew on a button.

Thank goodness my fears were all for naught. The dress still looked exactly the same, but it now fit as if it had been made especially for me. I thanked the cheerful lady and paid her modest fee.

One small problem solved just in time for a bigger one

to emerge. On Valentine's Day, my fiancé called.

"Sandy, I've come to the decision that I'm not ready to get married," he announced, none too gently. "I want to travel and experience life for a few years before settling down."

He apologized for the inconvenience of leaving all the wedding cancellations to me and then quickly left town.

My world turned upside down. I was angry and heart-broken and had no idea how to recover. But days flew into weeks and weeks blended into months. I survived.

One day in the fall of the same year, while standing in line at the supermarket, I heard someone calling my name. I turned around to see the alterations lady. She politely inquired about my wedding, and was shocked to discover it had been called off, but agreed it was probably for the best.

I thanked her again for adjusting my wedding gown, and assured her it was safely bagged and awaiting the day I would wear it down the aisle on the arm of my real "Mister Right." With a sparkle in her eye, she began telling me about her single son, Tim. Even though I wasn't inter-ested in dating again, I let her talk me into meeting him.

I did have my summer wedding after all, only a year later. And I did get to wear the dress of my dreams— standing beside Tim, the man I have shared the last eigh-teen years of my life with, whom I would never have met without that special wedding gown.

Sandy Williams Driver

Keepin' the Faith

Hope deferred makes the heart sick; but when dreams come true at last, there is life and joy.

Prov. 13

I always thought of the bridal gown as an extension of the bride.

It declares what kind of woman she is. It should knock the socks off of her groom, dazzle the audience and make the bride feel like the most beautiful woman in the world. It has to be perfect.

The dress shopping was to be all about me, the bride. After all, it was going to be my big day. However, I found that while I focused on myself, the strain blinded me from a bigger reality.

At first, the hunt was exciting. I spent hours trying on different styles. But as time wore on, nothing seemed right. No dress measured up. Could I settle for second best? The threatening thought nearly brought me to tears.

One Saturday afternoon, my mom asked if I wanted to shop. By this time, I was so disenchanted I wanted to stay home. Nevertheless, I went.

A bride on a budget, I dutifully stayed away from the more expensive, designer boutiques. Yet, we decided to enter one particular shop and look for sales. I chose three dresses. The first two were unsuitable. Donning the third, I walked out of the dressing room and approached the three-way mirror.

I blushed. My heart raced. I felt stunning.

I posed, preened and pranced, all the while picturing myself walking down the aisle. I was beautiful, confident, dazzling. This was The One.

I dared to look at the price tag—*ugh!* But there was a reason for its costliness. Duchess silk. Hand-sewn bead-work. Perfection.

Thoughts of "settling" crept back into my mind.

My mom shared my distress but wasn't ready to give up hope. She asked the owner if she would give us a price break since the dress was a display model. No luck. The next words, however, were unexpected.

"This particular dress will be $200 on our one-day sale a month from now," she said. "But, if it sells between now and then, or if someone gets here before you on the sale day and buys it, then you will lose the dress."

A price cut of $1,500? Was it possible? Could the dress last a month?

I fretted all the way home, imagining every possible sce-nario. *Should I have different people call the shop and put the dress on hold for an entire month? Maybe I should've hidden it on a back rack? If it sold, could I plead with the new owner?*

Could it last a month? Could *I*?

After explaining the situation to my dad, he and my mom agreed that it was the dress for me. We needed faith to believe it would still be there. We decided there was only one thing to do—pray.

Our wedding dress story spread. My church congrega-tion prayed. My colleagues prayed. My parents' friends, whom I had never met, prayed. My fiancé, who was living in Scotland, had his friends pray. My high school students loved the story and faithfully asked about it. Some told their parents and they prayed.

My father prayed that if anyone else tried on the dress, it would look ugly or make her itch. My three brothers offered to guard the dress with baseball bats. (I didn't take them up on this.)

More and more people became excited, nervous, anxious and delighted over the gown. I shared the faith of my growing supporters, but there were times when it seemed grim. When I wavered, someone assured me the dress would be there.

I realized a wedding, and the joy that accompanies it, is about more than just the bride and groom.

The day before the sale arrived. Petrified, I called once more to check on the dress.

"The dress has not been sold," the owner declared.

At four o'clock the next morning, my parents camped in front of the bridal shop. Armed with lawn chairs, Starbucks coffee and heavy winter coats to combat the Colorado freeze, they scoped out the position of the dress through the store window. I arrived and the moment the store opened, I raced in, followed by my cold parents.

I grabbed my dream dress off the rack, took it to the front and plopped down $200. And, all anxiety gone, I held a treasure in my hands. The perfect dress.

More importantly, I held a piece of the heart of all those who rallied behind me. A symbol of a vast community of people with faith to believe that even wedding dresses matter. And, all with part ownership in my bridal gown fantasy . . . which belonged to *more than* just the bride.

Greta Montgomery

4

THE BIG DAY

A wedding is just one of many stories in a couple's life together—stories of special moments . . . from the vows and the kiss . . . to laughing with family and friends . . . and especially those that weren't exactly planned.

Rosanna McCollough
editor in chief, WeddingChannel.com

Carolyn gets her first glimpse of the excessive frugality that would define the next 42 years of her life.

A Snow Cloud's Silver Lining

A father: The first man in your life to give you unconditional love, and the one who every man after is compared to.

Becca Kaufman and Paula Ramsey
creators of *WeddingQuestions.com*

It snowed like crazy on our wedding day. Not a piling up, traffic-paralyzing kind of snow, but the kind that leaves the trees sparkling and the streets looking like a river of licorice slush.

My mother closed all the drapes as if blocking the view would somehow force an end to it. But it didn't work. By the time my father and I were ready to leave for the church, the driveway and street were slathered with a generous portion of semi-frozen grayish sludge.

My father had cleared a path in front of the house but when it was time to go, Mom still insisted I wear plastic bags over my shoes to protect them "just in case." As luck would have it, the only two plastic bags in the house were empty bread bags.

Somehow my little-girl dreams of this day never

included parading to the church with bread bags peaking out beneath the hem of the gown I'd waited my whole life to wear. Still, snowflakes continued swirling down and no alternate plan prevailed. So, on went the bread bags over my shoes, and off we went.

Carefully we made our way out the front door and to the rented silver Mercedes waiting to take us to the church. Ed, the driver, never said a word, but the look on his face was priceless as he watched me approach with blue-and-yellow-plastic-polka-dot clown feet.

As we started out of the driveway, I realized that never before in my life had I taken a ride with my dad without him driving. Gripped by this moment of truth, I turned my head to look through the back window and watched our house—and my childhood—shrink slowly out of sight.

One lone tear trickled down my cheek while Dad sat quietly beside me. Then I felt him reach over and take my hand. This small, quiet gesture spoke volumes of what he, too, must have been feeling—but never said.

The freshly fallen snow transformed a relatively short ride into a slow and cautious journey through the landmarks of my youth. As we passed the playground, the schoolyard and even the corner candy store, each seemed to call my name and whisper good-bye.

As much as I looked forward to all the future held for my husband and me, this intense feeling of ending my girlhood pierced my heart. Sensing this, my father squeezed my hand and drew me close to his side. His warm embrace assured me everything would be all right.

While Ed parked the car at the church, Dad and I simultaneously looked at each other, then cast our eyes down to the polka-dot Wonder Bread "booties," which by now had taken on a role of their own and seemed to be staring back at us.

My father turned to me and said, "Do you really want to step out of this car with clown feet?"

"Well, not really, but what else can I do?"

The street and sidewalk surrounding the church had been on the receiving end of a barrage of galoshes, snow tires and shovels since early that morning. What started as a pristine blanket of white now appeared to be nothing more than a dirty mess that threatened to ruin my shoes, as well as whatever part of the dress and train that would end up getting dragged through it.

"Lose the boots," Dad said. With those words he got out of the car and walked around to the door on my side.

I leaned forward and slipped the bags off my feet to reveal lovely white satin ballet slippers with the pale pink satin ribbons that twirled about my ankles and came to rest in a delicate bow. I dreaded the thought of how they would look by the time I reached the church steps.

I methodically gathered up as much of the dress and train as I could, and stepped out of the car trying to keep it all from touching the ground. As I turned toward Dad, suddenly I felt my feet lift off the ground and in an instant I was swept into his arms. Just that quickly my dress and shoes were safely out of harm's way and my heart had wings to fly.

How many years had it been since Dad had carried me in his arms? How much like a princess I felt, and how appropriate it seemed to close the door on my childhood in such a poignant way.

Dad carried me from the sidewalk all the way up the steps and into the vestibule of the church where my mother and bridesmaids awaited our arrival. Setting me down in front of my mother he kissed me on the cheek and said, "Now that was fun. Wasn't it?" To which I replied, "Let's do it again!" We all laughed and a few moments later he walked me down the aisle where I joyfully stepped forward into the future.

Dad faced his own moment of truth that day. My husband and I were married on my parents' thirty-sixth wedding anniversary. I imagine walking his last baby down the aisle on this day surely brought home to his heart that life was moving on; no turning back the clock.

My husband and I celebrated our twentieth wedding anniversary this year. Life moved on for us as it did for Dad—who now smiles on us from heaven.

The warm memories of our wedding day remain with me, but few are as tender as that precious moment when Daddy's little girl was swept off her feet one last time.

Annmarie B. Tait

Kiss and Tell

Creativity requires the courage to let go of certainties.

Erich Fromm

Clink, clink, clink, clink, clink.

The sound of cutlery hitting the wineglasses grows to a loud pitch. The bride and groom rise from their seats and embrace with a warm, passionate kiss—much to the delight of their guests.

Most of us are familiar with the well-known tradition to get the bridal couple to kiss—"the clinking of the glasses." Half Italian, I have attended my share of Italian weddings and know full well that before the first course or antipasto plate, the *clinking* sound will be heard at least ten times.

When Michael and I were planning our wedding, there were two traditions he did not want to follow. "Theresa, I love to kiss you, but I don't want to hear the irritating sound of glasses clinking all night. And I won't do the Chicken Dance."

I had to agree with the latter. The Chicken Dance is silly enough, let alone trying to do it in a wedding dress.

However, the other would be expected unless we had an alternative. But what?

Some kissing traditions involved singing a song with the word "love" in the title. A good idea if your guests can carry a tune. However, if guests saw this as a "karaoke" opportunity, it could get out of hand. Another tradition would be to have guests give a "toast," but then who wants to listen to toasts all night?

As Michael and I wrote out our seating plan for the *fifth* time, an ingenious idea hit us. It would give an opportunity for our guests to interact and allow them to be creative. But best of all, they would have FUN in the process, which is really what attending a wedding should be all about. It was perfect.

Our reception night arrived, and no sooner had we taken our seats in the dining hall, than the *clinking* began. Before it reached a crescendo, our best man, Tom, announced, "There will be no clinking of glasses tonight to get Theresa and Michael to kiss. Instead, they ask that you each perform the unique request on your tables and they would then be happy to kiss for you."

On each table was the following poem:

> *The bride and groom will kiss for you*
> *Read on to see what you must do*
> *Each table has a unique request*
> *So get together and do your best!*

Each request was specifically chosen according to the guests seated there.

One table of Michael's old friends was requested to relate childhood stories about Michael. Laughter bubbled as they reminisced and shared tales about their high school antics. They debated which story would or could be shared with all the guests. The one chosen received chuckles at the expense of the sheepish groom.

A table of couples married thirty years or more were asked to recount their marriage proposals. Another group of friends present when Michael and I first met were asked to tell the story of our "beginning."

One of the more daring requests was a "celebrity impersonation." This group caught everyone's attention when, en masse, they proceeded to center stage wearing pristine white dinner napkins on their heads. Arranging themselves into a choir, they made the sign of the cross and sang their rendition of "How Do You Solve a Problem Like Maria?"

But, they altered it to: "How do you solve a problem like Theresa? How do you make Michael understand?" It was a creative collaboration in words, melody and choreography that kept the audience in stitches.

Looking back, Michael and I realize those moments of spontaneity provided memorable entertainment and made our wedding day both fun and personal. Friends and family members exceeded our expectations and we could do nothing more than sit back and enjoy their creativity and presentations of love.

As we promised, we returned our humble appreciation and thanks in the only way we could . . . with warm and loving kisses.

Theresa Chan

A Bouquet to Remember

You know, fathers just have a way of putting everything together.

Erika Cosby

"Where are the flowers?" My sister panicked pacing the living room dressed in her wedding gown.

"I don't know, sweetie. They were supposed to be here an hour ago. But don't worry; I'm sure they'll be here promptly," my mother assured Kathy to calm her down.

"Oh, no, the photographer's here. He's early!" the bride yelled hysterically. "I need my bouquet for the pictures."

I was seventeen years old and the bridesmaid. As a girl who always planned on getting married one day, I considered my sister's wedding day a learning experience.

That morning, Kathy was a wreck. She had planned every detail of her wedding carefully. The invitations, personalized napkins and matches, the bouquet with white roses, calla lilies and baby's breath. All planned a year in advance. The one thing Kathy didn't plan was the fact that something could go wrong.

We waited and waited for the flowers to arrive. My

sister looked enchanting with her classic fairy-tale gown and full skirt that gathered at the waistline. But for her, no flowers meant no sweet fragrance, no delicate decorations, no beautiful pictures, no mementos, no wedding.

The groom was often called "a romantic fool" in the good sense of the word. He was the kind of guy that would leave little notes saying "I love you" for no special reason. The night before the wedding, he gave my sister a bracelet proving he was a hopeless romantic.

But there was nothing romantic in the air the next day. Trapped in an apartment filled with desperation and nervousness, I noticed my father open a window to smoke. It was interesting to see how one stressful situation could drive a man who had quit two years before to suddenly go back to the habit.

The doorbell rang. *The florists,* I thought, running frantically to answer the door. Disappointed to find a young delivery boy, I asked in my annoyed voice, "May I help you?"

"It's a delivery for Kathy Lassalle from her future husband, Hernan," he said, trying to keep my attention.

He pulled out a huge floral bouquet of red roses. My father's lit cigarette fell to the ground. He immediately grabbed the bouquet and took off for the bedroom, leaving me at the door to sign the paper.

"Thanks a lot," I said to the delivery boy as I watched my father mysteriously disappear. "Dad, that's not for you. Give Kathy her gift!" I shouted down the hall, wondering what he was up to.

Minutes later, my father reappeared in the room where we all waited. He had a big smile on his face; his way of saying that things were going to be all right. He then presented to us three gorgeous bouquets he had arranged from the groom's beautiful red roses.

We couldn't believe it. Dad (and Hernan) had saved the day.

With little time to spare, the photographer took pictures of the bride, bridesmaid and flower girl as planned. Not with the wedding bouquets, however, but with bouquets made out of love, creativity and *urgency!*

The scheduled flowers finally arrived just before we entered the church. My sister was happy to have the bouquet she designed herself; and the flower girl had her basket of flowers. I, On the other hand, decided to keep my dad's lovely red-rose creation, giving my original white bouquet to my mother.

Ten years later, when we look at my sister's wedding pictures, we notice something that nobody else does. In fact, we think it's cute that some pictures show a red bouquet of flowers and others show a white one. But each time, we are taken back to that eventful day. A day of emotion and stress, but most importantly a day where a groom's romantic gesture and a father's hidden talent made a bouquet to remember.

Cindy L. Lassalle

Flower Princess

I patted the tulle clouds of my white dress as Mama brushed my dark hair. She clipped tiny ivory flowers to the top of my head, and I was complete—a real princess. Flower girl, they called me, but in my four-year-old mind, I was Cinderella.

We arrived at the church early to practice, and Bonnie, the bride, handed me the basket of all importance. Tucked inside lay dozens of crisp purple orchids. The outside was white wicker, adorned with bows and satin ribbons. It whispered to me, "Princess, princess, princess."

My turn in the rehearsal came, and Bonnie leaned over. "Now, don't put any of the flowers down yet," she said. I nodded, thinking Mama must have been wrong when she said my job was to drop flowers on the carpet. Poor Mama. She must have never been a flower princess.

I marched to the front of the church, clasping my basket, holding my head even and stiff. The prettiest bridesmaid, Josephine, winked and said how grown-up I was. My fingers longed to touch her long satiny skirt, but I stood tall and still, like a real lady.

Then the people came. Tall people, squatty people, people in hats and vests and polka-dot dresses. Men in collars and aloha shirts. Women in heels as tall as pencils. I watched the other kids in their suspenders and pigtails and long flowered muumuus. *Well,* I thought, feeling sad for them, *I suppose we can't all be princesses.*

They filled the church with their hushed laughter and rustling dresses and warmth. Up front, Mrs. Ayabe plunked beautiful music out of the old piano. Mama kissed my forehead. "You'll do just fine, sweetie." She put my hand in Bonnie's and left.

Bonnie and I waited at the very back in our matching Cinderella dresses. We waited through the music and the praying and the turning pages. We waited as the brides-maids in their satin skirts went before us—one, two, three, four. And then it was my turn.

Hundreds of eyes rested on me, but I stared straight ahead to the front of the church. Watching only the old man with the Bible, I slowly traveled the skinny aisle, just like Mama told me—first foot, together; second foot, together.

My fingers gripped the handle of the wicker basket as I guarded my treasure. I wished right down to my toes that I could sprinkle a few flowers, just to show everyone how purple they were. But Bonnie's words whispered in my head. *Don't put the flowers down yet.*

As I reached the man up front, I saw Mama smiling. It was a funny smile. The kind she gives when I mix the but-tons on my shirt, or forget which shoe goes where. I thought maybe her strange look was from being so proud, but a little part of my stomach tied worried knots.

After lots of talking and praying and singing, when I almost had to yawn, I saw one of the men kiss Bonnie smack on the lips. I didn't think God allowed kissing in church, but the man with the Bible was nodding, so I let it pass. Then everything was music and clapping and peo-ple swarming around Bonnie and the kissing man.

Mama found me after the wedding, and knelt down to

my size. She held both of my hands, even the one still clamped to the basket. "Sweetie," she said with that smile, "Sweetie, why didn't you put down the flowers?"

I opened my mouth to explain when Bonnie glided by, all lace and white and tulle.

"You were adorable, Nicki, absolutely adorable!" she gushed. "And it's okay that you forgot about the flowers." Then the sea of fancy people swallowed her back into their handshakes and hugs. I couldn't believe it.

I stood very, very still. I didn't look at Mama. The tears spilled down before I could stop them, splashing my cheeks, my dress, the rounded toes of my glossy white shoes. I wanted to use my screeching voice.

I had listened! I really had. I listened all perfect but I still did it wrong, and now I can't be a princess!

Mama hugged me close, saying, "It's okay. It's okay to forget. Everybody forgets sometimes, even Mama."

I made my body stiff in her arms. "But I didn't!" I protested between gulping sobs. "Bonnie said not to do the flowers! I didn't forget!" Mama patted and shushed and peppered me with kisses, but I knew she still thought I'd forgotten.

Then I felt a new hand on my back. I blinked up into the sunlight, and saw Josephine's soft smile. She whispered something to Mama, who nodded. Josephine took my hand and led me back to the sanctuary, her satin skirt swishing.

The church was empty and quiet and big as we stood at the wooden doors. I looked at Josephine. "Go ahead and put your flowers down," she said. "It's time now." She waited at the very back, and I walked slowly, carefully down the aisle of the empty church. I fingered the smooth flowers and dropped one here, then here, then here. The last orchid fell just as I reached the front of the sanctuary. Perfect. Just like a princess.

Turning toward the back of the church, I stretched my skirt wide and curtseyed deep to my imaginary audience. Josephine's laugh was like silver. When I looked up, Mama was standing beside her. She beamed my favorite smile, all shining and rounded cheeks—the kind that means she's so glad I'm hers.

I raced back over the trail of scattered flowers. Then we left the wedding, Mama with her smile, and me with my empty basket and a glow that rivaled Cinderella's.

Nicole Owens

What Could My Country Do for Me?

One of the best ways to persuade others is with your ears—by listening to them.

Dean Rusk, former U.S. Secretary of State

It was March 1963.

At nineteen, I was the first in my crowd to get married, certain this young sailor was the man with whom I was supposed to spend my life. Everything was arranged. I could hardly wait to see my fiancé, Robert Frisch, when he came home for the first time in seven months, just a few days before our wedding.

He called Sunday evening. "I won't be there for the wedding."

My heart did a loop-de-loop.

"I'll be in the middle of the Pacific," he explained. "All military flights from Hawaii have been canceled."

"Can't you find another way back?"

"I wanted to get a commercial airline ticket with the money I've saved for our honeymoon, but they said 'no exceptions.' So, cancel the wedding and we'll get married later."

"Cancel the wedding? I can't just cancel the church, the flowers, the caterer—everything." Panic crept into my voice. "They can't do this. I'll find a way. I'll call someone in Washington. I'll call, um—I'll call President Kennedy!"

"Well, you could try, but I doubt it would do any good," Robert replied. His lack of surprise at my idea was a reminder that he accepted me and loved me just as I was—impetuous, stubborn and perhaps a bit eccentric.

The next morning I told my mother about my plan and phoned the information operator. (This was before the days of Directory Assistance.)

"I want to speak to the president."

"The president of what?"

"The President of the United States, of course." I tried to sound business-like, yet nonchalant. I was neither.

She hesitated. "I'll have to call you back. What is your name and number, please?" One long hour later, the phone rang. "Please hold for Washington."

"Y'all are callin' for President Kennedy?" The voice drawled across the line. "He's not in Washington right now. This is George Lusk in Vice President Johnson's office. How can I help you, ma'am?"

I took a deep breath and poured out our desperate story of canceled flights, changed orders and the impossibility of postponing a big wedding only days away.

". . . And he offered to buy a ticket on a commercial flight, but they refused to let him do that," I finished.

"Y'mean he's got the money and they won't let him go?" Mr. Lusk sounded indignant. "I'll see what I can do, ma'am."

Again I waited for the phone to ring. This time, however, it didn't.

At three o'clock, I called the naval base in Hawaii, anxious to speak to Robert.

"Frisch isn't here."

"What?"

"Frisch isn't here." The phone connection was quite clear.

"But, he has to be. . . ." I clutched the receiver.

"No. His girlfriend called somebody in Washington. Frisch is on his way to the Honolulu airport. He's gone home."

"Home?"

"Home. Home—to get married."

Smiling my thanks, I cradled the receiver. We would both be at the church on time.

Carlienne A. Frisch

Dismally Late

What do we live for, if it is not to make life less difficult for each other?

George Eliot

My husband and I were driving across our state to the wedding of my cherished friend's daughter when we had a flat tire on a country road. While he changed the flat, I worried. I wanted to arrive early at the church I once attended. Friends since we were young, I was "Auntie Jeanne" to her Beth and she was "Auntie Ruth" to my three youngsters.

It was devastating when Ruth Ann's husband had died suddenly four months prior, but she'd insisted Beth go ahead with the wedding as planned. Although she'd suggested her daughter choose another relative to give her away, Beth had decided no one should take her father's place walking her down the aisle. Knowing today would be difficult, I hoped to hug each of them before the ceremony.

So I was chagrined when we were dismally late.

Barely inside the open sanctuary doors, we slipped into the last two vacant chairs ushers had added beyond the back pews. For an instant I enjoyed the lovely organ music and the heady fragrance of orange blossom boughs decorating each pew. Then, with a heavy heart, I saw that the groom, his best man and three of the four bride's attendants were already down front by the altar. Shortly, the last bridesmaid glided past us and on down the aisle.

After an especially long passage of music, I saw the organist look expectantly in our direction toward the open sanctuary doors, watching for her cue to start the wedding march. No cue came. Where was the bride?

Fifteen minutes passed and murmurs of concern stirred the audience. Her mother, seated up front, couldn't go check but I was in the perfect position to do so. I slipped out of the sanctuary doors.

Once into the narthex, I ran down the hall. As I remembered, there were two quick turns to the bride's dressing room. On my first turn, I heard faint hammering of small fists against a door. On my next turn, I heard Beth calling, "Let me out, somebody! The doorknob came off in my hand and I can't get out! Help me!"

I ran to the door but I couldn't open it. "Beth, it's me—Jeanne. I'll go get help."

"Oh, Auntie Jeanne! Thank heaven!"

When we got the door open, I complimented Beth on how in-control she looked in spite of the situation. "I wasn't at first," she said. As she gathered her satin skirts and ran through the hall beside me, she told me how she'd started crying but soon felt her father's hand on hers.

"I know it sounds crazy but I heard Daddy say, 'Don't cry, Bethie, everything is going to be all right.'"

Moments later Beth triumphantly marched down the aisle to "Here Comes the Bride." I sat in the back row giving thanks for a flat tire that had put me in exactly the right chair at the right time. Dismally late? More like providentially late.

Jeanne Hill

My Love Is Like a Mountain

Ever has it been that love knows not its own depth until the hour of separation.

Kahlil Gibran

The fog was so thick I couldn't see the mountain. But I knew it was there and my fiancé and his best man were somewhere on it. Not knowing exactly where filled me with a fear that was almost unbearable. It was our wedding day.

The mountains were in our blood. Living at the foot of the Adirondacks as we did, how could they not be? During our growing-up years, our families lived near the tallest of the Adirondacks—White Face Mountain—a few miles from Lake Placid, New York.

Bob and I loved hiking and one day decided to climb White Face to the top. Looking at the world below in all its peace was a surreal moment.

"This is the perfect place to share our vows," Bob suggested.

Not wanting the typical wedding with a church, gown, tuxedo and four-tier cake, we agreed on a nontraditional ceremony at a place where our hearts lived—on top of the world.

Our excitement grew as we planned for a September wedding. The fall colors, that no florist could ever match, would be in bloom; and no church could compare to God's mountains.

We found a justice of the peace in the small town at the foot of White Face and reserved cabins for excited friends and family. Everybody met at the local restaurant for dinner and celebrating the night before the wedding. Everybody except the groom.

Bob's testimony of his love for me was unlike any other. He had a plan to climb White Face in honor of his commitment to me. He and his best man would climb halfway that night, camp out and then finish the climb to the top the next morning, the day of our wedding. All in time to meet me at the top by one o'clock.

With camping gear on his back, Bob kissed me goodbye. My heart in my throat, I was worried and excited at the same time. I couldn't believe this man was climbing a mountain to show his love for me.

When morning came, I looked out the window and there it was—surrounding me like a large white blanket—fog. Although I knew the mountain was there, I couldn't see it. And Bob and Kirk were somewhere on it.

Frightening thoughts went through my mind. What if they're lost? What if they're hurt? What if they ran into a bear? The mountains were full of them.

I was so upset I couldn't think straight. Finally my maid of honor took me by my shoulders.

"God takes care of the pure of heart," she assured me. And that was Bob, for sure. Holding on to that thought, I calmed down—until I was faced with even more bad news. The state ranger closed the mountain to the public due to the thick fog.

"Closed to the public?" I screamed. "They can't do that! I have to meet Bob in three hours at the top. He's on his way and I'm stuck at the bottom with no way of letting him know. What do I do now?"

The park ranger was alerted that there were two men on the mountain climbing to the top. He told me they would be all right; there was a ranger at the top who would notify us of their arrival.

Gathered at the restaurant, the rest of us worried as hours passed with no word. By now I was a total wreck and didn't know how much more waiting I could take.

It was three o'clock and I should have been on my honeymoon. The ranger called: Bob and his best man had reached the castle at the top. While everyone else was cheering, I was tearing. A heavy weight lifted from my heart.

I asked if the ranger was driving them back, but to my surprise the answer was no! It was against the law. So after climbing all day in thick fog, the poor guys had to walk another two hours down. But I thanked God they were safe.

After I calmed down, a thought came to me. *The wedding! Where will we have the wedding? If not on top of White Face, where?*

Someone suggested Santa's Workshop, a tourist spot known as The North Pole, located at the base of the mountain. The village had a small chapel, too. Our wedding day went from "on top of the world" to "Santa's world" in one day.

To my surprise, I didn't even need to tell the villagers my story. They already knew and graciously opened the tourist attraction and the chapel to us at no cost. Now all that was missing was . . . the groom and his best man.

Five hours late to his own wedding, Bob finally made it—dirty, sweaty, bleeding, hips chafed from his backpack, toes raw and bleeding. This sight for sore eyes was my sight for complete joy. My knight in shining armor had returned and, to my amazement, in his backpack were flowers he had picked for me.

"All I could think of was you and our wedding," he told me.

The town was abuzz—a wedding at the North Pole! Santa's helpers embroidered *bride* and *groom* on red hats and the "elves" were all in attendance. A sight to behold, for sure.

We exchanged vows but to my surprise Bob had his own. "My love for you is like a mountain: strong, forthright and everlasting." My eyes filled with tears as his words echoed in my mind and heart.

After the ceremony we were whisked off to see Santa. Pictures were taken, jokes were made and Santa gave us a beautiful wedding candle. But our most prized gift was our wedding certificate. It reads, "Married at the North Pole. Witnessed by Santa Claus!"

We may have gotten off to a rocky start, but after almost thirty years of marriage, our love for each other is more like the mountain every day. Strong. Forthright. Everlasting.

Eileen Chase

At Ease

*P*eople who throw kisses are hopelessly lazy.

Bob Hope

Now in their late sixties, the widow and widower, long-time friends before their spouses passed away, chose to marry. The groom—a proud and valiant ex-Marine—arranged the wedding at the unobtrusive Marine Corps Chapel tucked over the gymnasium at Headquarters Battalion USMC, Henderson Hall, in Arlington, Virginia.

At the close of the simple ceremony, my cousin Larry—officiating chaplain—presented the couple to the audience and introduced them as "Mr. and Mrs." Then he suggested it was time for the groom to acknowledge his bride.

Larry waited expectantly. The bride looked up adoringly. And the small audience held its collective breath, eager to witness the traditional first kiss as husband and wife.

But guests collapsed into gasps and gales of laughter when the feisty groom snapped to attention and, in true military style, "acknowledged" his bride with a proper Marine . . . salute.

Carol McAdoo Rehme

Should We or Shouldn't We?

A kiss is a lovely trick designed by nature to stop speech when words become superfluous.

Ingrid Bergman

There are some decisions every prospective bride and bridegroom must make before the big day. First, will there or won't there be cake shoved in someone's face? And, secondly, what kind of kiss will be shared at the end of the ceremony?

Should it be soft? A light dusting of the lips, to avoid smudging lipstick?

Should it be passionate? A celebration of the moment, a true indication of the feelings involved?

Or should it be chaste? Quiet and sweet, a sign of respect to those in attendance?

Of course, having the conversation is only a good use of time if the arranged plan is actually followed.

In the days before our wedding, Travis and I discussed both questions: cake and kiss. On the first, I was adamant. If the cake wound up anywhere other than my mouth, our wedding night would be stormy. Although Travis agreed not to smash any cake in my face, his wide smile made me wary.

On the question of the kiss, though, we were in full agreement. Neither of us was comfortable with a public display of affection, so we agreed to share a soft, chaste one. This insured the added bonus that my lipstick would remain intact for the photographs.

Then the moment arrived.

"You may kiss the bride," the priest said.

Travis looked deeply into my eyes. I tilted my head. Our lips met.

But instead of the quick peck on the mouth we'd agreed upon, my groom gathered me in a very un-Travis-like embrace and gave me a passionate, lingering, breathless kiss . . . Hollywood-style.

I forgot we were in a church.

I forgot the priest was an arm's-length away.

I forgot a host of family and friends looking on.

I'm not sure how long we stood there kissing, but we paused only when the priest leaned toward us.

"Travis," he chided, "there are children present!"

To this day, those in attendance still tease us. But—I'm happy to report—our wedding photographs prove no cake was smeared on anyone's face.

Only lipstick.

Raegan Holloway

"Please, Fred—I have a headache."

He Completed Us

The most important thing a father can do for his children is to love their mother.

Theodore Hesburgh

My daughter Alyssa was born in 1992. I had just turned nineteen and was left to raise a daughter on my own. I was young, alone and bitter that her father wanted no part of our life.

I had a few boyfriends that did not mind that I was a young single mother, but I could never bring myself to include Alyssa in those relationships. It wasn't that I was ashamed of having a daughter; she was the first person to show and teach me what true love really was. I just never trusted a man enough to include Alyssa. That is, until I met Travis.

Travis and I met in the summer of 2000 and I think I fell in love with him the first time we talked. We had one of those conversations that seems to last forever and everyone else in the room seems to disappear. It wasn't until we were together for a few months and we were talking about moving in together that I felt ready to include Alyssa.

From the beginning they got along—not that it surprised me. He was the first person who actually got her to swim and get over many of her fears. Alyssa's dad has never played a role in her life and it was like a breath of fresh air to see Alyssa with a father figure.

The three of us grew as a family over the next couple of years. Travis's family accepted Alyssa and me into their family as if we had always been there from the beginning. I finally had the life that I had always dreamed of, except that it was missing one thing. Marriage.

Travis proposed on Valentine's Day that year and I could not wait. I wanted everything to be perfect. I planned for over a year, until I was driving everyone crazy, including myself. The wedding became my weekend project, and I made sure I included Alyssa from the very beginning. I didn't want her to feel left out. I expressed this to Travis to make sure he included her in everything as well.

Then he made a suggestion that confirmed how much I loved him.

The day of my wedding came and the sun was out. The stress and whirlwind of getting ready for the wedding had everyone running around freaking out, but Alyssa was the perfect princess all morning.

The church was beautiful and the bridesmaids made their way down the aisle followed by Alyssa and then myself. Travis and I said our vows to each other. It was a wonderful moment.

Our Reverend then asked Alyssa to step forward. It was then that Travis made his vow to my daughter.

> *I Travis, choose you, Alyssa,*
> *to be my family.*
> *I promise to honor and respect you,*
> *and to provide for you to the best of my ability.*

I promise to make our home a haven,
where trust, love and laughter are abundant.
I make these promises lovingly, and freely,
and vow to honor them all the days of my life.

He then placed a beautiful gold locket around her neck and gave her a kiss.

At that moment all the planning and worrying about how I looked didn't matter. I knew that God had sent the perfect man, a man who taught me the meaning of unconditional love, of trust and renewed faith. A man who, on this day, completed us.

Michelle Lawson

Coming Full Circle

I met Sara during preschool. I was three years old and she was four. We were kindred spirits, alike in so many ways—inseparable sisters who became family through our own self-created love.

But one thing that differentiated the two of us was the fact that my parents were still married, while her parents were divorced.

Jim and Teresa's divorce had shocked everyone who knew them. They were high school sweethearts who married right after graduation. Then two years later, shortly after Teresa gave birth to Sara, Jim divorced her and moved to another state.

"Why did your father leave?" I'd asked Sara.

"I don't know." She shrugged her shoulders and flipped her ponytail like she didn't care. But deep down I knew she did.

Although Sara did not see her father often, he called regularly, encouraged and rewarded her good grades, kept abreast of her activities, and provided the family with more than enough money. So in spite of the separation, she always felt he cared about her.

Teresa never discussed why she and Jim divorced. Family and friends reminisced about their once-passionate relationship. But Teresa's bitterness was apparent.

During her freshman year of high school, Sara met Brad, a sweet, smart and handsome young man who eventually won over all of us. All except her mother—who objected when Brad proposed four years later.

Teresa repeatedly explained how painful marriage could be, especially at such a young age. She did not want to see her daughter go through the same hurt she'd experienced. Sara insisted she loved Brad, and their situation wasn't the same as her mother's. Defeated, Teresa accepted Sara's decision to marry.

The day of Sara and Brad's engagement party, the couple's families and friends enjoyed meeting one another and celebrating the upcoming nuptials. Brad tried hard to entertain and talk to Sara's mother in spite of her persistent coldness.

Toward the end of the evening, Sara's dad startled everyone when he walked through the door. I watched Sara run across the room and throw herself into his arms. Surprisingly, even Teresa looked pleased.

After meeting Brad and congratulating the couple, Jim spotted his ex-wife and immediately went to her table. He kissed her cheek, gave her a lingering hug and sat beside her. The two talked away the evening.

The day of Sara and Brad's wedding was magical. As maid of honor, it was my responsibility to tend to my best friend. As I straightened her veil, there was a slight knock at the dressing room door.

Teresa walked in and quietly gave Sara her blessing, apologizing for being so doubtful in the beginning. Then she admitted to Sara that she'd been in regular contact with Jim since the engagement party. They had done lots of talking and, for the first time, Jim explained why he'd left, apologized for his immaturity, his panic as a young parent and his wrongdoings. More importantly, he begged for forgiveness.

Teresa explained how this conversation helped her deal with the resentment she'd felt and the lonely void caused by his absence. After all these years, she discovered she still loved him. Thrilled with the reconciliation, mother and daughter embraced.

Sara's father escorted her to the altar where she joined hands with Brad. Then Jim sat next to Teresa; they joined hands, too.

During the reception, everyone danced, ate and toasted the evening away. And Sara's parents did not leave each other's side. When a slow song began to play, Jim asked Teresa to dance. Suddenly he got down on one knee and took his ex-wife's hand in his. A clamorous crowd circled the pair.

"I love you," Sara's father began, "and I need for everyone to know how sorry I am for what I did to you and our daughter."

Sara's mother couldn't utter a word, because her other hand was covering her mouth in shock.

"And I want you to be my wife. Again. Will you marry me, Teresa?"

She pulled Jim into her arms.

In Sara's eyes, that moment made her wedding day perfect. Not only did she marry the man she loved but, after eighteen years of hope, tears and prayers, her mother and father reunited. Like the wedding band her husband slipped on her finger, Sara felt like her life had come full circle.

Denise N. Wheatley

Built on Love

Remember that the most beautiful things in the world are the most useless; peacocks and lilies, for example.

John Ruskin

"Is this a serious relationship with Matt?" I asked into the phone as I watched workmen nail drywall in our Florida home.

"It could be," Betsy answered from her apartment in Washington, D.C. When I heard the love in my daughter's voice, I knew there would be a wedding in her future.

Months later, Betsy called late one night. I could hear excitement in her voice. "Mom! Matt just asked me to marry him and he gave me a beautiful diamond ring. We're engaged!" She paused to catch her breath. "The wedding will be a year from now. That will leave plenty of time to make the arrangements."

As happy as I was for my daughter, I was relieved the wedding would not be soon. With our home under major construction, we needed to complete all the messy renovations before focusing on a wedding.

A few months later Betsy called with another surprise.

"Mom, guess what? Matt and I decided we don't want to wait a year. We want to get married in two months. A Christmas wedding . . . at your home."

Two months? Our home? A wedding at our construction site?

"Our home looks like a hurricane hit it," I alerted Betsy. "The 'curb appeal' includes an outhouse for the workers and a Dumpster overflowing in the driveway. Bricks and debris occupy our front yard. The indoor tile floors and electrical installations aren't finished. How can you have a wedding in all this chaos?"

"We'll manage somehow." Betsy, determined and undaunted, ignored my panic.

My stomach churned as we began to plan.

"There's going to be a wedding here in a few weeks," my husband, Jim, announced to the surprised contractor. "Complete as much of the construction as you can. Focus on finishing the tile floors." The workers shook their heads in disbelief.

I immediately contacted my friend, Lois, an experienced caterer. "I'll plan the wedding, make the cake and decorate your home the best I can," she promised with a sigh, "but it's going to be a challenge."

I quickly hired a photographer who stared in disbelief when he saw the rubble. "I'll have to avoid capturing construction eyesores in the wedding pictures. It won't be easy."

The day before the wedding, Lois and her assistant balanced boxes of decorations as they picked their way around piles of sand, broken bricks and discarded boards.

"Be careful to avoid the parts of the tile floor that were grouted last night," Jim advised as they stacked boxes in a corner. "There is nothing we can do to camouflage the exposed air-conditioning ducts."

"Let's hang garlands and red bows above the floor-to-ceiling windows to frame your view of the Intracoastal Waterway," Lois suggested, looking at the changing panorama of lazy sailboats, expensive yachts and squawking seagulls. "We'll intertwine garlands and bows on the spiral staircase and outline the steps with red and green poinsettias. Tall candelabras at the base of the staircase will add a formal touch." She stepped back to visualize her plans.

The day of the wedding, the sun cast early morning shadows on the overflowing Dumpster while dew clung to the outhouse.

"Welcome to our disaster area," we teased, as guests navigated a maze of construction obstacles. Inside, people sat on a hodge-podge of furniture. Outside the open glass doors, guests awaited the ceremony on a lone couch perched on a sandy knoll.

The music began and Betsy entered from a bedroom, a vision in white on her dad's arm. Her eyes twinkled as brightly as the lights on the Christmas tree. When she caught my eye, she winked at me with happiness. With the sparkling water and cloudless sky in the background, Betsy and Matt exchanged their wedding vows.

The photographer squatted in front of the tiered wedding cake positioned on a festive table in front of tall windows. He carefully aimed his camera and focused on the cake with the waterway, seagulls and sailboats in the background. With a quick snap of the shutter, he captured the scene.

"Let's eat by the water," guests suggested as they spilled out onto the deck and the dock. People were so impressed with the natural beauty of the waterfront they seemed oblivious to the tackiness of our construction zone. They enjoyed themselves as they feasted on fine food and a fine view.

Our wedding-under-construction was a success.

Years later, Betsy and Matt came to visit our renovated home. We reminisced about their wedding and decided to visit Lois at her bustling cake shop. She urged us to stay a few minutes so she could share her favorite story.

"Here is a book I show clients." She opened a bulging black binder. "Your wedding cake, with the cascade of red roses, is right here . . . number 32." Lois pointed at the picture. "This is a popular cake among my customers. They often linger and study the photo.

"They always ask, 'Where is this beautiful waterfront hotel with the tall windows?' And they say, 'Look at the view with the birds and the boats in the background! We want to make a reservation to have our wedding there.'

"I get a chuckle out of it every time," Lois smiled. "But I continue to keep your secret."

Betsy laughed at the irony and shared a thought. "I've come to realize a wedding is something you construct at the beginning of a relationship. A marriage is something you build over time."

Miriam Hill

With a typical wedding cake costing $300, Ed and
Linda opted for the more economical wedding pizza.

Raining Love

I found the music to her favorite song. I wore earrings that belonged to her. I searched out flowers that had grown in her garden to add to my bridal bouquet. Still, something was missing. Nothing could fill the space in my heart reserved for Nana.

During their nearly fifty-year-long marriage, my Nana and Granddad shared an unwavering love. A love ingrained in my own life. A shining love that made me hope to meet someone, someday, with whom to share a love as deep as theirs.

Now, it was really happening: The time had come for me to marry David, the love of my life. But Nana wasn't there to see it. Even the comforting knowledge that she and Granddad were dancing together in heaven couldn't soothe the pain in my heart. I missed her.

The morning of my wedding dawned gray. As I left for the hairdresser, rain drenched everything around me. It continued to rain when I left for the ceremony. Showers gently washed the church windows while we exchanged our vows.

Suddenly, the rain stopped, as we exited the church.

The sun peeked out.

And I felt my grandparents there with me.

Later at the reception, my godfather, Uncle Bob, walked to the podium. "With all this rain, I know the ladies feel like wilted flowers. Your Nana always said that tears were 'liquid love.' So it is my belief that all the rain that has fallen is your grandparents' love showering down. If you can embrace all that love you will have a very happy marriage."

I felt my own tears "falling down," and remembered the old adage, "Blessed is the bride on whose wedding day rain does fall." And I knew now that it was true. I was blessed this day. Blessed with Nana's liquid love.

Kelly Stevens-Hartley

5

WHO GIVETH?

You know what they say: "My son's my son until he gets him a wife, but my daughter's my daughter all of her life."

Stanley Banks in
Father of the Bride (1950)

A Tale of Two Fathers

Our parents divorced when Karen was a toddler, and a few years later we were blessed with the best of a complicated world—a father and a stepfather. The situation wound up a bit confusing later on down the road. Especially when it was time for Karen to get married.

As sometimes happened in those days, long before shared custody and divorce mediation, we didn't maintain much contact with our natural father. It was hoped that our new stepfather would grow to be the apple of our eyes.

Gordon was, in fact, a wonderful man. He accepted us as his children and went on to nurture, counsel and play a major part in the raising of my sister and me. He was the humor in an otherwise dry existence. He was the fun where there often wasn't any. And he was the true keeper of our hearts, with our best interests always at the center of his own.

I maintained ties with my natural father, too, although initially strained. I saw the situation for what it was and did my best to mend all wounds. Gordon supported this whole-heartedly. Karen, being years younger than me, grew up without really knowing our natural father.

When Karen was in high school and I was married, living far away from home, we went through a second divorce. This time, however, I was careful to maintain ties. Gordon remained the father figure he'd always been and even became "Grandpa Gordon" to my firstborn. Karen and Gordon grew apart some, but reestablished ties after graduation.

Gordon eventually remarried. Carol was ideally suited to him and understood the complications of our situation. When they both encouraged Karen to mend her severed ties with Dad, she bravely set about renewing a relationship she barely remembered.

Communication with Dad was, at its best, on the surface. We knew he loved us and he knew we loved him, but the words were seldom spoken aloud. And none of us ever mentioned our relationship with Gordon.

Before Karen announced her engagement, she voiced her concerns. "I want Gordon to give me away when I get married."

"Mm-hmm," I replied.

"But I want Dad to give me away, too. I don't want to hurt either one of them."

I knew Gordon would understand. My father, however, would be a little harder to convince. "Let me see what I can do."

A letter, I decided, felt right. Gordon, of course, was privy to my plan and supported it.

> Dear Dad,
>
> We were children when this all started, and the situation was completely out of our hands. As adults now, we need and want you to be our father. We love you and want you to be a part of our lives.
>
> But Gordon is a part of our lives, too. He has been a

*good man, an honest man, and has done everything a
father would do for his children.*

*Karen is getting married in a few months. It would
mean the world to her, and to me, if you would walk her
down the aisle—together with Gordon.*

*Loving Gordon doesn't mean in any way that we love
you any less. There is plenty of room for two wonderful
fathers in our lives. Gordon always encouraged contact
with you, never spoke a word against you or under-
mined our feelings for you. We respect the fact that you
never voiced negative feelings about Gordon.*

*Give this some thought. Remember both Karen and
I love you and want our family ties to be restored.
Remember that in your absence, we established strong
family ties with Gordon, and it would be unfair to all of
us to expect that to stop.*

*It would be a beautiful sight to watch Karen walking
down the aisle on her wedding day, flanked by two
wonderful fathers. It would be an answer to prayer.*

I love you.

Kim

A couple of weeks later, Karen received a phone call
from Dad.

"So where do I go to get measured for my tux?"

In late August, Karen walked down the aisle with a
handsome father on each side of her. They wore identical
tuxedos with matching smiles and radiated the same
fatherly love and joy.

The blessing to Karen and I was twofold. In addition to
ending years of confusion and estrangement, we learned
to share the joy of being the proud daughters of two
extraordinary fathers.

Kimberly Ripley

The Best One

Blessed indeed is the man who hears many gentle voices call him father!

Lydia M. Child

When I was a little girl, my father had a time-honored tradition of tucking me into bed. Following my bedtime story, he would give me a nose kiss, tickle my stomach and whisper the most wonderful words into my ear.

"Michelle, of all the little girls in the whole wide world . . ." he would pause.

"Yes, Daddy?"

"How did your mommy and I get so lucky to get the best one?"

Before he had time to finish, I would say, "You got me!"

And then he would continue, "The best little girl in the whole wide world, and we got you."

"You got me!" I would scream and clap.

"Yes, you, Michelle, and we're so lucky." He would end with a bear hug and another kiss to my forehead.

Years passed and my father never missed a night, even when I thought he should have. After my basketball team was defeated, he came into my room.

"Michelle, of all the basketball players in the whole wide world," he paused.

"Yes, Daddy?" I stared at the floor.

"How did your mom and I get so lucky to get the best one?"

"You didn't."

"Of course we did, Michelle. We have you."

"But, Dad . . ."

"Yes, you, Michelle, and we're so lucky," he cheered, as he gave me a high five followed by a bear hug and a kiss to my forehead.

I thought becoming a teenager would end the ritual, but it didn't.

"Michelle, of all the teenagers in the whole wide world . . ." he would pause.

"Dad, I'm too old for this," I would sigh.

"How did your mother and I get so lucky to get the best one?"

"C'mon, Dad," I grunted.

"We have you, Michelle, and we're so lucky." Then the embarrassing hug and kiss.

Following college, I became engaged. My father never missed a night to call or leave a message reminding me how special I was to him. I even wondered if he would continue calling after I got married, but he didn't.

The daily calls I had taken for granted all my life ended the day he died from cancer, only weeks before my wedding.

I deeply missed sharing the day with my father. Standing behind the white church doors with my arm in my brother's, I waited for the wedding march to begin. Before we began our descent down the aisle, my brother reached inside his pocket and handed me an ivory napkin embroidered with pink ribbon. Inscribed were the words:

Of all the precious wives in the whole wide world, how did Mark get so lucky to marry the best one? He married you, Michelle, and he is so lucky! I am so proud of you, my little girl.
Love,
Dad

Without a doubt, it was the best wedding gift I received. One I would never forget. My father showered me with his gifts every day of his life. How did I get so lucky?

Michelle Marullo

The Unconditional Step

I didn't just marry their mother. She had two young teenage daughters whom I loved dearly. For several years, I watched them grow from little girls into beautiful young ladies. We got along great, but I worried that things would change once I married their mom.

Having never been married before with no children of my own, I was concerned about taking on the role of "father." I read several articles on the subject—all contradicting one another and leaving me nothing but confused. I don't think I ever made a conscious decision on just "what" to be to the girls. Luckily I didn't have to—they made that decision for me.

Something wonderful happened. Without any encouragement from my wife or myself, the girls began to call me "Dad." Such a simple word, but an unfamiliar one that filled my heart with even more love for these amazing girls. By them reaching out, I realized that they needed a dad in their lives. And so the decision was made—I would be "Dad."

Several years passed and we made it through life with no major catastrophes. My marriage to their mother was a happy one and I was delighted that the girls and I had a strong relationship.

The older of the two, Veneta, was now eighteen and legally old enough to make her own decisions—and a *big* one she made!

On my birthday she presented me with a beautiful frame. This wasn't a picture or a piece of art, but a legal document protected by a beautiful casing. Veneta had given me the most precious gift—she had changed her last name to mine.

She told me that something was missing when she heard her name being called at her high school graduation. "It wasn't my father's name," she explained.

She continued by promising that the next time I was in a room where her name was announced, that it would be mine. "Everyone will know you're my dad."

I know grown men aren't supposed to cry, but I'll admit I did that day. This wasn't the last time she would make me cry.

Veneta graduated college, and along the way fell in love with a great guy who would become her husband.

After months of planning, the big day arrived and I would walk her down the aisle. I couldn't have been more proud of my daughter, who looked radiant.

As the music started, Veneta took my arm. "Are you ready, Dad?" she asked with poise.

I looked at her, trying to smile but feeling like I needed to cry. My quivering lips struggled with a humble, "Yes."

I kissed the top of her head—right through the veil—smiled and walked her proudly down the aisle. The ceremony was perfect.

At the reception, I heard the DJ announce the infamous father-daughter dance. Dancing not being one of my better attributes, I became consumed with nervousness. Scared to death, I put on a brave face, took my daughter's hand and led her to the empty dance floor.

While preparing to relax by taking a deep breath, I noticed someone hand Veneta a microphone and something in a frame. *Another framed gift? Is this déjà vu?* Not knowing what she was up to, Veneta kissed me on the cheek and stepped back. In front of everyone, she began to read a touching poem she wrote about our relationship. She called it "Something Special," and something special it was.

As she continued, I tried to block out everyone around us so I could just listen to her. Tears filled my eyes when I heard her voice quiver:

"Daddy, it is because of you and your love that I have the confidence and courage to stand here today as Mrs. Jeremy Veneta Novakovich Leonard. I hope that as you look upon me at this moment, it is with the same pride and unconditional love that I have always felt for you. As I begin my new life as Jeremy's wife, I hope you will continue to hold my hand 'in your heart,' offer me your guidance and advice, and continue to be my best friend. I will always be your little girl—and in your heart is where I always want to be. I am proud to be your daughter."

Mrs. Veneta Novakovich Leonard—always a Novakovich, I thought.

When my daughter finished, I thought about her promise to me years before. Hearing my name next to her new name took away all my insecurities from the past.

Then she took my hand for our father-daughter dance, and I suddenly realized that my fear of dancing had disappeared. As we swayed to the music with Veneta in my arms, she laid her head on my chest in a childlike manner. I told her I loved her and she simply replied, "I love you, too, Daddy."

Donald R. Novakovich

Bedtime Fears

He has no hope who never had a fear.

William Cowper

When I was a little girl, say four or five years old, there were many things that frightened me: Snakes, bugs, big older boys and *storms*. I remember the dark, rainy nights when a thunderstorm would roll into town and wake me from a sleep, in my childhood room at the front end of the house.

The rain would beat on my window as shadows played games on my bedroom walls. Tree branches screeched against the outside of the house making strange noises. I'd lay there, so afraid, nearly ready to cry. Poking my little foot out from under the covers, I'd slide out of my warm bed and tiptoe quietly into the next room where my mother and daddy slept.

And then, as I had done so many times before, I would crawl over the foot board at the bottom of the bed and make my way over the top of the covers between my mom and dad, looking for a secure place to lay my head between their two pillows.

Dad would roll over and say, "Hey, little girl, what's going on?"

"I'm afraid in my room. It's storming."

Then without another word, the three of us would snuggle close together and go back to sleep. Just my mom and my dad . . . and me.

Morning would come, the sun shining. A new day would begin.

When I was a grown-up girl, not quite twenty years old, there were many things that still frightened me: School, jobs, big older boys and *getting married*. I remember the days leading up to my wedding day. Parties, planning and packing for the honeymoon. Writing thank-you notes. Ironing my veil and cleaning out my closet for the last time. Last-minute lists. The rehearsal dinner.

It was finally here—the night before my wedding day. I went to bed, tired. *Very* tired from all the weeks of preparation.

I lay there, so afraid, nearly ready to cry. Poking my foot out from under the covers, I slid out of my warm bed and tiptoed quietly into the next room where my mother and daddy slept.

And then, as I had done so many times before, I crawled over the foot board at the bottom of the bed and made my way over the top of the covers between my mom and dad, looking for a secure place to lay my head between their two pillows.

Dad rolled over and said, "Hey, little girl, what's going on?"

"I'm afraid in my room. I'm getting married tomorrow."

Then without another word, the three of us snuggled close together and went back to sleep. Just my mom and my dad . . . and me.

Morning came, the sun shining. A new day in my life was beginning.

Charlotte Lanham

Going Home

Marriage is our last, best chance to grow up.

Joseph Barth

"Is everything okay?" Tim asks as we drive through the night's heavy rain.

"I'm fine," I say, staring out my window. "Just tired from the plane ride." The November downpour outside is a harsh contrast to the warm beaches we enjoyed all week on our honeymoon.

"If you want," he begins slowly, "we can probably stay with your mom and dad."

"No, that's okay!" I say quickly, half smiling. I turn to look at our backseat, piled with the wedding gifts we had picked up from my parents' house. The drive to our new apartment to spend the night for the first time is lonely.

"Are you sure you're okay?" Tim asks again.

I look at him carefully and I can picture him in his black tux at our wedding. I see us running hand-in-hand to our car while a row of guests on each side tosses tiny leaves into the air. I pass my parents without looking back.

"I just feel different," I say aloud.

Suddenly, I see my young self. I'm graduating from high school and picking a university 1,500 miles from home, not telling my parents until after making my first tuition payment. A year later, I don't have a dime for my tuition, but somehow manage without a single terrified call home. My junior year, I tell my parents about my boyfriend, Tim—whom I'd already been dating a year and a half.

Reflecting back, it's all clear now.

I wanted to do everything on my own and assumed my parents would accept and support the changes. But my independent spirit told me they would always be waiting when I decided to come back.

"You know," I tell Tim, my throat tightening, "up until a week ago I've always lived with my parents. I could leave home to do what I had to do, and then come back whenever I wanted." The reality of what I'm saying chokes me. "But now I can't go back to live in my house—I have to grow up!"

With surprise, I feel tears spilling down my face. In between sobs, I hear Tim dialing his cell phone.

"Hello, it's Tim. Can I speak to Mrs. Gomez?" A pause. "Hi, Mrs. Gomez. No, we're fine, but I think someone needs to talk to you." He puts the phone by my ear, and before I can think, I whimper, "It's just different, that's all."

Mom already knows.

"Don't cry!" she says, her timid voice unusually strong. "Don't you know I already prayed to God to give me the strength to let you go?" I wipe my eyes as her soothing voice explains, "That's just life, but it's all going to be all right."

She talks to me for a long time, and when I finally say good-bye to her, I'm no longer crying, just sleepy.

Thinking back at that first night in our new apartment, I smile. As I slept next to Tim, surrounded by boxes and empty rooms, I could not possibly know how easily and without notice I would begin to call our new place "home."

I sleep peacefully now, knowing I can leave and come back and everything will be all right, because I am always home.

Liza G. Maakestad

Angie's Wedding Day

A mother laughs our laughter,
Sheds our tears,
Returns our love,
Fears our fears.
She lives our joys,
Cares our cares,
And all our hopes and dreams she shares.

Julia Summers

Dawn is just beginning to show her soft pink face. My bedroom is dark except for a silvery wisp of light stretching a shadow across the floor. I'm awake, have been for a long while, consumed with details and anticipation. Edging quietly from the bed, so as not to disturb my aging mother, who snores contentedly, I tread barefoot on the cold tile of the hall and peek in on my sleeping company.

Aunt Nell and Uncle Mac curl together on the sofa bed, spoon fashion, while their baby granddaughter snuggles deep in Nell's arms. Five children—nieces, nephews and cousins all under the age of ten—are sprawled across the floor. Gently moving an arm here, a leg there, I cover them with warm quilts. Heading back up the hall, I pause to adjust the thermostat to offset the chilly October morning.

I pad down the hall and listen carefully at my daughter's door. My angel, my baby, my little girl. I want to see her in her buttercup-yellow bedroom, surrounded by childhood toys and record albums. I don't want her to grow up, but today she will.

Today is Angie's wedding day.

I grasp the cool doorknob, turn it gently and step quietly into her room where the pre-dawn light gives the room a luminous glow. One dainty foot protrudes from the blanket's edge; the rest of her is shrouded in covers, mummy style. Removing the pillow from over her head, I smile. Dark curls tumble and sooty eyelashes lie gently on her creamy skin. I caress her rosy cheek and nudge an errant lock lying across her eyes as she stirs slightly.

"Wake up, baby," I coo, settling myself down beside her. A slow smile spreads across her face then reaches her chocolate eyes as they flutter and focus on mine.

Angie struggles against twisted bed covers, gives a deep yawn and props herself on fluffy pillows. "Mama," she whispers, "I was dreaming about the time you taught me to dive into that pool in Ft. Lauderdale, the summer I turned seven." We laugh, for her words bring the moment immediately to mind. "Remember, how I kept saying, 'I can't do it'?"

"Yes, but you kept on trying."

"I was so tired, my eyes burned, but I had to get it right."

"Well, Angie, you are my determined little girl."

"Just like you, Mama," she giggled.

"Yes," I smile back, "just like me." We hug each other tightly.

We speak of silly things, tender things, things that

spark memories of the past and ramble through eighteen years of her life. Despite my wish to hold it back, the morning sneaks in to light her room . . . and all that's in it: Small posters with "This is my mess" and "A teen lives here" printed in her schoolgirl hand; a Dothan High victory banner waving from across the room; her doll collection dancing across the headboard; ridiculous hats and teen magazines; visible proof of her happy childhood; snapshot souvenirs within my heart.

Watching me eye the remnants of her youth, Angie sighs. "I should've packed this junk away by now, you know. But it just doesn't seem to belong anywhere else. I'm afraid my kid stuff will be out of place in our new apartment."

I hear the tears in her voice and can't help hugging her closer.

"Do I have to move them right away?" A sob catches her words; I know she is crying.

"Of course not," I say, determined to soothe her worry. "You don't have to move anything until you're ready."

She turns, takes my face in her small hands, and looks me straight in the eyes, "I love you, Mama, and I'm sure gonna miss you. But please, let's not change my room for a little while, okay? I need to know that sometimes, if I want to, I can be your little girl again." Angie's voice cracks and she leans her head on my trembling shoulders.

"Angie, you can leave your things here as long as you want, but you don't need to look at things to know you will always be my little girl."

We talk some, cry some, hug some—then laugh at our silliness. And before we know it, we start crying all over again. Long before either of us is ready, the rest of the household stirs and we know our private time is ending.

As I leave her room, I realize I'm not losing my little girl. She is changing and will continue to do so for the rest of her life. But—woman or child—she will always be mine, and our relationship will only grow.

As for today, I'm kind of hopeful she'll need me—at least as much as I need her.

Judith Givens

"Please excuse my mother, Reverend.
She always was a bit possessive!"

Reprinted by permission of Dan Rosandich.

The Music Played On

Youth fades; love droops, the leaves of friendship fall;
A mother's secret hope outlives them all.

Oliver Wendell Holmes

I stood on the sidelines and watched, unable and unwilling to take my eyes off him. He held her close and they danced under the moonlight to the rhythm of the song. The chill of the night wind brushed my hair while something damp ran down my cheeks. The cool breath of another breeze told me I was feeling my own tears. Were they sad tears or happy tears? I wasn't sure. My heart stirred with a mixture of emotion.

Why can't I let him go? I wondered.

I remembered the first time I held him. Our love was indescribable. Binding and strong. Each passing year gave me events to remember as well as memories to cherish. But now I had to stand back and simply watch their love in action. And there was absolutely nothing I could do, even if I wanted to.

And the music played on.

I knew Chad so well, I could read his heart. He pulled her closely to him and smiled as she gazed into his eyes. Their devotion was obvious. Their affection was radiant. Their love exploded like fireworks. The stars twinkled above and I marveled that several didn't sprinkle down on the couple.

Yet when he looked my way, I still melted. Our eyes met and a narrow smile crossed his face. My heart pounded, for I knew my life was about to undergo a drastic change.

How will I handle these emotions?

Chad was happy and his happiness meant everything to me. And, after all, wasn't that what I had wanted for him all these years? I wanted to cry and shout for joy, all at the same time.

And the music played on.

Quietly, I continued to watch while reliving recent events: the excitement, the plans and the preparations for their big day. And now, tonight, this final party before their sacred vows would be recited. The evening was drawing to a close. The music stilled, and I saw him kiss her cheek. When, hand-in-hand they walked my way, I quickly brushed away my tears before he saw the dampness on my cheeks. I wouldn't let him think I was sad.

They stood before me, Chad with his beautiful Lucy smiling beside him.

"I love you, Mama," he whispered.

"I love you too, son," I replied. "I love both of you."

At that moment it dawned on me that twenty-seven years earlier I had given birth to a little boy who, now an adoring man, had swept a lovely young lady off of her feet. They were so happy . . . too joyful for me to be sad.

And the music played on.

"You're pretty," I overheard Chad whisper to Lucy, as they walked away.

My heart smiled as I watched them gaze deeply into

each other's eyes and I was filled with abundant hope and joy. I prayed that—for the two of them—the symphony of love would continue a lifetime. A simple wish, really.

That the music plays on.

Nancy B. Gibbs

This Is Our Dance

Nobody cares if you can't dance well. Just get up and dance. Great dancers are not great because of their technique; they are great because of their passion.

Martha Graham

Jason and I were dancing before dating. During his first two years in college, Jason took dance courses and always kept an eye for partners to join him at local dances. We'd been friends for a year when he first asked me. I was thrilled, but nervous at the same time.

Jason first learned to dance as a young child at the polkas thrown by his German relatives. I'd missed out. My parents danced only when they were young, never passing down any styles or moves to their children. I'd seen Dad boogie to some rock 'n' roll music, singing along and clapping his hands. He had fun, but rarely could find the beat. Thanks to a few lessons in grade school, I at least had some practice. My knowledge was limited, but my interest was definitely high.

I took Jason up on that first offer and we spent the

evening swinging, waltzing and foxtrotting. I learned how to follow and pay attention to Jason's slight body movements to predict upcoming steps. With his arm firmly hugging the middle of my back, pulling me close to him, I relaxed, letting him lead me across the floor. My gaze locked on his bright-green eyes, softly squinted from his broad smile.

I couldn't resist those eyes, or the evenings we spent on the dance floors. Soon we agreed to date. Looking back, I think we already had been for months. The close contact, communication through movement and long evening talks allowed us to reach a new level of understanding and desire to be together.

We joined a college Newman Center church and soon found our true passion—swing dancing. Four times a school year the Newman Center held dances. In the tiny cafeteria, dozens of young people kicked up their heels to vibrant polkas, smooth two-steps and the wild melodies of modern swing bands. Energetic young men sent their ladies flipping, sliding and spinning with ease. We couldn't resist. There we learned to push aside proper rules and have fun, the way swing was intended.

Over the next two years we tried our moves at dozens of dances. Our friends and parents cheered proudly as we won a trophy in a talent contest.

"That was amazing!" Dad said, beaming and leaning closer to take a peek at the trophy. "I had no idea you could do all that. Congratulations!"

A few months after the talent show, Jason proposed. We had become a complete team, on and off the dance floor. Of course I answered with a joyous "Yes!"

We immediately chose the Newman Center to be married in, but were pretty flexible about everything else—except for the first dance. Jason and I wanted to share our love for dancing with our closest friends and family, so we found a hall with an excellent dance floor and hired one of the best six-piece jazz bands in town. My aunt even tailored my dress to my dancing needs, a slender skirt hemmed a few inches from the floor. I could do nearly everything—but a flip—without worry.

Following a romantic ceremony and dreamy horse and buggy ride to the reception hall, we enjoyed dinner until—finally—it was time. During "When You Say Nothing at All," Jason held me tight for our first dance. We couldn't stop beaming and it was over too soon.

I had eagerly anticipated the father-daughter dance as well. Dad and I rocked slowly to the music of "You Are So Beautiful." The smile never left his face and I held back tears as he kissed me on the cheek.

As I walked back to Jason glowing with love and excitement, I noticed he looked a little nervous and was trying to catch Dad's attention.

"I'll be right back," he said hastily and wove his way through the crowd.

Several friends called for me and I soon lost sight of Jason in a flurry of hugs, photos and shared college remembrances. My sister Nikki and I were posing for another photo when the band broke into a lively swing.

"Gotta run," I said, smiling at her and turning around to find my groom.

I nearly ran into Dad instead.

"This is our dance," he said.

On the dance floor, Dad smiled and took both of my hands in his as I stood motionless, eyes wide with wonder. He paused, ears and feet searching for the rhythm, then looked down at me with a twinkle in his eye and took a bouncy step with his right foot. We were swing dancing!

His steps were nervous at first, but accurate. They were slightly offbeat, yet filled with energy and love. I giggled out loud when he showed some moves, including a twirl.

The floor cleared, with just the two of us laughing, smiling and dancing.

As the song ended, Dad looked at me with pride and love. I hugged him tightly, still a little shaky and stunned.

"When? How?" I stuttered.

Dad pointed across the room to Nikki and Jason. "I asked them to give me secret lessons. I wanted to surprise you with a dance at your wedding. Sorry, I'm not very good."

"It was perfect," I said, trembling and hugging him. "Absolutely perfect."

Amanda Parise-Peterson

The Unlikely Best Man

*Age does not protect you from love. But love, to
some extent, protects you from age.*

Jeanne Moreau

Day after day, I saw life at its loneliest—elderly men
and women wasting away to nothing with no one to visit
them. I was interning at a public healthcare facility, and
the loneliness I witnessed was sad.

Then I met Sophia.

Despite her deteriorating physical condition, Sophia
was an assertive little lady who proved to the entire nursing facility she was still full of vitality, humor and—most
importantly—romance. She would often weave tales to
the staff and fellow patients of her Romeo-and-Juliet-
esque relationship with her husband Carl.

One of her favorites was the story of two hearts.

As young Depression-era lovers, Carl and Sophia were
in love, yet extremely poor. But Carl didn't let that shake
their love. On bended knee one Valentine's Day, he asked
Sophia to marry him. Unable to afford an engagement
ring, he presented her with a small brooch with two
rhinestone-covered hearts.

"A woman needs two hearts," Carl said. "One to love, care and live with; the other for the man of her dreams to steal."

They had been married thirty years when Carl died of a heart attack. On his deathbed, he gave her his last wish.

"Sophia, you deserve to be taken care of. I want you to move on and find yourself another husband."

Shaking her head in denial, Sophia cried until she couldn't speak. Carl grasped her hand.

"Don't worry. I'll be watching you from above. I'll send someone to take care of you." A few minutes later, he passed away.

Sophia's eyes brimmed with tears each time she repeated his last words. I'm not sure what pained her more—Carl's short life or that, after all these years, no one was sent to take his place in her lonely heart.

Then a new resident was admitted to the nursing home.

Like Sophia, John lost his spouse unexpectedly. The two clicked immediately and were often seen dining and visiting each other's floors. They were like two love-bitten teenagers, holding hands in the television lounge or headed out "on pass" for a date in the city.

Now, Sophia's eyes sparkled with refound youth. And the health of both drastically improved.

Sophia's ninetieth birthday was celebrated by all the residents at the facility with a special dinner cooked by the staff. When John was asked to give a speech, the twinkle in his eyes hinted he had something up his sleeve. Before Sophia could comprehend what was happening, he handed her a small jewelry box.

"Sophia, will you marry me?"

An emotional silence filled the room as she opened the box with shaky hands. Her mouth dropped and tears streamed when she revealed a ring with two heart-shaped diamonds.

"Every woman should have two hearts," John declared. "One is for me, and one is for Carl."

The couple married a month later. The nursing home chapel brimmed with staff, patients and local news crews elbowing each other to cover this sweet "December" romance. Gowned in scrubs, nurses served as bridesmaids. Sophia's daughter gave her away. And perched on a pedestal next to John was a large portrait.

A picture of Carl.

"The best man is supposed to give the couple his blessing," John said. "Carl gave his when he sent me to her."

Jenn Dlugos

Given Away

I cannot think of any need in childhood as strong as the need for a father's protection.

Sigmund Freud

There really is no use denying it. I've been given away. Sure I could attempt to hide it, make excuses for it, or just plain lie, but what's the use? The truth is, I am what is traditionally referred to as a "Daddy's girl."

Now, I know women today are supposed to be fiercely independent. We don't need validation from a man and are certainly more than capable of taking care of ourselves. We are supposed to be in complete charge of our own lives. And, although I might try to keep up a good feminist front, to be perfectly honest, my father has always been there to help take care of the major problems in my life.

As a child, I was a little shadow trailing behind the tall figure my father cast. I remained close to my father and even lived at home while I attended college. So when Mark and I discussed marriage, I must confess to being a little worried about my father's reaction. I knew losing the little girl he had so carefully protected all these years was not going to be easy for him.

I, too, was apprehensive. I loved my boyfriend, of course, but I found the idea of losing the most dependable person in my life a little bit unsettling. Getting married required me to leave his protective wing and face day-to-day life with Mark—with whose track record I was unfamiliar.

After our engagement was announced, long weeks of wedding plans followed. During this time, my father remained conspicuously quiet. Not that he was ever in the habit of discussing his feelings at great length. And anyway, it was a noisy, busy time with little opportunity to dwell on emotions.

When the wedding day finally came, I was in a state of panic. Until then, marriage was only theoretical—full of hopeful what-if and could-be scenarios. Now marriage was in the present and it was real.

What was I doing? Did I know how to be married? What if I was making a mistake? What if I couldn't handle all the things that marriage and married life threw at me? And how could I get through it all without my father to smooth out the edges?

Would my husband accept my attachment to my father? Would my father accept my attachment to my husband? Would there be rivalry between the two men in my life?

As we stood at the entrance to the church, I knew an entirely different life waited inside. I took deep breaths to calm my nerves. The Wedding March came on cue, infinitely appropriate. I was a soldier reporting for duty and the army had no idea I was too young and inexperienced to handle the battle.

I leaned over and whispered, "Dad, I'm scared."

He gently took my arm and escorted me into the church. We slowly walked the aisle together and he gave me away.

And it felt perfectly natural. My father had been there for all the major moments in my life, quietly guiding and leading me, knowing instinctively when to pull or when to push. His constant but gentle nudging had gotten me through every meaningful transition in my life.

At the reception, Mark and I made the rounds, greeting and thanking everyone in a whirlwind of smiles and hugs. When we started to drive away toward our new life, I realized I had forgotten something.

I turned to Mark. "I didn't get to say good-bye to Daddy."

My new husband instantly pushed on the brakes, turned off the car and got out. He yelled into the crowd and, after a few moments, my father stepped out from among the guests with a puzzled look on his face.

Mark opened the door so I could jump out and give Daddy a good-bye hug. At that moment I felt I had really been "given away." I realized my father had given me to my husband and, in turn, my husband had given my father back to me.

This, then, was the purpose of all those years of leading, nudging, pushing and pulling—to make me an adult who uses her heart generously. Who loves big and who loves in all directions. I finally understood what it meant to be truly given—to be loved yet never held back.

Renata Waldrop

6

FOR BETTER OR FOR WORSE

What greater thing is there for two human souls than to feel that they are joined for life—to strengthen each other in all labor, to rest on each other in all sorrow, to minister to each other in all pain, to be one with each other in silent unspeakable memories at the moment of the last parting.

George Eliot

"I hope this is a typo; it says
the reception is Open Bra."

That's Entertainment!

You give but little when you give of your posses-
sions. It is when you give of yourself that you
truly give.

Kahlil Gibran

I always loved December. Mystical December with its
mysterious gray skies, its magical lights, its air of anticipation. What a perfect month to celebrate a marriage.

Maybe that's why I wasn't disappointed when a winter
snow softened the scenery on our wedding day. Although
we originally planned for a horse-drawn carriage to transport us to our reception, neither of us objected to a limo
ride instead. Those floating flakes of fantasy were definitely worth the trade.

The same snow that dusted our wedding path was
falling heavier on the highways, but we were oblivious to
those concerns. After all, everyone we cared about—
friends, family and even the students from both of the
classes that we taught—had already arrived. So this winter wonderland only heightened the excitement of our
day. Besides, thoughts of nesting in a cozy Vermont

honeymoon cabin with smoke curling from its chimney warmed our minds.

Soft snow swirled around the crowd of well-wishers who encircled us as we left the church in the stretch limo. Perfect, just perfect. *Everything is magic,* I thought. *Now, for the perfect reception.*

But it was there, at the reception, that I noticed peculiar things beginning to happen.

It all started when I heard my aunt warming up her vocal cords in the bathroom while she clutched a half-empty glass of scotch. She smiled warmly as she patted my cheek.

"Lucky for us, dear, that I have talent . . . considering the circumstances." She coolly patted my cheeks and sailed out the door. Speechless and confused, I stared after her as she breezed by me, scotch in hand.

What did she mean, "Lucky for us?" What circumstances was she referring to? And, even more importantly, *what* talent?

Then the receptionist from my mom's office tested the microphone on stage—by belting out a few chords. And she was gamely singing . . . "Joy to the World"? That was a real stretch, considering she was Jewish.

Next, my aunt—obviously feeling quite confident at this point—commandeered the mike to regale everyone with Frank Sinatra hits (the only tunes she knew). And she eagerly shared them all, song after song after song, with *my* wedding guests.

I glanced at her two daughters. Their hands held their heads and they wore looks that said—more eloquently than any words could—they wished the performance would mercifully end. My dad watched helplessly, his own face slightly drawn.

As the events unfolded, I heard my mother-in-law whisper to my father-in-law. She requested another drink.

And, when he headed to the bar, she added, "Eddie, hold the ice." She settled down to watch the show.

Meanwhile, Grandpa—beginning to get into the spirit of things—headed to the stage to teach everyone an Irish jig. Mom intervened just before it got worse, and enlisted the aid of my two brothers, who descended upon him. Flanking him on either side—not unlike bodyguards trying to control an unruly patron at the local bar—they discreetly led him back to his table.

After witnessing what appeared to be the onset of a karaoke free-for-all among my friends and family, it occurred to me: *The band! Where is our band?*

They were M.I.A.

En route to our reception, the Irish band we'd engaged had gotten stuck in the snow.

Still, the reception went on. Certainly not as I planned. But it was even better. The brave people in our lives created unforgettable memories when they stepped up to sing their hearts out for us on our wedding day.

Oh, yes, the Irish band did finally show up—a bit harried, but quite amused by the impromptu entertainment. In fact, everyone did a collaborative and uniquely spontaneous rendition of "My Way" before the band took the reins.

And we all raised our glasses to the gift of the unexpected—to laughter, to song.

Maryellen Heller

Reprinted by permission of Bill Canty.

Of Blue Jeans and Buttons

Love cures people—both the ones who give it and the ones who receive it.

Dr. Karl Menninger

I'm a jeans and T-shirts kind of girl. Always have been. Born and raised in a small town back East, I loved riding four-wheelers and snowmobiles and hiking in the woods. Other than special occasions like school pictures or a wedding, you'd rarely find me in a dress. It just wasn't my thing.

But, like most girls, I dreamed of a fairy-tale wedding with my future husband and wearing that long white dress down the church aisle. Now I was about to live it.

I was engaged to an incredible man who truly showed me a Cinderella life. I went from fast food and macaroni-and-cheese dinners to dining in five-star restaurants. I grew accustomed to fine wines and having my chair pulled out for me. Ward made me feel like a princess.

But there was another reason I wanted to be that princess for him on our wedding day. Ward and I chose to remain pure until our wedding night. Both in our late thirties, this was quite a testimony to many of our friends.

With the wedding approaching, I was hesitant to go dress shopping, as I knew I would feel out of place in the bridal shops with all the fancy silk and lace. *Will they laugh at me? Will I look awkward?*

My fear fell aside when I stepped into the first dress. Lined with pearls and satin, it fit just right. I looked into the mirror and couldn't believe how wonderful and special I felt. *Why, I'm beautiful!* I envisioned our wedding and couldn't wait to walk down the aisle to Ward. I couldn't wait to show him I was his princess.

Indeed, our wedding day turned out to be a fairy tale. After the beautiful ceremony, we held our reception at a harbor where we ventured down the boardwalk with the photographer for black and white shots on the Ferris Wheel.

It was a whirlwind day. Deliriously exhausted, Ward and I said goodbye to our friends and family for a sunset cruise along the coastline. As we sat in the limo on the way to our bed and breakfast, we anxiously awaited our wedding night.

But there were other plans in store for us.

Soon, the excitement of the day's events came to a screeching halt. Reality bit hard. Sudden nausea overtook me; my chest felt tight and I was having trouble breathing.

"I'm carsick! No! This can't be happening!" I cried.

In the midst of everything, I forgot that I shouldn't ride backward in a car—and now it was too late. I felt awful. My husband suggested I put my head between my legs. I leaned down, folded in half like a chair. The weight of a long bridal train crammed my head and squeezed my bodice even tighter.

"I can't breathe. I think I'm going to be sick! Ward, please unzip my dress!" This was not how I envisioned our first night together. He graciously unzipped my dress, but it didn't help.

"You're going to have to undo my bra, too." My head,

veil and all, was hanging out the car window.

"Shall I pull over?" the driver politely offered.

"No! Just get to the hotel . . . quickly."

When we arrived, the limo driver opened the door to . . . me, dress practically hanging off.

After Ward graciously placed his jacket over my shoulders, I grabbed his hand to attempt to exit the limo. Suddenly everything went white and my legs gave out. Holding my dress with one hand, I clung to Ward's neck with the other while he literally dragged me through the lobby. Pin drops could be heard as hotel guests stopped what they were doing to witness the "passed-out bride."

Sprawled on the bed in our room, I still felt nauseous.

"Could you please get me some Mylanta?" I asked Ward. "I'm so sorry."

"No worries," he said. "I'll be right back."

I soon fell asleep and awoke feeling better. With Ward not back, I looked down to assess my condition. I still wanted this night to be romantic. Determinedly, I decided to put my dress back on.

It had taken three bridesmaids to get the back buttoned earlier that day. *How can I do this alone?* Realizing the dress was not going back on, I slipped it off and put on Ward's tuxedo jacket. I positioned myself on the bed in a sexy pose, waiting for his return.

And promptly fell asleep.

When I awoke, Ward was sitting on the bed next to me, Mylanta in hand. I sat up and downed a mouthful. Lying across his lap, I began to cry. He held me, comforted me.

"I'm so sorry. I wanted to be beautiful for you." Tears rolled down my face as I told him how much I wanted our first night together to be special.

As we sat talking, I glanced up and saw myself in the mirror. There I was—in a wrinkled tuxedo jacket, veil cock-eyed, hair a mess and black mascara smearing my face.

All the while, picking bobby pins out of my hair, Ward was telling me how I was his beautiful princess.

Maria Nickless

House to Home

Snowflakes are one of nature's most fragile things, but just look at what they can do when they stick together.

Fay Seevers

"Mike, you need to leave work right now. I can see your house on the news and it's on fire." My friend's voice on the other line was filled with concern.

This cannot be happening to us. This is not happening to us, I thought. I was getting married in four days and the reception would take place in the backyard of our home.

I had met Lorena three years earlier and immediately developed a wonderful friendship. I soon knew my best friend was going to be my wife. A couple of years passed and after purchasing a home together, the conversation of getting married came up in passing.

"We should just do it," I impulsively suggested. Lucky for me, she agreed. With money tight, we planned a simple courthouse ceremony and a nice reception at our house. Little did we know our life plan would be turned upside down.

The wildfire started on a nearby hillside. Although we heard different updates, the final outcome was not good. "Your house got hit pretty bad," a friend informed me. I headed home from work as fast as I could.

My fiancée and I drove up at the same time and we couldn't believe our eyes. *Why are all these people here? And the news media?* I thought. *The house doesn't look that bad.* The tall trees in the front yard hid our view.

The short walk past the people and media was the longest of my life. Despite the chaos surrounding me, my world fell silent. There, barely standing, was our only possession—our future. The one thing we owned as a couple, the one thing that held our belongings and sheltered our lives. Totally destroyed.

We hesitantly approached what was now walls and mortar and looked in the window to our bedroom. The entire roof had collapsed on our bed; embers and charcoal engulfed every surface; water-drenched belongings still dripped. Lorena's eyes filled with tears. *Why did this happen?* I thought. *We have no money and no house.* I was numb.

Bewildered, Lorena and I rummaged through the house. Suddenly, all I could think about was the wedding. Would Lorena still want to marry me? What if she wanted to postpone it or maybe even call it off? It dawned on me that, with time, the fire would be a mere memory. But if we didn't get married, it would affect the rest of our lives. We'd lost our home; I didn't want to lose Lorena, too.

A reporter began interviewing me. I told him about our upcoming nuptials and admitted my apprehension of Lorena's unwillingness to go through with it.

Little did I know the same reporter approached my fiancée and told her I had mentioned we were getting married on Friday. Moved, she looked at the grinning reporter, smiled and started crying in relief. In the midst of our crumbling world, we each thought the same thing—

we didn't want to postpone our marriage.

As the day's mayhem settled, we were left alone to search our soaked, burned, broken belongings, looking for anything salvageable—including our wedding rings. By 3:00 A.M., hungry and heartbroken and with no rings in sight, we clung to a few salvaged photographs as if they were gold.

The days to follow were surreal.

We were bombarded by an outpouring of donations, support and kind wishes. Neighbors and strangers alike brought gifts, money, food and knickknacks. A local television station organized an on-air donation fund.

Having always worked hard for what we had, it was difficult to accept money and gifts from strangers. But with everything gone, Lorena and I knew we had to set aside our pride and let others help. The simple act of a pizza delivery woman giving us a blanket from her car filled our hearts.

And then the irony hit. In spite of our losses, we realized how lucky we were. Our newfound perspective left us thankful for community support and grateful to be alive and together.

The wedding was scheduled for Friday. Although the media asked to attend, we wanted this special moment alone. My mom and the priest were the only people present. Having no idea of the week's events, the priest commented that we seemed happy. After explaining why we were so emotional, he cried along with us.

We *were* happy. Happy for a new beginning and happy to move forward without looking back.

The day before the wedding, I received a call from the owner of a local café. George offered to host our reception at his restaurant after the wedding. Although it seemed a bit much, we accepted his offer to invite our closest friends and family for a small get-together.

Once again, I was shocked and overwhelmed to see the crowd that awaited us. Outside the restaurant we found reporters, news anchors, firefighters, Chamber of Commerce representatives—well-wishers wanting to congratulate us.

As reporters approached me, I thought, *The real heroes are the firefighters. The real heroes are the community.* I encouraged them to interview those who stepped up to the plate during a disastrous and wrenching time—the people who put their hearts first to help out a couple of strangers.

Inside the restaurant, we were overwhelmed with love and cheers from friends and family. We discovered generous donations: a keyboardist, a wedding cake, a honeymoon train trip to Arizona and a limousine ride to a night's stay at a local Hyatt.

Just when we thought it couldn't get any better, a stranger who noticed our party approached us. "Will you please accept this for your wife?" she asked. "It belonged to my grandmother." The sweet woman slid a beautiful ring on Lorena's finger and the three of us tearfully embraced.

Now we see our tragedy as a blessing in disguise. God intervened during a difficult time and gave us a fresh start. Not only are we more stable financially, but we've been blessed with a closer, stronger relationship.

Next, we plan to rebuild our house. After all, how could we leave a place filled with people who loved and supported us? More than ever, we look forward to the day that our house is our *home* again.

Mike Zeballos

Princess Bride

Brooke was our little princess. She was spoiled not only by me but by her father and four older brothers as well. She was beautiful and intelligent, but also compassionate and loving. She never put herself first; she lived to make others happy. She made our souls sing.

Brooke met Dan in her junior year of college. I loved her phone calls even more now. Her laughter and giggles when she talked about Dan made my heart smile.

But when he graduated, Dan took a position two states away with an esteemed accounting firm. Over the next year Dan and Brooke kept in constant contact. I could tell my daughter was in love so I prayed nightly their hearts would remain strong and true, and would someday be united as one.

Brooke graduated with honors and applied for several jobs near Dan's home. It didn't take her long to be offered one. Now they were not only close in heart, but also close in proximity as they shared day-to-day life. Two years passed before I got the phone call I dreamed of and prayed for.

My princess was getting married!

They set a date for the following summer. Since it was

already January, we had a year and a half to prepare for this joyous occasion. Brooke and I began planning a fairy-tale wedding—the only kind fit for a princess.

But on December 2, the fairy-tale world came crashing down. A simple yearly exam revealed horrifying news: Brooke had breast cancer and it was already quite advanced. We cried for hours.

Why was this happening? Why Brooke? Why my baby? Why not me? I just didn't understand. I was terrified, confused and angry all at the same time. But I soon brushed all my emotions aside to put Brooke first.

I assured her we would beat this thing and life would go on as planned. She would grow old with Dan and the children they would one day have. I knew my princess would be okay. She had to. She was my baby and I would not say good-bye to her. After all, this wasn't the way things were supposed to happen.

But the doctors were honest from the beginning. They only gave Brooke a 20 percent chance of survival. Because of her cancer's advanced stage, a regimen of drugs and chemotherapy began immediately.

After only a month or so of treatment, the disease spread and my daughter got weaker. We knew Brooke had only a short time left. My heart was broken and beaten.

Throughout, Dan remained strong. He was there for Brooke every step of the way. She had lost all of her hair, dropped so much weight she couldn't even sit without help and could stay awake no longer than ten to twenty minutes at a time. Yet Dan was there to love and support her.

One day, Dan asked for our blessing to marry Brooke before she passed away. He had loved her so long and only wanted one thing in his life: Brooke as his wife. Even if her days left on Earth were uncertain, he wanted them to be spent as a married couple.

We knew she still dreamed of the fairy-tale wedding she would now never have. But we also knew she would not want Dan to marry her when they both knew she was dying. So, we decided the wedding would be a surprise. With help and cooperation from the hospital staff, Dan secretly arranged a lovely ceremony.

When Brooke first realized what was happening, she strongly objected. But Dan explained the most important thing in his life was *her*. And all he wanted was her as his wife—be it for fifty years or for only a day. Brooke sobbed, but agreed. It was her dream, too.

Dan brought a simple but beautiful white gown, delicate lace scarf and sheer veil to her hospital room. The nurses and I dressed the fragile bride, using the scarf to cover her smooth head and draping the veil gently over it. Even pale and broken, my princess daughter shined. This was her day, the day she had dreamed of and planned for.

There was no elegant church as we'd once imagined. None of her family and friends were in attendance as we'd once hoped. But her beloved Dan was there, they were getting married and that was what mattered most. The two exchanged vows and a touching, sweet wedding kiss. It may not have been the fairy tale, but it was still a dream come true.

Brooke spent sixteen days as the wife of the man she adored and loved. And it wasn't until after she passed away that I found a letter tucked into her hospital nightstand.

In it, Brooke wrote that she had only ever wanted to love, be loved and to matter to others. She expressed her gratitude for wonderful brothers and loving parents. The day Dan married her, she said, all her dreams came true. She had truly lived her life's dream. Brooke felt her life was complete; she was neither afraid nor disappointed. And, compassionate to the end, she wished only that none of us had to suffer her loss.

Today, we often see Dan and we love him as our son and Brooke's husband. After all, he made our daughter a princess when she most deserved to be.

Veneta Leonard

Te Amo, Te Quiero, Cariña

Love is composed of a single soul inhabiting two bodies.

Aristotle

They met in the dawn of their childhood.
As kids they would play man and wife.
And they knew even then, before they were ten,
They'd share the rest of their lives.

They played in her tea-castle garden,
'Neath the shade of an old tamarind tree.
In his poor Key West clothes, he gave her a rose
And whispered these words tenderly:

"Te amo, te quiero, cariña"
He said as he whispered her name.
"I love you, I want you my precious one."
These words set her heart all aflame.
And they danced 'neath the stars to the sound of guitars,
"Te amo, te quiero, cariña"

In the noon of their lives they courted,
No longer young children at play.
And they spoke not a word, only heartbeats were heard,
As they kneeled to worship and pray.
They married in an old Spanish churchyard,
'Neath the shade of an old tamarind tree.
In his best Key West clothes, he gave her a rose
And whispered these words tenderly:

"Te amo, te quiero, cariña"
He said as he whispered her name.
"I love you, I want you my precious one."
These words set her heart all aflame.
And they danced 'neath the stars to the sound of guitars,
"Te amo, te quiero, cariña"

In the twilight of life she goes walking,
To where their song was first sung.
And she sees his sweet face in memory's fond place,
In a time when they were both young.
Now he sleeps in an old Spanish churchyard,
'Neath the shade of an old tamarind tree.
In her old woman's clothes she brings him a rose
And whispers these words tenderly:

"Te amo, te quiero, cariño"
She says as she whispers his name.
"I love you, I want you my precious one."
These words set her heart all aflame.
She can't hold back the tears after all of these years,
"Te amo, te quiero, cariña"

Patrick Mendoza

In the End

To love and win is the best thing. To love and lose, the next best.

William M. Thackeray

After struggling for twenty-two years to make an unhealthy marriage work, I walked out and, without any intentions of doing so, walked right into another relationship. That relationship, through twists of fate, lasted only one year. But it was a year I will never forget. It changed the direction of my life and taught me what a healthy, mature union was really like and that they do exist.

On May 1, 1996, I left my first husband and a marriage that had been "existing" for far too long. I met Chuck only four weeks later and soon after, we started dating. I quickly learned the difference between being with a man who wanted to remain a child and being with a man who was young at heart. There was maturity, a strong sense of self, a love for life and communication. Very important communication. Something lacking from my past.

A whirlwind courtship began. A finding and coming together of two soul mates and hearts. Healing started to take place within me.

He was someone strong enough to handle my residual anger and resentment. His love, caring and sense of humor would help me through my healing times—and through his limited time here on Earth.

You see, after we decided to get married, we learned Chuck had a brain tumor. He was slowly becoming paralyzed on his right side. Fortunately, Chuck was left-handed.

We planned our wedding day; we planned a battle with cancer. It was the happiest time of my life; it was the saddest time of my life. I had finally met someone who opened my heart, someone I wanted to spend the rest of my life with . . . someone for me to love only a precious, short time.

Chuck's sense of humor gave me strength to face each day. As his paralysis worsened, he would lose his balance and fall. There were times I returned from work to find him face down on the floor. So we developed a code. If he was in bed, he was "sunny side up" and if he was on the floor, he was "over easy."

When I came home, he would always call out, "Hi, beautiful!"

"Hi, handsome," was my usual response.

The day of our wedding, April 26, 1997, was a spectacular spring day. The sun was shining. The sky was the bluest it could possibly be with white puffy clouds. The air was warm with a slight breeze.

By now, Chuck was in a wheelchair. When we said our vows, he struggled to stand by my side. To dance our wedding song, "Every Time I Close My Eyes," I sat on his lap while his best man pushed us around on the dance floor.

The first night together as husband and wife, our feelings for each other were stronger than ever, but physically, Chuck was weak. I lay on top of him so he could hold me with his left arm. We fell asleep embraced.

The following week, we watched the video friends took of our wedding and reception. We looked at photos friends felt compelled to get to us as quickly as possible. Chuck turned to me and told me what a great time he had and how happy he was.

Exactly one week after our wedding, we awoke to a Saturday the exact opposite of the week before. Cold drenching rain fell on a dreary day. We watched old John Wayne movies (Chuck's favorite), and just enjoyed our time together.

That night, while I was preparing a special one-week anniversary meal, Chuck fell and was having difficulty breathing. By 10:30 P.M., the paramedics were trying to resuscitate him.

But I knew he was gone. I knew his essence was already in a peaceful place. All that was left was the shell he had lived within.

"Life is so unfair," friends and family said as they comforted me.

But I believe otherwise. Life would have been unfair had we not met. Life would have been unfair if our lives and hearts had not touched. Life would have been unfair if Chuck had no one at the end to be loved by . . . and to love.

Life is very fair.

Barbara M. Johnson

A Second Chance at Remembering

"I think patience is what love is," he said, "because how could you love somebody without it?"

Jane Howard

The day we married, January 14, 1984, dawned crisp and beautiful. A florist delivered long-stemmed roses with a card from Tom.

"I can't wait to see you at the end of the aisle."

I knew when I read those words that Tom would love me forever. What I didn't know was he would soon forget having written them.

Our wedding was huge and joyful. Pretty much everyone we knew helped us celebrate. We danced until we got kicked out of the reception hall.

After our honeymoon, Tom and I settled into a new townhouse. I was only twenty-three and Tom was twenty-five, so it was exciting to be on our own. We put away gifts, invited our folks for dinner and settled to begin our new life together.

Twenty-two days after our wedding, we were heading home from the mall. It had snowed and the road was a little icy, but otherwise it was a bright February Sunday. When the car in front of me hit the brakes, I tapped mine, too. The next thing I remember was waking up in the emergency room with a nurse asking if I knew my name and where I was.

Our car had skidded onto the wrong side of the road, where another car hit the passenger side head-on. I had minor cuts and bruises, but Tom was flung seventy-five feet from the car. Although he was declared dead on arrival, the emergency-room doctors restarted his heart.

I was stunned when I saw him. His face was covered with bruises, and his broken jaw hung sagged to his chest. He was on a respirator and hooked to monitors, with tubes everywhere.

He lingered in a deep coma for an unbelievably scary two weeks. Overwhelmed, I couldn't digest what the doctors said.

"As each day goes by, it's less likely Tom will ever open his eyes."

"If Tom wakes up, he's unlikely to be the same man he was."

"Tom could end up with the mental capacity of a child."

"You may have to institutionalize your husband."

My mom wrapped her arms around me, coaxing me to focus on the here and now: Tom was alive. That's what mattered. We'd deal with the rest when we had to.

I spent hours by his side, hoping for a miracle. I chattered about little things, my new computer-support job and how I couldn't believe I was back at home with my parents (they wanted to keep an eye on me). I joked that he had to wake up so I could get out of there.

One morning Tom flinched when doctors pricked him. Bit by excruciating bit, he moved a little, then a little more, staying awake longer each day until, after a week, he was fully conscious.

Tom couldn't move most of his body and he couldn't talk because of his broken jaw. He knew we were engaged, but he didn't remember the accident or our wedding. Worse yet, he just wasn't "Tom."

He'd entered the coma a twenty-five-year-old man but came out like an adolescent, with an inappropriate, twelve-year-old-boy sense of humor. The doctors assured me this didn't mean he'd stay that way. As his brain healed, he might slowly return to being himself again.

The question was: Would his brain fully heal?

Surgery repaired his jaw. But it took physical, occupational and speech therapy to help regain his motor skills. In March, he moved into my childhood room with me so my mom could take care of him while I was at work.

It was a confusing time. Tom was improving, yes, and I never really doubted he'd recover, but I'll admit I felt more like a caregiver than a wife. One day, Tom was struggling to do a small motor-skill exercise, picking up a nickel off the counter, and I wanted to scream, "Just grab it!" But then a few days later my mom called me at work to say Tom had mastered the challenge, and the pride and hope I felt was indescribable.

Gradually Tom regained his strength, speech and motor skills, and after about six months we moved home. Signs of his brain injury continued to show up occasionally. By our first anniversary, he was nearly 100 percent better. Tom was himself again—the man I depended on.

As the years passed, our memories of the accident slowly faded into the background of our jam-packed lives. We had three beautiful children. But it was clear Tom would never remember the time around our wedding. We leafed through photos but nothing helped.

The hardest part for me was Tom couldn't remember the small, private things we shared: the spider that fell in my soup on our honeymoon and the first time he called me his wife. These moments, the intimate details that make up the fabric of a marriage, were locked away somewhere in Tom's brain—and I couldn't pry them loose. In the great scheme of things, Tom's memory loss seemed a small price to pay for his life.

Then an opportunity to renew our vows came through a contest with *Redbook* magazine. When I learned that my entry won, I immediately called Tom to tell him all five of us were going to Disney World to get married again.

The day of the ceremony, Tom and I saw each other at a morning rehearsal then parted to separate hotel rooms. As I was getting ready, I heard a knock at the door—it was our twelve-year-old, Jeffrey, holding a bouquet of long-stemmed red roses with a card from Tom.

"I can't wait to see you at the end of the aisle," I read.

The vows we exchanged were simple and traditional, a cherished opportunity to recommit to the man I came so close to losing.

That night our kids were whisked on a VIP tour of the Disney parks so Tom and I could have a romantic dinner. After nearly two decades together, we felt like newlyweds, holding hands and kissing all night—a night that, this time, we'll both remember.

Becky Knutson
As told to Jeannie Kim

"For richer or for *what*?"

Reprinted by permission of Martha Campbell.

What Matters Most

Trouble is a part of life, and if you don't share it, you don't give the person who loves you enough chance to love you.

Dinah Shore

The day before the wedding, Travis and I were both sick with the flu.

However, I pushed myself to tie the final ribbons and fold the final programs. I had instructed my planning crew about exactly what went where, at what time and how. I made list upon list, envisioning every detail. I drove and drove—delivering, directing and reconfirming. When it was time for the rehearsal, I was lying on the front pew, fighting waves of nausea and diarrhea, but still trying to direct the proceedings.

No problem, I thought. *I'll get some sleep and be fine for the big day.* I said good-bye to everyone, and went home. I'd allowed myself six hours of uninterrupted sleep, and then the wedding schedule would begin. I laid out the papers and directions, took an antacid and went to bed.

Shortly after midnight, I awoke with a knife-sharp,

crippling pain in my lower back. I rolled awkwardly out of bed, and crawled up the stairs. Every second step, I stopped to catch my breath.

My mother and stepfather rushed me to the emergency room where I was promptly admitted. At 2 A.M., Travis arrived with his mother and father. The nurse gave me pain medication, scheduled me for X-rays and suggested I try to get some sleep.

All I can clearly remember is the concern on Travis's face while he held my hand. Our mothers were in the next room, frantically trying to create a contingency plan for the wedding. Postpone? A ceremony in the hospital? I vaguely remember those concerns, too.

The on-duty physician—a friend of both families—told me my pain was probably a kidney stone. I was incredulous. A kidney stone? The night before the wedding? Something so small could cause so much pain?

I didn't care, I told them weakly. I was getting married in a few hours. I had a schedule to keep.

The nurses on staff chuckled and rolled their eyes. But they called the X-ray technician early, scheduled me first and rooted for me to make it to the church on time.

At 7:30 A.M., the doctor made his diagnosis; at 8 A.M., I went to X-ray; at 9 A.M., the results came back: kidney stone-free. It had passed! At 10 A.M., I was released—just in time for a quick shower before my hair appointment en route to the church.

Travis drove me home from the hospital. I was disappointed he'd seen me before the ceremony, tired and miserable. I felt weak, weary and un-wedding-like. He looked at the "Bride" T-shirt I still wore from the rehearsal the night before and told me I was beautiful. It was at that moment—leaning on him as I walked to the car in my faded pajama bottoms—that I felt "married" for the first time.

Because of the medical fiasco the night before, I don't

remember much about the decorations or the food or the placement of all the items that I was oh-so-focused on just a few days prior. I forgot about schedules and details. I didn't care about the music, or who sat next to whom, and honestly, I don't even remember how everything worked out.

What I do remember is the face of my husband at the end of the aisle. I remember him holding my hand in the hospital. I remember the look in his eyes when we spoke our vows.

He was there, I was there—and nothing else mattered.

Shonna Milliken Humphrey

Old Love Turned Brand-New

Vicki gripped the steering wheel of her car, trying to control her anxious excitement. Twenty years was a long time—what would he look like? Would she recognize him? As she began her three-hour drive to the airport, it all came flooding back.

Vicki met David in 1975 at a campfire party in Georgia. They were sixteen and instantly fell in love. Not long after that, David's stepfather, who was in the military, received orders to move the family to Oklahoma. David asked Vicki to marry him and go with him, but she was simply not ready to leave home. Instead, her father retired, and she moved with her parents to Mississippi. Tearfully, the young lovers went their separate ways.

Soon after, Vicki discovered she was pregnant. Then she heard David had a new girlfriend. Not wanting to get in the way of what she perceived as his new happiness, Vicki decided not to call him. Rumors of a baby and pressures from their families frightened David as well. Broken-hearted, and in a desperate attempt to find himself and some sanity, he joined the Navy.

In January, Vicki gave birth to a baby girl and named

her Tammy Lisa. By now, she and David had lost all contact. As more time passed, they both married other people. David became the father of two more daughters. Vicki had a son.

Six years passed, and Vicki worried that if something happened to her, Tammy would never know the real story of her father. So she wrote a letter explaining everything, included the only two pictures she had of David, and stored it all in a safe deposit box.

As the years passed, Vicki never forgot David and the love they shared. When Tammy turned sixteen, Vicki gave her the letter she had written ten years earlier.

After reading it, Tammy looked up. "Momma, it's time to find my daddy."

The search began. For the next three years they hunted for David Garcia. They tried agencies, libraries, police departments, even old military records, with no luck. After they placed an ad in the *Army Times*, the father of David's best friend saw the ad, and his son called Vicki. She learned David was now using his birth father's last name, Frizzell. A new search began, and twenty years after they had parted, Vicki held David's phone number in her hand.

With trembling fingers, she dialed. When David heard her voice, he was overwhelmed, shaken and—to her delight—thrilled. He told her he had longed to know how she was doing and yearned to see and know his daughter. Ten years earlier he had tried to find Vicki but with no success.

David was alive, well and happy to hear from her. He told her he would come to Mississippi to meet Tammy, the daughter he had wondered about all these years. Vicki shared with David what had been in her heart for so long.

"David, I promised myself that if I ever found you I'd tell you this no matter what. When we were kids, I loved you. All these years I've loved you. Even through my marriage, I loved you. Every man I've ever known, I compared to you, and not one ever measured up." Her words left him crying as he began to share his own, similar feelings. He had never forgotten her, never stopped loving her.

Tammy decided she wanted to greet her father privately, so she anxiously waited at her apartment while Vicki made the three-hour drive to pick him up—alone.

At the airport, Vicki's anxious excitement grew. Each minute seemed like an hour. She paced back and forth and touched up her makeup three times. David was also nervous. As the plane landed, his heart started pounding. Once on the ground, he was impatient to find Vicki, to see her again.

As David walked off the plane, they recognized each other instantly. Amazingly, they saw each other as if through a tunnel, and the rest of the airport went white and grew silent. With smiles of joy on their faces, they gazed at each other in wide-eyed amazement. David slowly drew her into his arms and kissed her. Time stood still as the past and the present collided in one dramatic moment.

The drive home passed in no time, as they talked about their lives and all that each had done. During short silences, they would glance at each other and whisper, "I can't believe it's really you."

When they arrived at Tammy's apartment, David immediately recognized the beautiful young woman waiting outside as his daughter. Sharing their first hugs, they began talking and laughing at the same time. That night, they watched home videos of Tammy growing up, and all three cried as the history of Tammy's life that David had missed rolled by on the screen.

Two days after arriving in Mississippi, David realized that the only place on Earth he wanted to be was with Vicki and Tammy. He proposed, and Vicki excitedly accepted.

"If I wasn't living it, I wouldn't believe it!" she exclaimed.

As they planned their wedding over the next few weeks, they easily rediscovered their love for each other. Vicki's parents were overjoyed to have David back in their lives, treating him as if he was a son who had finally come home.

The following June, Vicki's parents gave them a traditional southern wedding. The invitation showed a fairy-tale castle with the words "Dreams Come True." Tammy was maid of honor.

Arriving in a horse-drawn carriage, the bride wore the long white gown of her dreams. During the ceremony, David sang a song he wrote for Vicki that told the world the miracle of their love story: "Old Love Turned Brand-New." At the end of the ceremony, David gazed at his daughter and sang a special song he'd written called "Daddy's Little Girl—Tammy's Song."

It took twenty years to fill the empty space they'd all had in their hearts. Now their family circle was finally complete.

Vicki Frizzell
As told to Janet Matthews

Got Match?

Brides dream of a wedding day heralded with pomp and circumstance: a beautiful venue with acres of flowers, just the right music wafting through the rafters of the church, and gorgeous attendants and handsome groomsmen bedecked in the most expensive gowns and tuxedos available. They imagine themselves in the perfect wedding dress with sparkling rhinestones and sequins. They see the guests waiting in awe of their grand entrance while they delicately take steps in time to the music toward their handsome intended waiting with a smile at the end of the aisle.

In their dreams, everything is perfectly planned and perfectly executed . . . for the perfect day.

Perfection took on a new meaning the day of my wedding. I had planned so efficiently that everything was finely tuned six months before the ceremony.

My friend Allen, who was giving me away, greeted me at the door of the ballroom. The music, performed by George and Diane, professional musicians, was perfect. I stepped in time to the Wedding March up the aisle. At one point I lost my balance and had to hang on to his arm for dear life. A friend on the end of a row cheered me on. "Steady. . . S-t-e-a-d-y!"

The ceremony began, and was going smoothly until I noticed the judge skipped over the "Ave Maria," which Diane was to sing . . . and he kept going, blasting right past the "Our Father" that was supposed to be sung next. I quickly glanced at the musicians as they turned the pages of sheet music like expert speed-readers. The ceremony was becoming a blur. My plans—the program—what had happened?

". . . And now, they will light the unity candle," said the judge. He stepped to one side. Jim and I stared, dumb-founded. One unity candle with two smaller candles—and none were lit.

Motionless for what seemed like eternity, Jim finally leaned over and whispered, "What are we supposed to do now?"

Quickly, like wildfire, a hushed, mild panic spread through the wedding party.

"Do *you* have any matches?" someone whispered.

"Not me!"

"Where do you think I'd put them if I did have them?"

"I have a lighter but it's in my purse in the back."

Now, as a professional speaker and trainer, I'm accus-tomed to thinking on my feet and quickly solving prob-lems as they arise. I calmly and gracefully turned to the entire congregation.

"Does anyone have a match?"

Instant laughter erupted.

An usher, Ron, held his arm up like the Statue of Liberty. "I have a match!" He charged up the aisle to the rescue, only to stop short when he got to the candle table. Confused, he turned to my maid of honor.

"Which one do I light?" he whispered.

"The outside two!" she answered.

Obviously still confused, he lit the unity candle.

Jim leaned over to me and announced, "Congratulations. You're now married—to Ron!"

Then a playful argument erupted between my maid of honor and Ron.

"Not *that* one. The *outside* two."

"You said the inside one."

"I did not!"

"Yes you did!"

"Blow that one out and light the other two!"

At this point I was crying—from laughter. And from the roars in the ballroom, you would have thought they were witnessing a comedy act.

Once all was settled, the judge pronounced us husband and wife, and presented us to our friends who stood—still laughing—and applauded loudly. Jim turned to me again.

"Are we done, now?"

"Yep, we're done!"

"Good—my shoes are too big!"

We triumphantly marched down the aisle together, knowing that the events at our wedding would be the first of so many humorous moments we would share.

At the reception, all the guests freely mingled and shared laughs about the ceremony. I realized my nonchalant request for a match had eased the situation and made everyone feel at home.

The definition for a "perfectly planned wedding" was suddenly redefined. In my reality, everything was perfectly *un*-planned and perfectly *un*-executed. And, yet, I found the best match and married my best friend. And my day was indeed . . . perfect!

C. Capiz Greene

7

TREASURED MOMENTS

Sometimes I would almost rather have people take away years of my life than take away a moment.

Pearl Bailey

A Bridesmaid's View from the Altar

I would expect to see her walk through any doorway but this one.

As I stand by the altar in black satin shoes, clutching my calla lily bouquet to fight back the tears, my thoughts run back to a hundred other doorways we've walked through together in our lives.

Valerie and I were five years old when we met, so my memories of her stretch back nearly as far as memories of my own family. Back to the time when we filled long summer days with the busy work of children: swapping ghost stories on the garage roof, dressing up in my mother's old prom gowns or sitting on the swing set eating Cheetos and wiggling our baby teeth to see whose would fall out first.

We crossed all our doorways together back then. Passed through a hundred rites of childhood in tandem. We stood side-by-side on strangers' doorsteps in Girl Scout beanies, peddling Thin Mints and Shortbreads. We ran shivering from door to door on Halloween, ragged hobos and red-lipped gypsies clutching plastic pumpkins full of candy. We scrambled over mountains of snow on Christmas mornings to bounce impatiently on each other's front porches, breathing the icicle air and fogging the storm door in anticipation.

A few years later, I grew into an awkward chubby pre-teen standing on that same front porch every morning dreading elementary school. I learned how cruel fifth-graders could be as I struggled through that painful phase. But Valerie met me faithfully outside my classroom every afternoon, oblivious to the welcoming arms of cliques that shunned me. She stayed as unquestioning and loyal a friend as any child could want.

Summers and winters passed by and led us through the doors of junior high, into the world of adolescence. Still side-by-side, we wrestled with our first pairs of nylons and fumbled through orchestra try-outs on second-hand violins. My ugly-duckling phase faded mercifully away and we began showing up on each other's doorsteps for our annual Christmas present exchange, carrying rock records, sweaters and new pairs of Levi's instead of toys.

Then, one chilly fall night in high school, I rounded the corner to Valerie's house to ask a question about algebra and found her leaning dreamily against the doorframe, twisting a green carnation around her fingers. Instead of sharing my anxiety over logarithms, she told me about the boy who had given her the flower. I stood at the bottom of the porch tracing imaginary patterns in the cement, and watched uncomfortably as she leaned in the doorway, ready to enter a new phase of life.

Soon, and without asking for my advice, Valerie had a serious boyfriend. I took up with other friends and dated here and there, but always dug in my heels and clung to childhood more fiercely than she did. Our friendship drifted to a looser one of casual calls and shared rides to school. But the thread that bound us together proved stronger than first loves or teenage heartbreak. Like signals from a car radio winding through the countryside, it faded in and out, now strong, now muffled by static, but always there in the background.

So many thresholds we crossed together. So many years. They slipped by silently, and now I realize the door leading back is all but closed. The vivid colors of those days have faded to the pastels of memory. They rush by in a blur of brilliant ribbons until I come to where I stand now, holding my breath as the music plays.

I see Valerie round the corner confidently, her arm through her father's. And it seems to me that instead of an aisle adorned with white bows and green leaves, as I watch she has passed quickly through each doorway of our lives, intertwined for the past twenty years. Far away, I see a tiny Valerie reaching up for her father's hand. Then she approaches and steps into focus in cream satin, pearls and white lace.

It hardly seems possible that this is the same Valerie who braved the first day of kindergarten with me, hit me in the mouth with a Zodiac ball in junior high and gave me a fat lip. The same Valerie who scolded me for singing Girl Scout songs off-key, stole Smirnoffs from my parents' liquor cabinet with me to make our first Vodka Collinses. Shared my life. Grew up alongside me. Two doors away.

As she unties the ribbon holding her fiancé's ring to a velvet pillow, her nephew's tiny hands stretch up, tightly clutching the lacy edges. His small, earnest face is crossed over with concentration on his task. I am struck by what a long time it's been since we held objects up, stretched on tiptoe, so adults could reach down for them. And I long to have those small hands again, to be that child just for a day.

As I watch her fiancé's eager shining eyes at Valerie's approach, I can hardly fight the tears. If my heart breaks, it's not through sadness. It's only that I feel the small hands of childhood tugging at my memory. It is a childhood I had forgotten, left lying just under a layer of dust in some happy back room in my mind, long neglected. I am momentarily aware of its existence very close: a small warm flash and then it expires. The door closes with a whisper.

And I am twenty-six again, holding my best friend's bouquet as she turns to face her husband on her wedding day. I force the lump out of my throat, squeeze my eyes shut. Force the sun-touched picture in front of me to soften back into focus, and chase away any selfish longing for the old days.

I know that for Valerie this doorway leads to many more happy rooms. To summer afternoons and backyards and childhood memories of the future. Sun streams through the stained glass, onto the pews and the rapt congregation as the organist hits her first booming notes. As Valerie turns away from me and reaches out to take her husband's arm, a cloud of triumphant recessional music filling the church, I close my eyes and let the tears roll. I wish her all the luck in the world as she passes through this doorway and on to the new rooms that lie beyond with her husband.

Kathy Passero

At the Ritz

*I awoke this morning with devout thanksgiving
for my friends, the old and the new.*

Ralph Waldo Emerson

My cousin Toni was my best friend growing up. I had
two brothers but no sisters, so she and I were especially
close. Our favorite times together happened when she
would spend the night. Sneaking Ritz crackers to my
room, we nibbled and watched TV in bed until the wee
hours of the morning. The next day, we always woke to
find the bed full of crumbs. No wonder we didn't get any
sleep, we exclaimed!

Years passed and we remained close. When I married
and had two daughters, Toni became their favorite sitter. I
was thrilled when she met the man she knew immediately
was the love of her life. After a couple of years, she and
Chris decided to marry.

Toni and Chris hoped to have a big wedding and nice
honeymoon, but their budget didn't allow for either.
They thought about waiting and saving but decided
they'd rather be married. The wedding didn't have to be

big to be nice, and the honeymoon could wait.

I wished I could afford to give them a honeymoon as a wedding gift, but that was out of the question. Nevertheless, I wanted my gift to be extra special and memorable. When I heard they were planning to spend their wedding night in their new, sparsely furnished apartment, I decided to give them a night they would never forget.

In a simple but gorgeous gown, Toni exchanged vows with Chris in her parents' backyard under a trestle covered with hundreds of fragrant, climbing roses. As the evening drew to a close, a small group of friends and family watched the happy couple open wedding gifts.

Then, I took an envelope out of my purse and handed it to them. Inside the card, they found the key to a hotel room I rented for their wedding night. It wasn't a honeymoon suite, but it was nice and came with a restaurant for breakfast and a pool for swimming.

Thrilled, the newlyweds shared hugs and kisses and headed for the hotel.

No one knew I had spent my morning at the hotel. No one but me knew they'd find a nice room with two king-sized beds, the comforter turned back invitingly on one. No one but me knew they'd find a rose and a chocolate on each pillow. On the table a bottle of sparkling wine beside a tray of cheeses, olives and crackers. On the nightstand, goblets engraved with their names and the date. And on the second bed they'd find a special nightie for the blushing bride and a robe for the groom.

Consequently, no one but me received a phone call at 2:00 A.M.

Toni was laughing so hard she was crying—or maybe crying so hard she was laughing! They had found the wine, the glasses and the roses. She slipped into the nightie and Chris modeled the robe. Then they slid under the comforter—and found themselves in a bed full of cracker crumbs!

Fortunately, the other bed was waiting for them, fresh and clean. But twenty years later, we still laugh about her unforgettable "wedding night at the Ritz." And we exclaim that, of course, the crumbs were the reason they didn't get any sleep!

Cathy L. Novakovich

"If there are any among us who know of some reason why Dave and Lynette should not be joined together, let them speak now or forever . . ."

Chain of Love

A wise lover values not so much the gift of the lover as the love of the giver.

Thomas à Kempis

Ron's eyes brightened when I walked into the restaurant. Always attentive, he took my coat and pulled out my chair. I avoided his eyes and wondered how to start.

We had dated for two years before getting engaged a week earlier. During that time we had decided to avoid physical intimacy. We wanted to remain objective about the relationship and thought this would help. And we were true to our agreement even though it became increasingly difficult as we fell more deeply in love. Now that we were engaged it seemed silly to continue our abstinence.

Yet I wanted to do just that.

How would Ron react when I told him? Would he think I was hiding something? Would he think I was afraid of intimacy? Worst of all, would he think I didn't love him?

Setting down my glass of water, I reached for his hand across the table.

"Ron, you know how much I love you," I began. "And I

think our 'agreement' has both tested and strengthened our relationship."

I faltered. Ron sat, silent. Waiting. My eyes focused on our clasped hands, then rose to meet his.

"I . . . I want to continue this way." I took a deep breath. "I want to wait until our wedding night."

Ron was grave as he pondered my request. I shredded the corners of my paper napkin—and waited. After a long pause, he looked up and met my anxious gaze.

"Agreed."

"Really?" I gasped.

"Really."

My heart filled with new respect and appreciation for the man I was going to marry. Yet, as we left the restaurant, Ron seemed distracted. In the parking lot, I suggested dessert at the local ice cream parlor.

"I have something important I need to see to," he declined. He had already started driving away when I realized he had forgotten his coat. I tried to flag him down but he didn't even see me.

Why was my attentive fiancé suddenly so absentminded? I returned home uncertain where we stood, not sure I had really gotten what I wanted.

Later that night the phone rang.

"I need to see you. I need to come over." There was urgency in his voice.

"Why? What's wrong? Ron?" He had already hung up.

Fifteen minutes later Ron arrived carrying a large cardboard box. My heart sank. Was he returning all the gifts I had given him? I twisted the week-old diamond ring on my finger. I started to slide it off.

Ron held out the box. "Open it."

I swallowed hard and lifted the lid. Inside the box was a paper chain.

I pulled out length after length after length. On each

link was a date, beginning with the current day and numbering into the future.

I knew my face mirrored the questions churning inside me. I looked at Ron.

He smiled at my puzzlement but quickly grew serious.

"I thought about your decision," he said. "And I plan to honor it—although it will be a great sacrifice." He nodded at the chain draping from my hands. "The chain represents that sacrifice."

Ron asked me to hang it in my bedroom and tear off a link every night. As our wedding neared, the chain would shrink and so would the sacrifice.

"With each torn link, pray for me to have the strength to be true to this commitment." Ron gazed into my eyes. "Will you do this for me?"

Tearfully, I accepted the chain and the commitment. All the love I felt poured forth when I kissed him like never before. Ron pulled away.

"If you want me to keep my promise, you had better stop giving such wonderful kisses," he teased. I laughed . . . and blushed . . . and showed him to the door. With my heart still racing, I suddenly recognized this would be a sacrifice for *me*, too.

The chain circled my bedroom three times. I delighted in the evening ritual as I tore a link, thought about Ron's— *our*—sacrifice, and said a prayer just as he'd asked.

Soon only seven links remained. Then three. And, finally, the day before our wedding, only one. I didn't tear the last circle; I packed it in my suitcase.

On our wedding night, I showed Ron the final link of the chain. Smiling, we each took one side . . . and pulled. Then, together, we offered a prayer that our love—rooted in mutual sacrifice—would blossom and flourish.

Kathleen Happ

"I still want to take a European honeymoon."

Reprinted by permission of George Crenshaw, Masters Agency.

Through the Beholder's Eyes

A friend is someone who knows all about you, and loves you just the same.

Elbert Hubbard

Have you ever looked at a couple and asked, "What exactly does she see in him?"

Shane Davis was a handsome enough young man, a broad-shouldered teddy bear of a guy. He had a winsome smile, a quick humor and a swagger in his step. Not a cocky walk, but a gently swaying gait.

His bride-to-be was a petite woman of forceful intelligence. Melissa didn't hold back her opinions; she was quick to speak her mind even if Shane disagreed. But when she talked, he looked deep into her eyes and smiled. It completely disarmed her.

I guess I could have surmised that his affable character was enough reason for these two to fall in love, but I suspected she saw something the passive eye would overlook. Naturally inquisitive, I wanted to know what it was.

Shane and Melissa were in my office for premarital counseling. Like most pastors, I knew I had a captive audience in the young couple. If they wanted me to perform the ceremony, they were obligated to spend at least six hours with me. I usually told couples, "I don't do weddings; I do marriages. If I'm going to be part of your ceremony, I want to be part of your lives first."

I knew this couple was different when they scheduled their meetings with me a year in advance of their wedding. That won my heart.

As we spoke over that year's time, the petals of their lives pulled back and I watched love bloom before my eyes. I saw it in their gentle unassuming touch. They didn't need to maul each other to express their love. It was often a look, a wink or a hand reaching out to pull back a stray hair off the forehead.

I spoke to them of family history and love's everyday choices. At every turn, their participation and earnestness encouraged me. Mostly I listened; and at times I felt like the student. This is where a story began to unfold that would take my breath away.

When Shane was in third grade, he met another child named Ryan who attended every neighborhood baseball game. His health precluded him from physically participating, but not from being the play-by-play announcer, supplying a voice of enthusiasm. Ryan and Shane hit it off, the root of a friendship that would blossom over years.

Ryan did not have the athleticism Shane possessed. His twisted, contorted body suffered from the spinal atrophy of severe muscular dystrophy. Limbs underdeveloped and fragile, Ryan was unable to move on his own, mobile only by wheelchair.

Theirs was not a relationship built on activity, but truly an event of the heart. They loved each other through junior high and high school and even into college. In a twist, Ryan went to college while Shane stayed home and worked. But it would not be long before their friendship brought them back together.

A very intelligent Ryan faced incompetent caretakers at college. Ryan's mother, in an unusual request, asked Shane to consider attending Indiana University to take care of Ryan while he attended classes. Not even enrolled in the school, Shane immediately quit his job and moved to the college town of Bloomington.

Each counseling session with Shane and Melissa revealed a bit more of this incredible friendship story. Shane was reluctant to share the details of his and Ryan's relationship because people's admiration made him uncomfortable.

"I'm not a hero; I'm just a friend," he said quietly.

I was beginning to see more of what this young woman saw in Shane.

As the wedding day approached, I had one last form to fill out and needed the attendants' and groomsmen's names.

"Shane, who will be your best man?"

The answer came in a need-you-even-ask tone. "Ryan, of course."

"Yes, but will he be able to do all that is required?" I felt almost ridiculous asking. My question unmasked some of my own prejudices and betrayed my handicap of mind more than exposing any of Ryan's limitations. Shane responded like the friend he was.

"He'll do just fine."

I knew Shane was right.

The day of the wedding, Ryan traveled down the aisle in his motorized wheelchair to meet the maid of honor. She took his arm and the two made their way to the front, preceding a beaming bride and groom. But the best these two had to give each other was still waiting in the wings.

In order for the union to be complete, I needed the sig-natures of the participants on the marriage license. I approached Shane and asked him who would be signing. My assumption that Ryan was incapable of signing the license was clear.

Shane's response was the same as before. "Ryan, of course."

I had no idea I was about to witness something sacred.

Shane took the license and walked over to Ryan. He gently wedged the pen between Ryan's stiffened fingers. Then Shane propped the license against the pen. As Ryan moved his hand ever so slightly up and down, Shane moved the paper in perfect rhythm. They had danced this dance many times before. To the final stroke, they coaxed the signature from the pen in a waltz not of pen and paper, but of hearts. Ryan's signature appeared in beautifully smooth script.

A tear trickled down my cheek and soaked a line on my tux. I could now clearly see what this young woman saw in Shane.

The Bible says, "the two will become one." Few people ever achieve this wonder. Only a few even glimpse its awe. But before my eyes, I realized this young man already knew what it took to share one's life to the extent that two become one.

Mrs. Davis, you are a very lucky young lady.

Keith A. Wooden

Arm-in-Arm

"Who will walk you down the aisle?" my mother worried.

My fiancé and I had been planning this wedding for months. I had taken care of the dress, the flowers, the hall, the catering and even the cake. Our invitations proclaimed, "Dreams do come true." But to my mother's question, I had no answer.

My father died about a year before I started dating Lou. I was haunted by the thought that Lou loved golf, my father's favorite pastime, but they never had a chance to play a single round. Sadly, they never even knew each other.

I thought about walking down the aisle alone. But I wanted it to be a happy occasion, not a reminder that I no longer had a dad. I didn't want people to feel sorry for me.

"What about David?" my mother suggested.

My brother? Maybe he could!

I sensed a glimpse of hope—until all the obstacles surfaced. He'd have to fly in early to rent a tux and make it to rehearsal, but because his work required him to be on call, it would be difficult for him to request time off. I was reluctant to ask.

"Mom, you know David is very busy."

"If you want him to do it, you should ask," my mother encouraged.

I knew I wanted my brother by my side during the most important time in my life. He always was in the past. Together we'd endured a traumatic accident, Dad's battle with lung cancer and, finally, his death. No matter what, David was there. It seemed only right for him to take my father's place. I decided to place the call.

When he answered the phone, I asked, "D-David? Do . . . do you think you could walk me down the aisle?"

"Yes," he said without hesitation. "It would be an honor."

"You mean it?" my voice escalated like a shy school-girl's. "You'd . . . you'd have to come a couple days early for a tux fitting and to make the rehearsal."

"Hmm," he said. "Now that's a problem. I'm not sure I can get more days off. I'll have to speak with my boss and get back to you."

"That's fine. If you can't, don't worry about it," I said in a rush, hoping my voice didn't betray my disappointment. I decided his response was a kindhearted excuse for "No." Maybe I was asking too much. My heart sank.

And the weeks passed without another word from David.

Four days before my wedding a strange car pulled up in the driveway. I went outside and saw my brother standing before me.

"Are you that blushing bride I've been hearing so much about?" he asked, with a proud grin on his face.

I ran and threw my arms around him. "But what about work?"

"I found a new job. This one pays better and gives me more free time."

Knowing my brother, I had a funny feeling that wasn't the only reason he'd switched jobs. "Really?"

"Yes!" He quickly changed the subject. "Now what size tux do you think I wear?"

The next few days passed quickly leaving me little time to spend with him. But when the famous strains of "Here Comes the Bride" cued him, David knocked on my dressing room door.

"It's time."

I swung the door open and stood in front of him in bridal white.

"Wow!" he said, offering his arm. "You look beautiful!"

At that moment, I saw my father's pride beaming at me through David's eyes, the same shade of blue as my father's. I realized that in many ways Dad was with me on this important day. And so was the brother I had always relied on. David and I walked down the aisle, smiles gleaming and tears flowing, but most importantly, arm-in-arm.

Michele Wallace Campanelli

Sisterly Love

For there is no friend like a sister
In calm or stormy weather;
To cheer one on the tedious way,
To fetch one if one goes astray,
To lift one if one totters down,
To strengthen whilst one stands.

Christina Rossetti

My sister Jayne and I were as close in age as we were alike in looks. In fact, as teenagers, we liked to pass ourselves off as twins. We adored *Fantasia,* our mum's stories and each other. We were best friends and close companions.

So when Jayne got sick I was devastated. It was a long time before she was diagnosed: a rare and deadly blood-vessel cancer. Jayne was tired and lethargic and tried to put on a brave face, but the fear showed in her eyes.

There were specialists to consult, tests to run, treatments to endure and decisions to be made. Naturally, the family spent most of their time going to the hospital. So it was that, with my wedding approaching, I found myself on my own—alone with all the arrangements it entailed. I had no one to help with the myriad details and, more importantly, no healthy sister to share my excitement.

Finally, doctors decided surgery was the answer. They removed both the tumor and an entire muscle from Jayne's leg. Due to a serious infection, it took many months for my sister to become well enough to leave the hospital, unable to walk or even stand.

At last my wedding day arrived. As our limousine slid to a stop at the church, I peered out the window. I saw my entire family waiting outside and felt a pang that Jayne wasn't among them, wasn't well enough to share this big moment with me. It was the only dark spot on the happiest day of my life. But she had survived the ordeal and that was enough for now.

Stepping from the limousine, I rearranged my gown and entered the church. I swept down the aisle to the traditional bridal march . . . and then I saw her. Jayne!

Jayne smiling. Jayne standing. Jayne—supported by crutches.

Dreamily, I paused in the middle of the bridal march to walk over and kiss her on the cheek. I recognized the pain, what it cost my sister to be there, to stand, to even walk a little. She could not manage it for long, yet she did it for me.

Now, several years later I thumb through my bridal book and turn to the page listing presents. Among the entries a special one reads: "Jayne's gift: My sister walked on my wedding day."

Hers is the gift I treasure most.

Ann Cooke

Heart of Friendship

Sometimes our light goes out but is blown into flame by another human being. Each of us owes deepest thanks to those who have rekindled this light.

Albert Schweitzer

For some reason, Melisa, a popular player on our junior high softball team, took awkward, unathletic me into her heart and under her wing. Fast friends from then on, we grew up together. Those early years passed quickly and, when Melisa got married, I served as one of her bridesmaids.

Then one day the phone rang.

"I just came from the doctor's office," Melisa's voice quivered. "Remember when I told you about all those headaches and how my vision sometimes got dark? My neurologist ran a CAT scan." She paused. "I'm going blind."

Blind? Melisa?

Melisa . . . who traveled the road with her trucker husband to soak in the sights across America?

Melisa . . . who contacted me monthly by letter or phone to describe those breathtaking views?

Melisa . . . who was only twenty-three?

"It's only a matter of months, two years or less. Retinitis pigmentosa they call it," she explained. "I'll lose up to 85 percent of my sight. The specialist recommends that I stop trucking and attend school for the blind. To learn Braille. . . ."

Both of us were stunned. Not knowing how to comfort her, I told her I would keep her situation in my prayers.

As time went on, letters I sent to Melisa went unanswered. When I called, her voice didn't sound the same; she seemed bewildered and despondent.

"Cursive is difficult. Please make your print larger," she advised, "so I can read your letters. Try using black ink on white paper . . . and type it."

I continued reaching out, printing my letters in a large, size 20 font. My typing improved over those weeks but her writing got increasingly more scribbled and illegible.

After months of exchanges, Melisa expressed her feelings about her new schooling. Learning how to use a cane, to command a guide dog and to read Braille was taking its toll. It wasn't easy; reality was sinking in. It was only a matter of a few short months before she would depend on these skills permanently.

Depression overwhelmed her. Melisa spent hours crying and often refused to leave her house.

By now, Louis and I had finally set our wedding date and I wanted Melisa to be my matron of honor. But, was it too much to ask? Would she be willing to stand up with me? Would she compare it to her own wedding when she had perfect vision?

I wasn't sure I should ask. But then, it didn't seem right to ask anyone else. No one meant as much to me as Melisa.

I broached the subject during one of our phone calls. "I have a question for you. But if you say 'no,' I really will understand."

"Sure, what is it?"

I took a deep breath. "I'm getting married in a few months and I was wondering if you would be my matron of honor?"

"No," she replied without a second of hesitation.

"I understand." I paused. "So. What did you learn in school today?"

Melisa described a stove that "spoke" the temperature it was warming to and told which burner was hot. Although tears threatened, I tried to be supportive.

Suddenly, her voice trembled. "I'm sorry I can't be your matron of honor. I just wouldn't want to trip down the aisle and . . . embarrass you."

"Mel, you could never embarrass me, ever! Do you understand? Ever! I am so proud to have you as my friend."

"But I wouldn't be able to find where to stand."

"I could have a groomsman walk you down the aisle directly to the spot. Either way, I'd love for you and your husband to attend even if you don't feel up to being an attendant. Let me know if you change your mind."

During the following months, Melisa helped me plan everything. Even though she couldn't see them, she suggested just the right napkins, table decorations and linens. She helped select the design for the invitations. When I panicked about arrangements, she calmed me.

Though she never confirmed her part as matron of honor, hopeful still, I left the spot open.

On the day of the wedding I was surprised and thrilled to discover Melisa waiting for me in the dressing room. My courageous friend, wearing her becoming turquoise dress, was ready to set aside her fears and fulfill her role as attendant. Tenderly, she helped me into my wedding gown. Her fingers fumbled awkwardly with the intricate buttons. Together, we lifted the pearl veil to my hair. Lovingly, she lowered the delicate lace over my eyes.

A short time later, I watched Melisa start down the aisle. My heart pounded in my throat. Not because I would be embarrassed by a stumble, but because I knew she wanted to perform perfectly for me. Poised, arm-in-arm with the groomsman, Melisa walked to her spot at the altar. And, as if she had done it a million times before, she turned gracefully to face the audience.

Then, as I strolled down the aisle to the traditional wedding march, I saw her waiting, saw her squinting desperately to see me. Tears and a smile spread across her face . . . to match my own.

The day was perfect.

And, now, in spite of her vision impairment, Melisa and I continue to see each other the same way as we did from the earliest days of our friendship: with our hearts.

Michele Wallace Campanelli

Guest of Honor

Think of him still as the same, I say,
He is not dead, he is just—away

James Whitcomb Riley

"I declare you husband and wife." My cousin Joan placed her own rings on our fingers. "You are officially married," she added, holding our hands together.

Robert and I were thrilled to hear these words; although we knew it was just for fun—a make-believe rehearsal for the real wedding scheduled a year later. As we gave Joan her rings back, I sensed her sadness. I pretended not to see her watery eyes and trembling hands; I avoided bringing up the obvious.

Leukemia was slowly killing Joan, robbing her of optimism and spirit. Avoidance was my way of handling it. I ignored signs of her deterioration, hoping to tether her to the physical world.

"I just know I'm not going to be able to attend your wedding," Joan said, grabbing Robert's hands to apologize. I felt suffocated, knowing she was right. I realized our mock ceremony was the wedding Joan wouldn't live to see.

"Are you kidding? You're here now! You're the guest of honor at this special ceremony," I chimed in with an optimistic tone. "As a matter a fact, you're the only guest—the only witness." She smiled and her big dark eyes glowed.

Months later, I dreamt I was walking down the aisle in my beautiful ballroom gown, holding a delicate bouquet of white roses and baby's breath. Nobody was there, not even Robert. I felt sad and betrayed. Then a noise came from the back of the room and there stood Joan, arms wide open. She hugged me and we cried, not letting go of each other. I woke up that morning terrified of losing her.

A week later my aunt called to tell me Joan had died. I immediately recalled the dream and knew it was Joan's way of saying good-bye and reassuring me she'd be at my wedding.

A year later, my "real life" wedding day arrived. As I looked in the mirror, I admired how the love I was feeling made me look beautiful. I closed my eyes and remembered the day Joan declared Robert and I husband and wife. I remembered the special sound of her voice. The memory made me feel rejuvenated and happy.

Our wedding was my little girl dream-come-true. We were all happy knowing Joan was there—in every song, every dance, every flower. She was there sharing my hopes, my tears, my fears . . . and my love. I know she was holding my hand, caressing my hair, comforting my soul.

I know now that expensive gowns, endless invitation lists and wedding gifts don't make a perfect wedding. The perfect wedding happens because loved ones are there, to physically and spiritually rejoice in your love.

My wedding was perfect—*thanks to my guest of honor.*

Cindy L. Lassalle

The Look

We grew up viewing the documentation of our parents' love. Every year on their anniversary a white twin bed sheet pinned to brocade drapes served as our improvised movie screen. We sat mesmerized by the sight of their 1947 wedding. Live. On film.

I loved seeing Dad's thick wavy black hair and strong athletic build. Mom was more beautiful than Cinderella or Snow White, possessing the aura of a princess. They filled the screen with glamour, excitement and fairy-tale magic.

And then there was that look. The expression on Dad's face as he beheld his bride taught me to search a man's eyes for that same glowing reflection of devotion, awe and pride.

The images on our homemade screen reinforced in our minds the daily affection they demonstrated for us. The secret winks Dad sent Mom's way were intended to fly over our heads, but of course we always caught them, and they brought a sense of security. I identified his conspiratorial wink as a sign of their complete solidarity. They were an inseparable twosome moving through life as one.

So I began a quest for the real-life personification of the

images I viewed on a plain bed sheet. My dream man was crystal clear in my mind. I wanted to find a husband to love me the way my dad loved my mom. I would recognize him by the look in his eye.

Of course, it is one thing to know what you are looking for; it is quite another to find it. But miracles do happen.

Like my parents, we met at a party. Bob spotted me—as the romantic cliché goes—across a crowded room, and asked his friend to introduce us. Frank dutifully steered me over. As soon as I saw him, my gaze locked with his. I was unaware of how gorgeous he was; I was far too distracted by his eyes boring into mine.

This look belonged to me.

If it was the look in his eyes that rocked me, it was learning about him and getting to know the depth of his character that steadied my feet. He was solid, loyal, witty, compassionate and charming. He was my dream come true.

I wanted desperately to introduce Bob to my parents—my role models for love. Unfortunately, by this time Dad was deeply immersed in his battle with Alzheimer's and was, for the most part, nonverbal. Locked away in his private world, he seldom even made eye contact.

But I needed him, in whatever limited capacity he could command, to meet and get to know Bob. I sought his approval for the biggest decision of my life. I knew Bob was the right man for me but I yearned for Dad's recognition, too.

The first time I introduced them, Dad cursed. His hand was caught between the edge of the kitchen table and the arm of his chair. It's funny how profanities survive in an otherwise frozen mind. I had hoped for a more tender meeting.

As we sat at the table, we watched for any sign of acknowledgement from Dad. He, however, was far too busy inspecting the tablecloth to notice us—absorbed, repeatedly rubbing his fingers along the stitched hem.

Bob said softly to me, "Honey, I think your dad may need his chin wiped clean."

I blotted Dad's chin with a soft cloth. His eyes lifted to rest briefly on mine and the gratitude in them squeezed my heart. In those precious fleeting seconds, I had my dad back. Then he cast his eyes downward and was gone again. I remember that moment precisely because the feeling was so overwhelming.

I was consumed with love and admiration for the indomitable, yet gentle, strength exuding from *both* sides of the table.

The second time Bob and I visited, we helped Mom put Dad to bed. As we lowered him down, he grabbed Bob's arm and in hushed, slurred words requested: "Come back." We were making progress.

The third time these two men of mine met, Dad sat in his usual silence. Not so usual was that Dad's eyes fixated on Bob with a calculated intensity. Then for the first time in longer than I could remember, my father spoke clearly and loudly.

"Marry her," he said to Bob. Bob was only too happy to comply.

My dad passed away shortly after speaking those words. Yet even though he was physically absent, I snatched glimpses of him at our wedding. In my mind, he was there at my mother's side gazing at her with love-filled eyes. And when I observed my new husband across a ballroom overflowing with family and friends, Bob gave me *that look* I so dearly remembered, and softly sealed it with a secret wink.

Patty Swyden Sullivan

Stepping In

To a father growing old nothing is dearer than a daughter.

Euripides

"I feel sad that Dad won't be able to walk you down the aisle." I swallowed the small lump in my throat as I glanced at my sister.

Before our father had Alzheimer's disease, I could never imagine saying this to my sister, but a possible wedding was only one thing that had changed now. Dad's frequent hospitalizations that spring kept our entire family in a state of tension. We began rotating shifts, doing all we could to help on the home front, preparing meals, answering phone calls and making hospital visits while telling Dad repeatedly where he was and why he was there.

Cara and I had left our parents' home that evening and stopped at an intimate café to unwind. As we listened to the outdoor music, I thought briefly about my own wedding day.

I remembered that just before we stepped down the aisle, Dad whispered, "You look beautiful, just like your mother."

I remembered how special I felt at the reception when it was time for him to dance with the bride. I remembered.

And I regretted Cara would never experience it.

When Cara and Greg decided to marry three years later, Dad's illness had progressed. His walk was as unsteady as his memory. With his shoulders slightly stooped and his head bent downward, he had to concentrate on each step he took.

With the big event only a week away, my mother and I excitedly discussed plans for the ceremony and reception. Dad repeatedly asked, "Now, who's getting married?" Yet Cara valiantly insisted it wasn't a time for regrets; it was a time for laughter and dancing.

At the wedding, Dad sat next to Mom in the front row. He wasn't capable of escorting Cara down the aisle. Instead, it was Greg who took her arm. It was Greg who turned to her and whispered, "You look beautiful."

And, when they spoke their vows we all fought our tears, trying to respect Cara's wishes: to find and focus on their joy in the moment.

At the reception, guests gathered and the orchestra played. Since group conversation was too much for our father to follow, we hoped he'd sit comfortably and enjoy listening to the music.

Everyone smiled and applauded when Greg twirled Cara onto the floor for their first dance. Afterwards, Cara motioned to me.

"Will you ask Mom to come to the dance floor? Greg's going to stand in for Dad and dance with her."

Since Dad isn't capable.

Cara didn't have to say the words. After all, Dad hadn't been able to dance for nearly ten years. How thoughtful of Greg to step in for him.

I nodded agreement and hurried over to Mom. Just then, my father stood. He reached out for Mom's hand—

and asked her to dance. Stifling her surprise, she took his hand. Shoulders back and head erect; he walked my mother confidently onto the dance floor. In an instant, he swept her into a jitterbug.

The room hushed. Time stopped. Quietly, everyone stepped closer to watch. And none of us held back our tears. My eyes sought my sister's as, in that magical moment, Dad let himself go and danced joyously.

Then, before his memories slipped away again, he held out his arms to Cara and danced gracefully with the bride.

Penny Perrone

Joan's Bouquet

I remember my mother's prayers and they have always followed me. They have clung to me all my life.

Abraham Lincoln

We hurried to our gleaming limousine parked at the curb outside the church. Smiling, cheering and blowing bubbles of congratulations, guests lined the sidewalk. It was a sunny July afternoon—our wedding day.

Mark and I waved our good-byes, while the big car headed for the reception. I turned my attention to my wedding bouquet of delicate pink and ivory roses and thought of the printed words on the program: "The bride's bouquet is dedicated in loving memory of her mother, Joan Miller."

My throat tightened again. I took a breath of the roses' scent and then smiled at Mark.

"On to the party!" he called to the driver.

After a festive reception featuring a prime rib buffet and dancing, I felt the need to spend a private moment with my father.

"Thanks for everything, Dad. It was more than wonderful!" I gave him a lingering hug.

Mark and I slipped into the white limousine to leave. He wrapped his arm around my shoulder and pulled me close. Pastel balloons crowded my side of the seat, but I didn't mind. The young driver started for our destination, forgetting about our special stop. Mark spoke up to redirect him.

"Oh, yeah, you wanted to make a stop. Just tell me where to go." Mark gave him the location.

"It's a cemetery," I said softly. There was silence in the car. "My mom is buried there."

"I bet you don't get many requests like this," Mark chimed in.

"No, sure don't," the driver replied, glancing through his rearview mirror. "But I understand. I lost my mother when I was thirteen."

At the cemetery, I clutched Mark's hand. How could my heart be filled with so much happiness and so much emptiness at the same time?

There we were—me, a bride in long white gown, and Mark, a groom in handsome black tuxedo—strolling on the sun-scorched grass, gazing at tombstone after tombstone, caressed by the summer evening air.

One hand held my husband's and the other gripped my bouquet. My chin quivered as we neared my mother's gravesite. We stood prayerfully above it in the dusk. Then, without saying a word, I bent and tenderly laid my bridal flowers on her headstone. Lightly, lingeringly, I stroked the carved letters of my mother's name.

I just had to come here on this special day, Mom, I thought. *How you would have rejoiced at our wedding. The guests, the smiles, our joy.*

Mark held me to his chest while, together, we read the etched scripture my mother had chosen for her marker: "I know that my Redeemer lives." (Job 19:25) Next to those words lay the elegant bouquet that symbolized the most important day of my life.

Julie Messbarger
As told to Charlotte Adelsperger

Pennies from Heaven

Children and mothers never truly part
Bound in the beating of each other's heart.
Charlotte Gray

My friend Jill and her mom had a very close relation-ship. Of the many things they enjoyed together, they often talked about Jill's wedding day and what it would be like to plan together. But losing a battle with cancer would keep Jill's mom from ever seeing her daughter get married. Her death was devastating.

A few years later, Jill got engaged and began to plan her wedding. Every nuptial detail brought mixed emotions during this bittersweet time. Yet, despite her loss, Jill amazed me with her strength and faith.

Soon after her mom's death, a peculiar thing began hap-pening. Jill would find pennies at odd times in familiar places.

Sometimes she would go to shops and restaurants where she and her mom had spent time together. Miracu-lously, she'd find a bright, shiny penny. Occasionally she'd leave a room only to come back and find one right in the middle of the floor, knowing it wasn't there earlier. In the midst of stressful situations or struggles with her grief, a penny would pop up.

Jill believed they were signs from her mom.

"They're her way of letting me know she'll always be with me. They're my 'pennies from heaven.'"

On the day of the wedding, the bride, her other attendants and I went to Jill's favorite salon to get our hair done. The stylist did Jill's hair first, creating an elegant "up-do" with her blonde locks. The rest of us followed, taking turns in the stylists' chairs. The morning was pleasant with lots of laughter, smiles and even a few tears of love and happiness.

While Jill was in another room getting her makeup done, the stylists softly asked how she was holding up, knowing it was an emotional day.

"She's doing great," I said, "thanks to her 'pennies from heaven.'"

The two stylists looked perplexed, so I explained the phenomenon.

Astonished, one replied, "You're not going to believe this. But when we opened the shop this morning, there was a single, shiny penny in the middle of the floor. I know it wasn't there when we closed up the night before."

He directed us to the corner where he had swept the untouched penny. As he placed the polished copper coin in my hand, we stared at each other. All of us decided we would plan a special moment to present this token to Jill.

After the wedding reception, we anxiously waited for all the guests to leave.

"Close your eyes and stretch out your hand," I nervously asked. Grinning from ear to ear and with goose bumps tracing my spine, I gently placed the symbolic coin in Jill's palm.

She opened her eyes and stared in amazement.

While we explained where we found the penny, tears welled in her eyes. Jill squeezed the comforting coin and brought it close to her heart. Then she smiled and opened her hand again to admire her wedding memento.

"She's been here all day, hasn't she?" I fondly asked my friend.

With remarkable calm, Jill answered, "Yes, Mom didn't miss a thing."

Holly Jensen Hughes

Silverware and Sauces

Spice a dish with love and it pleases every palate.

Plautus

"How long has your grandma been senile?" my fiancé asked, after his first dinner at her house.

Truth is, while I made no excuses for my family, I had to feel pretty secure about someone to introduce them to my gene pool. The word "eccentric" doesn't really describe them, but it's more polite.

Still, I was startled by those words. If Grandma had turned senile, I couldn't tell. For as long as I could remember she'd been this way. Actually, she was spoiled. Her diminutive stature, soft chin and thinning white curls were misleading. While family members often sneaked around her, no one ever dared oppose her.

On the afternoon I asked to bring Wayne to dinner, Grandma perked up, turning away from her game show to regard me carefully. Bringing a man to the house was serious business. Grandma figured this was my last prospect for silverware and china. I was nearing thirty, after all, and had no property and way too much education.

"What does he like to eat?" She was intent on impressing this man on my behalf.

"Oh, I don't know, anything." I tried to be casual. Actually, he was something of a gourmet chef who cooked almost all the meals we shared, but I didn't dare let Grandma know that.

"He likes regular food," I said, "you know, just meat, potatoes and a vegetable. Green beans, maybe." This is what Grandma fixed every Sunday.

"But what do *you* fix for him?" Her eyes narrowed.

I made some vague answer. I'm sure she was suspicious, so I mumbled that he was fond of sauces.

"You mean gravy?" She was confident now.

"No, Grandma," I said, "not gravy. He likes sauces, on all kinds of things."

Grandma, of course, taught me what little there was to know about gravy; but I was thinking more along the lines of chasseur's sauce, teriyaki, Dijon and hollandaise, delicacies that required shallots, imported mushrooms and wine. Such ingredients never saw the inside of Grandma's kitchen.

So, the great and terrible Sunday came. Grandma arranged her good china on the carefully ironed linen tablecloth. She prepared meat, potatoes and green beans but, strangely, no gravy. I could tell by the thin line of Grandpa's mouth that he was holding his tongue about the lack of gravy.

By way of instruction to me, Grandma added an orange gelatin salad on iceberg lettuce, ice tea and a pickle tray. She made a big deal of having me help her in the kitchen, hoping my fiancé would be duped into believing I had cooked the meal.

Wayne was seated next to Grandma. Now, no one in the family actually remembers ever seeing Grandma eat. Normally, she perched on her chair, offering seconds way too early and commanding Grandpa to pass the white bread. With my future hanging in the balance, she was especially keen to her duty.

Within minutes after the meal began, Grandma sprang into the kitchen and returned with a bottle of steak sauce, which she placed strategically in front of Wayne. A few minutes later she went to the kitchen again, this time returning with a bottle of Worcestershire sauce. Before long, arrayed before the plate of the man I really wanted to impress, Grandma had arranged the ketchup, soy sauce, mustard . . . and just about anything else she could dig out of the cupboard. Judging from the crust around the caps, the bottles looked to be about twenty years old.

My fiancé threw me a puzzled glance.

"Grandma, what's with all the bottles?" I ventured, breaking with required etiquette.

"Well, didn't you say he liked sauces?" she whispered fiercely.

Much to his credit, Wayne didn't laugh out loud but only thanked Grandma for her attentions. He even put a little steak sauce on his meat to satisfy her. By the time Grandpa was served his traditional dessert of white balloon bread smothered in clear corn syrup, my friend and lover didn't even blink.

Our wedding was a few months later, and Grandma enjoyed herself while feeling helpful serving coffee from her own crowd-sized coffee maker.

Grandma is gone now; but I hope she knows I married well. We're not rich, but we're happy. It's a good partnership—he makes the sauces and I make the gravy.

Carol Mell

Budding Hope

There is no medicine like hope, no incentive so great, and no tonic so powerful as expectation of something better tomorrow.

Orison Marden

"Will you hurry up?"

I don't actually say it, but I'm sure thinking it. Sitting here on the front steps of my parents' house, I'm waiting for my new husband, Jim, who's still inside packing a few last things. We've been married for a week and a day.

This morning, we're going to swing by the hospital to visit Dad, say our farewells, climb into our car and head to Colorado from New York. This is such a wonderfully exciting time for us. Everything is brand-new, and we've decided to begin our married lives in a new state where I've never been before.

But for the moment, I have to wait. My mind wanders.

I glance over at the rose bush my father gave my mother on their twenty-fifth wedding anniversary. It was a grandiose gesture then, but what a sad-looking bush it is now. It's scrawny with a few buds scattered across its branches. I have no idea what color it's designed to produce because it's never bloomed. It just keeps hanging on year after year, budding out but not going any further until the leaves fall off each autumn. It's such a stubborn plant, sticking it out, determined to live.

Stubborn.

Suddenly this rose bush reminds me of an argument Dad and I had about a month ago. We had both been so stubborn over something that seems, now, so petty.

A few weeks before the wedding, I brought my wedding gown home along with a beautiful veil I had found. The veil coordinated perfectly with the gown. Okay, I admit, buying it was a bit extravagant because the veil actually cost more than the dress.

Later that night, about 1:00 A.M., I woke up because I heard a noise downstairs. I walked down to the kitchen to find Dad sitting at the table holding my veil. Before I could even ask why he was awake, he began criticizing the cost of the veil.

"I can't believe you'd spend that much!" He slammed his fist on the table.

Startled by his unexpected outburst, I reacted with my own angry protest. "It's made for the dress. Don't you want me to look great on my wedding day?"

Then came my ultimate hit-below-the-belt comment. "But what do you care? You might not even be there!"

Whoa. That one hurt. Especially because we both knew it was true.

Seriously ill, Dad was scheduled to have open-heart surgery on the Thursday after my wedding. He was pretty weak by this time (although you couldn't tell by his yelling) and was supposed to be resting in preparation.

Dad would enter the hospital for two weeks of testing prior to the surgery—and my wedding fell right in the middle. We all hoped the surgeon would "let Dad out" to attend and give me away.

But the fear hung there: Dad might not be strong enough. And, as the yelling showed, it was a sensitive issue.

I had grown up feeling very close to Dad. Yet here we were, hollering at each other, neither of us willing to give in. I would wear this veil no matter what. After all, it was my wedding.

We stood in silence, fuming, glaring at each other because there was no more to say. I stomped upstairs to my bedroom and broke down.

But this time it wasn't about the veil. I was scared and so was Dad. Scared he really wouldn't be at the wedding. Scared he could die. Scared to admit how much we loved each other, knowing I would be moving 2,000 miles away to start a life he couldn't be part of every day.

I slipped back to the kitchen and gave him a hug, a wordless "I'm sorry" for both of us.

On the evening of my wedding, they released Dad from the hospital (with lots of "dos" and "don'ts") for four hours. While we sat in the brides' room for a few last moments together, he took my hands lovingly in his.

"Hello, Beautiful."

He was too weak to walk with me down the aisle, so my brother did the honor. But Dad waited up front by the minister and gently put my hand into the hand of my new husband.

Now, a week after our wedding, Dad has had his surgery and is in critical condition. But we'll head over to see him in just a few minutes . . . if Jim hurries up. After all, it's almost 10:45 A.M. and we have to get on the road to Colorado and our future.

I catch a whiff of something sweet. Like a rose. It is a rose.

That scrawny bush is blooming! I stare at it, hardly believing what I'm seeing. Right before my eyes, one of the buds bursts into a full white blossom—like a film in fast motion. Beautiful.

"Jim!" I call out. "You've got to come and see this."

"Just a second, I have to get the phone," he answers from inside the house.

I watch the rose, amazed, until he comes out. I feel him sit down next to me. I pull my gaze from the rose to his face because he isn't saying anything. A long pause.

"I'm so sorry, Elaine, but your dad passed away a few minutes ago."

Dad died that morning at 10:44 A.M.—the exact minute the rose bush bloomed. I'm sure it was his special goodbye to me.

Yet, in my mind, that rose is not about goodbyes. It's about *hope*. The hope a wedding brings. The hope loving parents leave with their children by giving their very best. And the hope that comes from knowing this new man will take me "from this day forward" to help me blend new memories with old ones.

Elaine G. Dumler

Grandpa's Gift

If we really want to love, we must learn how to forgive.

Mother Teresa

My grandfather was a dirt-under-the-fingernails blue-collar worker all of his life. He provided for his family and never complained but, in his heart, he fancied himself a writer.

Grandpa would sit for long winter evenings in his rocking chair in the kitchen—writing, laughing, erasing and rearranging until he was satisfied. He didn't want to be just any writer; specifically, he dreamed of being a joke writer for Bob Hope.

While growing up in his house, I thought that was the funniest joke of all—Grandpa, a writer for Bob Hope. But, whenever he brought out his boxes of jokes, I laughed with Grandma . . . assuming they were funny merely because *Grandpa* thought they were funny.

Every so often he rented a typewriter and, using the hunt-and-peck finger system, sat at the kitchen table diligently transferring his hand-written creations onto index cards. More than anything in the world, I wanted to be big enough to learn to type so I could type Grandpa's jokes for him.

Several years later, I elatedly interrupted Grandpa— who was still writing jokes—to show him the glistening engagement ring I'd received the night before. Slowly and somberly, he removed his glasses, folded his paper and carefully put away his pencil. There was no laughter in his voice and his only words were: "I hope you know what you're doing."

I knew Grandpa didn't dislike the man I was betrothed to; they got along quite well. What he could not accept was me marrying someone of a different religion.

After that day, Grandpa didn't write any more jokes. In fact, our once loving home was suddenly filled with angry words and tears, and now I couldn't wait to move out of the home I had grown up in.

Instead of anticipation, I despaired over thoughts of my wedding day. Of Grandpa not only refusing to walk me down the aisle, but refusing to step foot in my fiancé's church. The stubborn man made it quite clear that although he couldn't stop me, he didn't have to condone it, either. I was determined to marry even without my beloved grandfather at my side.

Preparations for our modest wedding were made out of Grandpa's sight and hearing. Grandma worked on my dress during the day while Grandpa was at work. We prepared invitations at my in-laws' home. At night, I stitched my dress behind the closed door of my bedroom to spare us all uncomfortable silences. Even though we didn't have a lot of money, I refused to let Grandma ask Grandpa to share in the expenses. I could be just as stubborn as he was and I was determined to let him know it.

The day before the ceremony, I set my pride aside and pleaded with Grandpa to be part of my wedding. He refused to attend. I had never known him to be so unbending. I always knew how he felt about this particular religion, but I never dreamed my final days at home would be so horrible.

That night, tears of frustration and pain soaked my pillow. My last night in this room, in this bed and in this house should have been filled with joy. Instead we were strangers on separate planets—a universe apart. *How could he do this? How could I be married without Grandpa beside me?*

My wedding morning dawned cloudy and dismal, a mirror image of my gloomy heart. I lay quietly looking around the room of my childhood, remembering the many times when Grandpa sat on my bed reading night-time stories, soothing me after horrible nightmares and kneeling beside me for prayer.

I dreaded facing him at the breakfast table. Disheartened, I rolled over, sliding my hand up and under the pillow. Suddenly I felt something strange. An envelope? With a pounding heart, I carefully opened it and removed a letter written in Grandpa's familiar feathery script.

"My Dearest Child . . ."

Grandpa apologized, pouring out his heart in the most moving, heartfelt way he knew. He was sorry for spoiling my joy the past months, ashamed of his dreadful, selfish behavior. He explained his feelings and beliefs and said that, although they were his, he realized he had no right to impose them on me. He went on to ask forgiveness and—at long last—promised to welcome my new husband into his home and his heart. Just as he had welcomed me all those many years before.

As I continued to read, I saw a change in the handwriting and noticed blurred ink where a teardrop had fallen onto the paper in a splatter. Suddenly tears filled my own eyes. But I wept for joy, not sorrow, when I read his humble plea, begging the "honor" of walking me down the aisle.

Grandpa never did sell any jokes to Mr. Hope, but the greatest thing he ever wrote was that single cherished letter to a beloved, grateful granddaughter.

Nicolle Woodward

Oh, What a Catch!

Children are an anchor that hold a mother to life.

Sophocles

Our home bustled with last-minute details that crisp, sunny September morning. This was a family affair. Our oldest daughter Christina was the gorgeous bride, middle daughter Jennifer a bridesmaid and ten-year-old Melissa a junior bridesmaid. Bride and bridesmaids shared a mirror, the flash of a camera adding its sparkle to capture the moment in history.

We loved our son-to-be, and we eagerly anticipated the ceremony that would make his entry into the family "official." With the father of the bride preparing for his role and me taking it all in, the day was off to a wonderful start.

The wedding went more beautifully than we could've ever imagined. The love in Christina and Wes's eyes provided warmth and romance to the setting that flowers alone could not. And the unexpected presentation of a candy Ring Pop by the best man, when the ring was asked for, added a touch of lightheartedness to the occasion.

Throughout the planning of this unforgettable day, our middle daughter, Jennifer, was sure she was also dating the man of her dreams, Bo. He wore his tuxedo proudly as one of the groomsmen.

At garter-throwing time, the line of male would-be catchers swarmed to the challenge. Pure grit and determination got Bo to the front of the crowd to snatch the garter. Soon afterward, it was time for the bouquet to be thrown. Poor Jennifer, sardined into the crowd of single hopefuls, didn't stand a chance. Yet—somehow—she managed to catch it. Everyone thought it was a little fishy. But Bo and Jennifer beamed as the photographer snapped pictures of them holding their "trophies."

A few weeks later, we were invited to a fish fry at Bo's family's lake house. At dinner, Bo startled everyone.

"There was more than one fish caught for this occasion," he grinned, "but I made the best catch." Then he turned and asked Jennifer to marry him. With the first wedding still a warm memory, we began planning the second.

The following autumn found us again pinning hair, zipping dresses and flashing cameras. It was the September wedding of Jennifer's dreams. It was also an anniversary month—Christina's first and our twenty-fourth. What a celebration!

At the reception, we teased again and again, "Our hearts are full . . . but our pockets are empty. Just don't let Melissa near the bouquet!"

But fate—and Melissa—had other ideas. Don't ask me how, don't ask me why, but our youngest daughter managed to catch her sister's bouquet.

Thank goodness we don't have to worry about our eleven-year-old getting married anytime soon. Nevertheless, we're saving her a date in September . . . for someday.

Kaylen Pierce

copyright kathy shaskan 2002

"And there's Charlene, my youngest.
She was all-state diving three years in a row."

8

KEEPSAKES

The heart
  hath its own memory,
  Like the mind,
  And in it are enshrined
  The precious
  keepsakes . . .

Henry Wadsworth Longfellow

The Ring of Love

To live in hearts we leave behind is not to die.

Thomas Campbell

Thirty-three years have passed and I've experienced much heartache since that day. But many wonderful moments have been mine as well—like the afternoon I walked down the aisle, arm-in-arm with my big brother, to wed my high school sweetheart. This was the day when all I had learned about love would come full circle.

My dad wasn't able to give his youngest daughter away, since cancer had claimed his life just three years earlier, so Tom, six years my senior, honored me that day.

It was essential, of course, that I have "something old, something new, something borrowed and something blue" on my wedding day. I wore the traditional new white dress and a garter of blue. A thin gold band my brother had given me six years before fit my left ring finger. It was "something borrowed" and "something old." It was my mother's wedding band.

Coming from a farm in Minnesota to the fast life of California with their three children, Mom and Dad often struggled. But she never complained. And soon a fourth child was born to the household.

Being the baby was a great position to occupy, especially since I came so much later than the other three. I didn't have to share. On top of it all, I was a tomboy, so my mother had her work cut out for her.

Like so many kids, I was caught up in my own plans and thoughts, and took it for granted that Mom would always be there for me. She sang goofy songs, made homemade cakes, sewed doll clothes and cuddled often. She was the warmth at the end of a cold day. It was impossible for me to ever lie to her, and I would find myself telling Mom everything in my heart. She was an amazing listener and my role model.

My father, although he drank daily, loved my mother immensely. Every Friday night, I watched him come home from work with groceries and a bouquet of yellow mums. Her face would light up as if it was the first time.

Mom had never applied for a driver's license, so she rarely left the house. Dad would make his daily trip to the local market, returning with just enough for supper that night. Sometimes he would get sidetracked, find himself sitting on a stool at the local bar near the market. Mom knew, and I guess I did too. But in those days we never spoke about it. She was committed to her husband and her family—no matter what.

From the time I was thirteen years old, my mom struggled with her health. One day, she finally told me that she had been diagnosed with congestive heart failure. Always in and out of hospitals, she fought the disease the best she could. She worsened over the next three years, shriveling to half her size. But her warm smile was as big as ever.

It was April 21, 1970, my father's birthday. A message received at my school office explained a family emergency.

Someone was coming to take me home. *No!* I screamed silently.

At the hospital, I held my mom's hand, as she lay comatose. I begged her not to leave me. I still needed her. Dad needed her. The fear of loneliness took hold of my heart. My mind could not fathom life without her. Sobbing profusely, I told her, over and over again, how much I loved her. With so much nervous energy, I found myself fiddling with her tiny wedding band, now loosely hanging on her finger.

My throat was thick with emotion as I thought of the thin golden symbol that represented the deep love and commitment she and my father had for one another. Now Mom lay there, motionless, connected to tubes and equipment. Suddenly, to my amazement, I felt her left hand squeeze my own, as if to tell me she loved me and to urge me to remember what matters most in life. She was saying goodbye.

Later that evening, the phone rang. Dad answered and, after a long moment, tears welled in his eyes as he muttered weakly, "Oh, no . . . my Evey, no."

The rest of the night is a blur, except for the coldness of the air stinging my tear-stained face as I ran down the street screaming, "Mom, I need you Mom, come back!" I was sixteen years old. And I felt lost.

At the memorial service, my brother Tom walked over to me and placed the ring of gold in my hand. He said nothing, but his eyes spoke volumes.

The days following the funeral were the hardest days of my life. Caring for my father, maintaining our home and focusing on school were all so difficult. Dad seemed lost, too. He missed his bride. He drank more. We both just did the best we could. I fiddled with the tiny gold band, rotating it repeatedly, reminding myself of the things that matter most—to love and be loved.

My father and I moved from my childhood home to start a new life. Soon Dad began his own battle with cancer. I was holding his hand when he finally lost. He fumbled for my ring finger and, holding fast to that tiny wedding band, he breathed his last breath, as if saying to my Mom, "I promised till death do us part, but I meant forever and a day."

My father died on their wedding anniversary.

That small ring of love has graced my finger for thirty-three years. It appears overshadowed beneath the beautiful diamond ring given to me by Mark, my high-school sweetheart, twenty-seven years ago. Yet, like its message from my past, it shines clear and bright.

Love endures all things. Love never fails. Mom and Dad were not with me physically on my wedding day, or at the births of their grandchildren, and that saddens me. But they left me a priceless gift expressed through a band of gold. A circle of love that lives on forever.

Ginger Boda

Kitchen Cache

It was a big step for Chet to give me free rein in his mother's kitchen. After all, he had lived there with his parents for more than thirty years and was comfortable with the way things were.

But, since his father died years earlier and his mother passed away months before we married, we chose to move into their fully furnished house. Although the cupboards and closets contained a lifetime of memories and possessions, we were eager to use the beautiful wedding gifts we had received—treasures that would make this family house our own unique home.

I was particularly eager to tackle the kitchen—all twenty-four cabinets and drawers. Like other newlyweds, we had registered a favorite pattern of china; our lovely set of swirl-rimmed Regency White was unwrapped and ready to be put away.

Chet was a trouper. He gave me free rein to make changes. Soon after the honeymoon, he devoted an entire Saturday to helping. We stretched. We strained. We cleaned. And cleaned. And cleaned.

We loaded, ran and unloaded the dishwasher over and

over. We ripped out and replaced sticky, aged shelf paper. We sorted the treasures we found. Things to discard; things to use; things to store.

By early evening we were exhausted and tense. But we were determined now to complete the project and have everything cleaned and put away before we dragged ourselves into bed. We delved into the deepest, darkest, dustiest cabinet. We pulled out antique appliances, several serving pieces, and even a bulky bowl—grubby gray—with clumsy handles and a ladle protruding under the lid.

Once again, we filled the dishwasher and turned it on for the umpteenth time. This would be our last load.

After we ate and rested a bit, we headed back to the kitchen to finish. I pulled out the bottom rack of the dishwasher and unloaded the large, gray—

No, it couldn't be! The once gray bowl was now solid white. Delicate swirls edged the rim. I gingerly turned it over and read the bottom.

"Regency White."

It was expensive. It was elegant. It was a two-handled soup tureen complete with matching lid and ladle. And it matched *our* wedding china.

Where did it come from? Had it been a gift to Chet's mother? Or did she special order it? How did it find its way to the secret depths of her kitchen? How long had it been there? Chet couldn't recall ever seeing it before.

To this day, the mystery remains unsolved. But we like to think it has special significance. Chet's mother graced us with a lasting treasure from her "old" kitchen to our new one. A divine wedding gift that will always remind us of her love and her eternal presence in our hearts.

Lucy Akard Seay

A Tradition in the Waiting

A promise made is a debt unpaid.

Robert W. Service

Tucked snugly in Gram's bed, I watched Sunday morning dawn. I loved the way the light sidled in around her vinyl shades to dance with the weightless dust that floated in its path before falling, silently, upon Grandma's braided rug. I could smell fried bologna and eggs and knew Gram would soon collect me for breakfast.

I crawled out of the bed to explore.

Across the room stood her dresser whose drawers, I knew, were full of cosmetics and perfumes and a jar of cold cream all mingling into the fragrant scent of Gram. But my attention focused on the unassuming jewelry box perched on top. Standing on tiptoe, I lifted it to the floor and knelt before it.

As quietly as my clumsy young hands would allow, I slid the top off the box and worked my way through all the things I deemed less valuable: bangles and baubles; costume jewelry; an old photo of a much younger Pop on his Harley. . . . And then I found it—the small blue box that seemed to call to me on my Sunday morning visits.

Despite its lackluster plastic facade, it contained the most beautiful ring I had ever seen. Reverently, I took the delicate circle from its nest of blue velour and slid it on my finger. Turning my hand this way and that, I admired its sparkle and pretended I was a bride.

I counted the small, crudely cut diamonds surrounding the large solitaire. Eight little ones circled one big one. Nine diamonds that looked just like a crystal flower. My young eyes didn't recognize the handcrafted workmanship. They didn't appreciate the intricate filigree of the band. But I saw it was worn and very old, and I could almost hear it whisper romantic stories from the past.

Gram found me gazing dreamily into her large mirror.

To my surprise, she didn't scold. Instead, she gathered me back to her bed.

"Sweetheart," she explained, "your grandfather gave me this ring as an engagement gift."

My eyes grew big. I *knew* it had a story. Listening intently as Gram continued, I reveled in the rosy glow of yesteryear.

"It was a tradition in his family for generations. A father would pass this ring to his eldest son when he decided to marry. And he, in turn, would pass it to his firstborn son."

From son to eldest son. Wow. I knew the ring represented the past—our family's past. It connected me backward through time to my ancestry and heritage. It told me something of who I was and who *we* were.

But Gram wasn't finished.

". . . However, your uncle seems quite content to remain a bachelor. So, I'll make a deal with you." She leaned closer and whispered, "If he's still single by the time you get married, the ring is *yours*."

Mine!

"Now if you don't mind," she slipped the ring off my finger and back into its soft nest, "the eggs are getting cold."

Thirteen years passed.

At last, and never having forgotten Gram's promise, I was ready to announce my own engagement. Although my uncle remained single, it felt strange to ask for the heirloom ring. But Gram saw that I didn't have to.

As she hugged me in congratulation, Gram pressed the well-remembered box into my hand and smiled.

"Now you don't have to make believe."

Lorraine Cheeka

Golden Slippers

*In every conceivable manner, the family is link
to our past, bridge to our future.*

Alex Haley

After the funeral, the family made its way from the
cemetery back to the house. Ladies from the church had
arrived early, uncovering casseroles and platters of sand-
wiches and desserts. Nobody talked much. Poppa
mumbled that he didn't know how he was going to get
along without Mama around anymore. We all agreed it
was going to be hard.

After lunch, we just sat there, all out of tears . . . not
really knowing what to do without Mama there to orga-
nize everybody. I forget who it was that broke the silence.

"Well, we need to make some decisions soon about
dividing up Mama's things."

There were furs and furniture, photos and antiques,
crystal, handmade quilts, hats and shoes, rockers and jewelry. It all needed to be divided between the four children
and their families.

Suddenly, from the adjoining room, my thirteen-year-old

daughter came running. Her ears had perked up when she overheard the conversation about dividing a household of her grandmother's belongings.

"I know what I want," she said boldly. "I want Grandmommy's dancing slippers!"

"Dancing slippers?" I asked in surprise. "But Grandmommy doesn't have any dancing slippers."

"Oh, yes she does. I'll go get them and show you."

I followed closely as she hurried down the hallway—straight into Grandmommy's bedroom. Not the pink bedroom where she slept every night, but the rarely used guest room at the far end of the house.

It was a stately room, featuring a four-poster bed and an antique washstand draped with linens. In the corner was a vase full of peacock feathers from Uncle Henry's farm. Granddaddy's Bible lay open on the marble dresser, his reading glasses folded and resting somewhere in the Book of John. And sure enough, beside the bed, on a hand-made wooden shoebox, sat a pair of golden slippers with pixie pointed toes.

My daughter picked them up and held them out for me to observe.

"Honey, why do you call these Grandmommy's dancing slippers?" I asked. "Grandmommy didn't dance."

A look of disbelief swept across her face.

"Oh, yes she did! Grandmommy always danced in these shoes!"

As quickly as she spoke the words, I remembered. My mother had, indeed, danced many times. I had forgotten about the earlier years when we visited. She took my two children back into her special guest bedroom and closed the door. And there, before her private audience, she would put on her golden slippers and dance the Charleston.

Often I would sneak a little peek. My children would sit

on the floor, wide-eyed and watching, as my mother crossed her hands over her knees, twirled her invisible string of pearls and danced so fast she would fling her golden slippers aimlessly into the air.

Laughing as they watched her dance the jitterbug, the children cried, "Do it again. Dance again!" So out of breath she could hardly speak, she would find the golden slippers, slide them onto her feet and start the performance over.

Twenty-five years after Grandmommy's death, my daughter got married. She arrived at the chapel wearing a shoulder-length veil and a white satin dress accented in butter-cream lace and pearls. A boys' choir marched before her in the processional and as the organist played the first notes of "Trumpet Voluntary," she took hold of her father's arm and began her long walk down the aisle.

Snug on her feet, sliding across the stone floor, was a pair of aged, worn-out golden slippers with pixie pointed toes. And in the air was the feeling that somewhere up there, part of a private audience, was Grandmommy, wide-eyed and watching, smiling . . . and dancing the Charleston.

Charlotte Lanham

The Wedding Gift

A gift, with a kind countenance, is a double present.

Thomas Fuller, M.D.

I had picked out the flowers in my wedding bouquet carefully, with thought for the meaning of each one. There was blue iris, my fiancé's favorite flower; white roses, symbolizing purity; and strands of green ivy, to represent faithfulness.

Midway through our wedding reception, I found myself breathless and happy, chatting with friends and juggling a full champagne glass and my flowers. Suddenly, I felt a hand on my shoulder. I turned to see a woman I had met only briefly, a friend of my new mother-in-law. In her hand, she held a tendril of ivy.

"This fell out of your bouquet when you were on the dance floor," she said. I thanked her and began to reach for it, when she added, "Do you mind if I keep it?"

I was startled at first. I hadn't even tossed my bouquet yet. And I barely knew this woman. What did she want with my ivy?

But then practicality kicked in. I was leaving on my honeymoon in the morning and certainly wouldn't take the bouquet along. I had no plans for preserving it. And I'd been given so much today.

"Go ahead. Keep it," I said with a smile, and congratulated myself for being gracious in the face of a rather odd request. Then the music started up, and I danced off in the crowd.

A few months later, the bell rang at our new home. I opened the door to find that same stranger on my porch. This time, I couldn't hide my surprise. I hadn't seen her since the wedding. What was this all about?

"I have a wedding gift for you," she said, and held out a small planter crowded with foliage. Suddenly, I knew. "It's the ivy you dropped at your wedding," she explained. "I took it home and made a cutting and planted it for you."

Years ago, at her own wedding, someone had done the same for her. "It's still growing, and I remember my wedding day every time I see it," she said. "Now, I try to plant some for other brides when I can."

I was speechless. All the quirky thoughts I'd had, and what a beautiful gift I'd received!

My wedding ivy has thrived for many years, outliving any other effort I made at indoor gardening. As the giver predicted, a glance at the glossy green leaves brings back memories of white lace and wedding vows. I treasure the ivy's story and have shared it many times.

Now, nearly twenty years later, I'm the mother of three growing sons. Someday they'll be married, I know. And although I don't want to be an interfering in-law, surely the mother of the groom can suggest that the bride's bouquet contain a bit of ivy?

I know just the plant to cut it from.

Carol Sturgulewski

Keeping the Tradition

We cannot really love anybody with whom we never laugh.

Agnes Repplier

The year was 1972. Noel and I had just gotten married in southern California and were traveling—by car—to our new life together in Pennsylvania. My in-laws offered to pack the top layer of the wedding cake in dry ice and mail it after we got settled in our attic apartment.

Sure enough, a few weeks later the package arrived. We eagerly unpacked it and placed it in our "freezer," a small metal box mounted inside the back of the refrigerator. The cake filled the entire compartment. Now we had a serious choice to make.

After some thought, a little deliberation, and a lot of conversation, we decided to forfeit ice cube trays and ice cream for the next twelve months—in honor of tradition. It was a big price to pay, but eating the cake top on our first anniversary would make it worthwhile.

One year later our anniversary arrived. I gently removed the package from the freezer and was relieved to see that our perfectly preserved top layer looked as fresh as it had on our wedding day. I made a nice dinner while it defrosted and Noel prepared for our celebration. When the meal was over, I ceremoniously handed the cake knife to Noel and asked him to do the honors and cut the first slice.

Noel pressed down on the knife.

"Something doesn't feel right," he said, pressing harder. We heard a strange noise, a squeaky crunch.

"Something doesn't sound right."

What was wrong with the cake? Noel slid the small piece onto a dessert plate. We stared in disbelief, caught each other's eyes, and burst out laughing.

Styrofoam! Our "cake" top was iced Styrofoam!

And, to think, for an entire year we had sacrificed cold drinks and frozen desserts in anticipation of this traditional event. After we finally quit chuckling, we raced straight to the store. Now we would *really* celebrate . . . by stocking the freezer with ice cube trays and our favorite ice cream.

Dr. Denise Enete

Showered with Love

Creativity requires the courage to let go of certainties.

Erich Fromm

"Stacy, you are my rock, my one true friend who never judges me, is always there and loves me unconditionally."

These were the words I wrote for my best friend at her wedding shower. It was my gift. In fact, it was everybody's gift—written pieces of memories, stories, insights and prayers for Stacy's future.

When Stacy asked me to be matron of honor, I was thrilled and couldn't wait to host her shower. I had my own opinions of traditional wedding showers and had decided on a nontraditional one for myself. Although I stressed to her that her shower could be any way she wanted, I was happy when she told me she liked what I had done for mine and wanted hers the same.

Relief and elation danced harmoniously inside me; I couldn't wait to give Stacy a wedding shower with meaning.

A few years ago, several months before my wedding,

three dear family friends wanted to throw me a shower. I was both touched and panicked. Touched because these women had known me since infancy and panicked because I was at the beginning of what is now my full entry into the simple living movement—I didn't want more stuff.

I thought long and hard about my quandary and went to the women with the idea of an alternative wedding shower.

Guests would be long-time friends and family. So, in place of a gift, I asked that they write a memory or story and read it at the shower. I knew this request would disturb some people. Write? And, read it out loud?

But, in the end, my belief that there's a writer in all of us was proven true. The final creations included kind, sentimental and humorous words read about me, to me. It was one of the most meaningful days of my life and everything was put in a keepsake book that I cherish to this day.

Remembering my wonderful experience, I couldn't wait for Stacy and her family and friends to experience the same. Stacy was showered with everything from handwritten words on plain paper to printed words on formal stationery. While I was pleased with my own piece, complete with blackmail pictures from our junior high days, the writings from Stacy's mother and future mother-in-law were the most moving of the day.

An only adopted child, Stacy and her mother held a strong mother-daughter bond that grew even stronger when her father passed away a few years ago. Her mother's memories—captured from the day she brought baby Stacy home to the present day—were something Stacy would treasure forever.

Her future mother-in-law brought tears to the room when she read a prayer written when her son was just seven years old. The prayer asked God to have her son's future mate in His care and bless her with wonderful qualities complementary to her son's. She concluded by sharing that God had not only answered her prayer, but had exceeded it.

Tissue boxes were passed as tears flowed and love filled the room. It was a touching shower. One filled with memories. I can't wait to give Stacy her keepsake book, a gift no amount of money can buy.

Lisa Solomon

$\overline{9}$

WELCOME TO THE FAMILY

As we are married, our families are united, the generations blended—all in a beautiful celebration of life.

Dean Walley

Our First Meeting

When you realize you want to spend the rest of your life with somebody, you want the rest of your life to start as soon as possible.
                    Harry to Sally in *When Harry Met Sally*

As a college student in the '70s, I belonged to a youth program called "Contact Canada," whose purpose was to attract potential college immigrants to Canada. I was one of only four Americans in an international group of two hundred young adults who toured in teams to several provinces.

Along the way, I met a lovely Brit, and we became friends. But our three weeks quickly came to an end, and we returned home to our respective countries. Sue and I exchanged letters over the next year.

The following summer, she flew to California to stay with my folks and me for a month-long holiday. I was immediately entranced by this exciting woman and asked her to marry me after two short weeks. We consulted an immigration attorney, who recommended that we marry on U.S. soil to shorten the laborious green-card process.

After six months, we could then have a formal church wedding.

With that, my best friend Joel, Sue and I drove to Reno for a one-day trip to tie the knot after a two-week engagement. We intentionally downplayed the ceremony, telling ourselves that this was only "for the government." We had no rings, no formal attire, and of course, no honeymoon. Aside from being love struck, our official marriage in the U.S. would shorten her request for residency to months rather than years.

The following day, I reluctantly watched Sue board a Pan Am 747 through tear-filled eyes. I hid in a corner of the airport lounge to compose myself. We would be separated for one hundred and twelve days—a time in which I would receive a letter a day from my long-distance bride.

I didn't have the courage to ask her how her parents handled the news that their only daughter was returning from a holiday married to an American. Somewhere in the hour drive between Heathrow and their home near Gatwick, she made the announcement. As much as I missed her, I'll admit I was relieved to have missed that awkward moment. Especially telling her father.

Each day seemed like an eternity waiting for the end of my college semester. My flight to England was scheduled two hours after my last final at San Jose State, but even that wasn't enough time. I would have to finish my three-hour test in only one hour. Nobody has ever whipped though an archeology final with such enthusiasm.

On the plane, I sat in my window seat in a complete daze. I was desperate to see Sue again and excited to stand before God and family to exchange vows in a real wedding.

But amidst the excitement, I was absolutely terrified—a nervous wreck, wondering what fate had in store for me when I finally met my *father-in-law*. After all, his daughter and I only dated a month before getting engaged for only two weeks. My worse crime, I was sure, was not properly asking him for her hand with European formality.

I pictured him basking in the same aura of anti-Americanism that was prevalent all over Europe in the mid-'70s. My stomach twisted and burned, and my excitement was waning as the fear grew.

After my plane landed, I found my luggage and stood in the long line at Immigration, in dread of *the meeting*. I prayed the drive to her family home would be quick and the impending explosion of anger even quicker.

As I cleared customs and entered the concourse, a sea of faces surrounded me. From the crowd, a gentleman broke free and raced towards me. Although I had not met her father yet, I knew who this man approaching me was. It was time. The long wait was over, and I was prepared for my fate.

He ran up to me, grabbed my hand and pumped it up and down in a warm handshake. His left hand slapped my shoulder as he said, "Thank God, lad. I thought she would never leave the house!"

And so began my relationship with a man that I've loved and respected for twenty-seven years. He's given me the gift of his daughter, my best friend and soul mate. Unexpectedly, he also gave me his gift of acceptance.

David R. Wilkins

Ode to My Mother-in-Law

I haven't spoken to my mother-in-law for eighteen months. I don't like to interrupt her!
Ken Dodd

A mother-in-law, the stories all say,
Is a thing to be feared by night or by day.
For you just never know when the man that you love
Will come out with the phrase
"Well, what my mother does . . ."

A mother-in-law is a fearsome thing.
But she's part of the package
When you take her son's ring.

She's your husband's mom—the woman who knows
How to bake lasagna and launder his clothes.
Her advice may be timely but not always loved
By the wife who must treat her with tender kid gloves.

Oh, a mother-in-law is a fearsome thing.
But she's part of the package

When you take her son's ring.
My husband is Randy; his mother is Rita
A woman who daily grows sweeter and sweeter.
She never butts in and she never takes note
Of the mess on my floors or pet hairs on her coat.
She's come to be part of my circle of friends
And her love for my son, well, it just never ends.
A half-century of wisdom is hers to impart
I've learned from her words and take them to heart.

A mother-in-law is a wonderful thing.
She was the bow on the package
When I took her son's ring.

V. J. Coulman

"Oh, calm down, dear! No one's looking! Just let me tweeze these little hairs you've got, so David doesn't think he's marrying Groucho Marx."

Final Approval

Am I not destroying my enemies when I make friends of them?

Abraham Lincoln

I rapped the serpent-head doorknocker, noting the uncanny symbolism when the door opened, creaking like Herman Munster's. There stood Miss Kay's father dressed in what looked like laboratory coveralls. It was a first date—the clumsy ceremony that begins with the dreaded handshake and introduction to "Daddy."

My grasp was dutifully subservient and his was firm enough to cause my knuckles to fuse. My fingers wrung red with pain, I knew it was just a form of punishment for requesting his daughter's company that evening. I remember thinking my black leather jacket probably sent the wrong message. But it was stylish, not the kind with excessive zippers.

As we left, I sensed Eddie's beady eyes following me, and even the clap of the heavy front door didn't free me from his stare. I looked back and saw the Venetian blind tilted up at one corner. His laser pupils pierced the darkness, causing the paint on my Chevy to sizzle and smoke.

Thus I survived the dreaded introduction to Mr. Eddie Banks.

Miss Kay and I dated nonstop for the next two years and I endured cold reception after cold reception from her father. When we had any conversation at all, it was like an oral exam. I formed each word carefully, not wanting to expose any unnecessary clues about my life that Eddie could probe.

I felt ashamed about my past. My parents divorced when I was an infant then went their separate ways, leaving me behind. Raised like an orphan—shuffled among relatives and living out of a footlocker—I feared my gypsy-like life wouldn't pass muster against the standards Eddie set for his daughter's beau.

So our courtship went by the book. Eddie's book.

I had Kay home by curfew and never called on the phone during mealtimes. I brought jonquils to Mrs. Eddie on her birthday, and once raked their yard while they were at work. I piled the leaves in two giant pyramids at the curb, and had them both burning when Eddie got home. He stood on the patio like General Patton—a Lucky Strike crimped between his teeth. The slight nod of his head was approval enough for me. It made me glad I had skipped fishing with my friends that day.

Then came the awful night when I asked for Kay's hand in marriage. The down-on-one-knee part went okay, but when I produced the rings of betrothal all hell broke loose in a mocking slur of my words.

"She can be 're-gaged,'" Eddie said, "but there'll be no ringely-dingelies on my daughter's hand!"

I snapped the ring box shut so fast I nearly lost a finger and stuffed it back into my pocket like a wary shoplifter. With his quivering finger pointing to the door, I left while Kay still pleaded for mercy. Obviously, there were few options left for two star-struck lovers.

I devised a plan. My brother lived in Florida and, through friends, got me a job. He even gave up his extra bedroom to help defray my expenses. I saved my first four paychecks for our nest egg, albeit meager, and sent for my bride-to-be. Ours was a whirlwind elopement.

Miss Kay packed a suitcase and left a note on the refrigerator saying she was spending the night with a girlfriend. With trembling legs and thumping heart, she took a cab to the airport and slumped down in the seat to avoid detection. Three hours later my brother and I met the plane and whisked Miss Kay away to Georgia where marriage was legal for eighteen-year-olds.

The sign read "Welcome to Donaldsonville." It was just a sleepy Georgia town but a noted marriage mill where required blood tests could be obtained at the Gulf Service Station. Our marriage was performed auctioneer-fashion.

For a twenty-dollar fee, we got a tinfoil-stamped certificate and a "honeymoon kit" from the judge. It contained samples of Midol, Tampax, Vaseline, Mercurochrome and Kleenex.

The phone was ringing when we got to my brother's house. It was Kay's frantic mother. She warned that Eddie, together with the Texas Rangers, had launched a manhunt. Whatever hopes I had for a boom-bah wedding night were dashed; instead, we spent it hiding under the bed and, in my new role as son-in-law, I slipped into an uneasy relationship with Kay's father.

The years zipped past like the jerky, hurried characters in silent movies, and the birth of our two boys formed the bookends of our lives together. Surprisingly, mutual respect replaced the simple coexistence that once had been the tone of my relationship with Eddie. Don't ask me how it happened. Maybe it was a byproduct of the peace grandkids bring.

We talked often about childhood experiences. In those conversations, I finally disclosed my past. Eventually, Eddie shared his. I learned that Eddie was only fourteen when his father died. He supported his mother and four sisters with meager earnings from the Depression-era Civil Conservation Corps. He, too, had had a rough boyhood and survived an austere, "foot-locker" existence.

Our exchanges revealed we had more similarities than differences. And the greatest similarity of all was our mutual love for his daughter.

In 1993, I was at Eddie's side when he died. That day he appointed me an honorary member of the Banks family. He leaned over in his bed to whisper a long-held secret in my ear:

"I hate to admit it," he said, "but you're my favorite son-in-law."

I told him it wasn't lost on me that his daughter was an only child. He closed his eyes, pursed his lips in a tight smile and took his last breath with my hand clasping his.

His grip was firm enough to cause my knuckles to fuse.

Lad Moore

Just Like Hazel

I was a nervous bride. I couldn't wait to be in my husband's arms and life, but I was leaving everything familiar. I was moving from the city to the country. I was leaving my small family behind and becoming part of an enormous, close-knit clan.

I stood at the reception while my husband made his way around the room. Another difference. I was shy, unsure. My husband had never met a stranger. His entire family was confident and outgoing. It was easy to get lost in a family like that when you're a person like me. I counted on two hands the people I knew well.

We decided to hold the wedding in Richard's hometown. His family accounted for most of the invitations we had so carefully inscribed. Plus his church friends and neighbors— the people who had known and loved him since boyhood. It was simply easier to transport my family of five and my closest friends to his hometown than to ship an entire community to my city.

Would we make it? Would I regret my decision the morning I woke up on a farm? Would I regret trading my slick green Mustang for a John Deere tractor?

The panic must have been marked clearly on my face.

Richard's grandfather slipped beside me and placed an arm around my waist.

"How are you?"

"Fine," I lied.

Digging in his pants pocket, he pulled out his wallet and held out a faded picture. "Isn't she beautiful?"

I studied the picture. She wasn't a classic beauty but I saw spunk in her dark eyes. Her hair was coiffed in the style of a long-gone past. And she was beautiful to Richard's grandfather. I loved that. "Yes, she's beautiful," I agreed.

"When we met we were just kids. We've been through a lot together."

I shook my head knowingly; Richard had told me all about them. They survived the Great Depression. They parented five children. They lost two teenagers—within three months of each other. He farmed and held a town job, working from dawn until sundown, to make sure his family was comfortable and cared for.

His voice cracked and he smiled—identical to the warm smile that had captivated my heart when I first met my husband. "Every year that goes by I love her more. That's what takes you through the hard times." He put his hand over mine. "If you will love my grandson just half as much as I love Hazel, you'll make it."

Tears dampened my eyes at the thought of this legacy. I could sit and worry about the differences between my husband and me. Or I could simply love the man that was my soul mate. I chose love.

Grandpa had a stroke in their sixty-second year of marriage; his Hazel nursed him. He couldn't speak but his eyes said volumes as she gently bathed and fed him. She took care of his every need, working from dawn to sundown to make sure he was comfortable and cared for until his death four years later. I wish I could talk to Grandpa Franklin once more. I'd thank him for comforting a nervous young bride. Then I'd tell him I love his grandson every bit as much as he loved Hazel.

T. Suzanne Eller

All in the Family

We are each other's business; we are each other's magnitude and bond.

Gwendolyn Brooks

"When you get married, babe, you marry the whole family."

That was my mother's caution to me as a young teenager. At the time I thought she said it to encourage me to get rid of my then-boyfriend, and maybe she did. In any case, it was a warning I didn't understand until my wedding day.

He was my best friend. He said he loved me when we were sixteen, and I laughed it off. At seventeen, he said he was going to marry me, and I laughed it off. At eighteen he kissed me, and I stopped laughing—but I didn't really believe he was serious for several more stormy years.

I wanted—in the tradition of my family—to move far away, start over, maybe visit my relatives every couple years. So I moved out west and went to school. He wanted, he said, to stay in Michigan for his family, but he was always there for me when I needed him, which was often.

After a few years I realized the kind of love we had was the kind I'd been looking for. The kind you keep, even if you don't really see the merits of staying in Michigan indefinitely. I returned home, convinced we could overcome any obstacle, and we made plans to get married no matter what.

But there was the matter of our families.

My family was small, suburban, a hardworking set of parents, my brother and me; we all accepted our new member without a hitch. His family, on the other hand, intimidated me. I strived to avoid them—and there were a lot of them to avoid.

Every holiday they converged in confusing, noisy crowds. They were rich and poor, black and white and Hispanic, city-dwellers or not, from every walk and in every stage of life. But they knew all about each other and hugged and laughed and talked at each gathering like they'd never been apart.

They scared me to death.

They ignored me, too, at first. But when I'd been to a few of the same special occasions, signifying I was more than just a passing fad, they started paying attention. I dreaded holidays. I would be patted, hugged, pinched, asked personal questions, given unsolicited opinions and expected to remember the names of five or six generations of people who looked and acted nothing alike.

My husband-to-be just smiled when I talked about it, and told me to give it time.

Even though I trusted him, I couldn't imagine staying in Michigan, within reach of the whole mad horde of them. But when we announced our engagement, I realized I didn't know the half of it. I learned the hard way that big families aren't just about holidays.

Suddenly I was an insider. That meant not just Christmas parties and weddings, but a whole host of new duties I'd never heard of before—all of which seemed dreadfully embarrassing.

There were funerals, baby showers, special masses and kids' birthday parties. Never mind that you didn't know the deceased or weren't religious or had never heard of the kid. You were family, so you went. It was as simple as that.

I found myself mumbling and patting the hand of a dying old woman (whom I'd only met once before) in a hospital bed, shedding real tears over the casket of an old friend of the family I'd only ever heard stories about, and holding a newborn (something I'd never done) while I asked, sheepishly, to be reminded of his mother's name.

Planning the wedding was like nothing I'd expected, either. Somehow I thought that my fiancé and I would do it, but I couldn't have been more mistaken. Everybody had an opinion, and it wasn't always phrased as an opinion, either.

I was lectured on religion, seating, clothing and just about every aspect of the ceremony and reception, and also on the zillion "traditions" that had to be in place, many of which I'd never seen or heard, or I secretly thought silly or humiliating. The guest list reached 400, and my family accounted for only thirty of those.

My fiancé was willing to let his relatives do whatever they wanted. "We'll enjoy it no matter what," he said.

So, on the wedding day, too far in love to pay attention to my misgivings about the family or my mother's reminder of long ago, I found myself standing at an altar (the mere idea of a secular wedding nearly caused fatal heart attacks of several older aunts), wearing a beautiful white dress ("But of course you'll wear white, dear"), and getting ready to swear my fidelity to Our Gigs: my best friend and true love on the one hand; their favored son on the other.

When he said "I do," a hush fell over the crowd. Every eye turned to me—most of them probing for any sign that what I was about to pledge wasn't the absolute truth.

I felt my stomach flip and my skin go cold as I realized every person in the church would take what I said next as a solemn oath sworn before *them*. But I did mean it—I really did—and so I took a deep breath and said it.

"I do."

Amidst the partying that followed, I most vividly remember slow dancing with my new father-in-law. He held my hands and with misty eyes welcomed me into the family. Him, the gruff, burly man who used to yell like a dragon when I kept his boy out too late.

I also remember seeing lots and lots of cheering people, faces I associated with Christmas. And I remember thinking none of them felt like strangers anymore. Not even the ones I didn't recognize at all.

My mother was right—I did marry the whole family.

But, instead of being the burden I'd imagined, they were by far the best wedding gift I got. Many of them I still don't know very well, and some of them will always be a bit unsavory or unscrupulous, but every single one of them—blood relations or not—is family. And they've given me new insight into what that means.

It means more than attending funerals or baby showers.

It means there are hundreds of people out there who are bound to me with a sense of love and duty so strong it doesn't even require knowing each other's names.

It means those people are there for me and, by extension, for my family.

I might still leave Michigan someday—for a vacation. But I'll have a whole lot of postcards to send home when I do.

Marie S. Lyle

My Big, Fat Pig Wedding

Bark and I planned a simple, elegant wedding. Since we'd already broken tradition by purchasing a house and moving in together, we also wanted to pay for our own wedding. Our budget was small, however, so we decided to hold the ceremony and reception at home.

The wedding would take place in mid-May. If our Pacific Northwest climate cooperated, we'd exchange vows in our backyard, amid fallen apple and cherry blossoms. If it rained that day, all sixty-five guests would end up crammed in our small living and dining rooms.

More worrisome than the weather, though, was family. Most of them hadn't met and we didn't know whether the elder members of my Caucasian family would mingle with my fiancé's Asian relatives. As far as I knew, my British-born grandfather had never socialized with anyone from China. Also, Bark's grandfather was only one of several Chinese relatives who didn't speak English.

Truthfully, not everyone approved of our marriage. I knew we couldn't hope to change attitudes at one wedding, yet if we could provide opportunities to break down some barriers, then it would be a start.

A few members of Bark's family were disappointed we

wouldn't serve the customary twelve-course banquet usually presented at Chinese weddings. Bark assured them, though, that the caterer would have plenty of sumptuous dishes.

On the morning of our big day, I anxiously looked at the clouds. As the day progressed, my plans unfolded beautifully, and by noon the house was spotless. Colorful flower baskets hung in our sunroom, red wine waited to be uncorked and Mozart tapes sat near the stereo. All I had to do was finish dressing before the guests arrived at 1:00.

When two cars stopped in front of our house shortly after noon, I was applying makeup in my underwear. Bark went to see what was going on. A minute later he returned.

"Deb, you've got to see this."

I peeked out the bathroom window and watched two unfamiliar Asian men lift a red wooden platform out of the trunk of their car. Lying on the platform was an enormous . . . roasted . . . PIG? My eyes widened in horror. The head was still on the beast, and they were bringing it up the steps to our front door.

Members of Bark's family emerged from the second car, carrying boiled chickens and roasted ducks. I didn't look to see if the heads were still attached. I didn't want to know.

"Where are we going to put the pig?" I asked Bark. "The kitchen counter isn't big enough and the table's covered with wine glasses."

"I don't know."

"We've already ordered tons of food."

"I guess they wanted to make sure pork, duck and pig would be served at the wedding," Bark replied. "Those foods are believed to bring good luck."

Funny, I wasn't feeling lucky.

More cars were arriving, I was still in my underwear

and my house was being overtaken by a fat, crispy, brown pig. What was I supposed to do? Hand everyone a bib and tell them to chow down? I hadn't even rented finger-bowls. I finished dressing quickly.

The pig wound up on our kitchen floor, surrounded by newspapers and pieces of cardboard. At this point, I desperately wanted a soothing cup of tea, but the porker was blocking access to my kettle.

More guests arrived, commenting on the delicious odor permeating the house. It didn't take them long to discover the uninvited guest on my floor. In fact, the pig rapidly became a conversation piece.

At 2:00, the ceremony began. As we were pronounced man and wife, the sun broke through and the afternoon grew warm, but few people stayed in the blossom-carpeted outdoors. They all went inside . . . to see the pig.

One of Bark's relatives, a butcher by profession, used his meat cleavers to cut with an expertise that had guests from both sides of the family spellbound. And pig grease splattered my once-spotless floor.

Business associates, friends and more relatives drifted to the kitchen to watch. As the meat was carved into bite-sized pieces and transferred onto aluminum plates, people smiled and began chatting with one another. By the time the butcher finished, the caterers arrived and our dining room was soon overflowing with food and budding friendships.

The new camaraderie gathered momentum all afternoon. Over piles of succulent pork, our accepting families were talking and laughing with one another like—old friends.

I guess that big fat pig brought good luck after all.

Debra Purdy Kong

Budget wedding photos

What's So Funny?

He who laughs, lasts.

Mary Pettibone Poole

It was a beautiful wedding. The dresses, the candles, the flowers—especially the flowers. They were wonderful. The candle glow and smell of roses heightened the intensity of the ceremony.

"And do you, Peggy, take this man . . ." the pastor began.

Yes of course I do. He's sweet and gorgeous and . . .

"I do," I said.

"And do you, Dickey, take this woman, Peggy . . ."

Yes, of course he does.

"Please kneel. Father, we ask your special blessing on this husband and this wife," the pastor continued.

Wait, is someone giggling?

"Bless their union . . ."

Who is giggling?

It's his mother! Why is she laughing? What does she know that I don't?

"And all of us gathered here promise to offer support . . ."

Now his mother's laughing out loud. And so is everyone else. Wait! May I ask a question before we continue?

"I now introduce Mr. and Mrs. . . . ," the pastor concluded, although he seemed a little confused, too.

They're still laughing.

But the music swelled and this man I was no longer sure of whisked me out of the church.

"Wow!" I said with a catch in my throat. "They all seemed to enjoy the service." I turned to Dickey, fishing for an explanation.

Dickey had a look of suspicion on his face as he leaned against the wall. He lifted one shoe and then the other.

"My little sister! I'm going to get her!" he groaned, shaking his head. Then he showed me the bottom of his shoes.

Written in big red letters were the words "HELP ME!"

Peggy Purser Freeman

10

TIMELESS WISDOM

Even for two people who are very much in love, learning to live together is full of challenges. How comforting it is to discover that the conflicts we face are not unique to our own relationship!

Marilyn McCoo
singer, actress, TV host,
married thirty-four years

His 'n' Hers

People shop for a bathing suit with more care than they do a husband or wife. The rules are the same. Look for something you'll feel comfortable wearing. Allow for room to grow.

Erma Bombeck

A marriage merges two lives, two hearts and two minds—that's the easy part. What people don't tell you is that marriage also merges two sets of household stuff—and that's where it gets tricky.

Take Person A, who has been trekking through life, collecting his own set of stuff for many years. Now add him to Person B, who also has her own set of perfectly good stuff. What you end up with is a lot of duplicated, uncoordinated, mismatched stuff . . . and the overwhelming need for a garage sale.

So that's exactly what my new husband Tom and I decided to do. And for about five minutes, we were as cute and nauseating as we could be about it.

"Ah, our first garage sale together," we cooed. We'd get up early. We'd buy doughnuts. We'd sit in lawn chairs and collect our money in a shoebox. It would be great. I ran the ad in the newspaper. Tom bought the signs pointing people to our driveway. All that was left to do was collect our stuff, price it and pile it on a card table. Easy enough.

Obviously, *his* things deserved prime billing in the driveway. That hulking artificial plant was ugly enough to scare the cat. We didn't need stereo speakers bigger than a foreign car. And then, there was the floor lamp with its glass-table tutu.

But, according to him, this was his *good* stuff.

And he showed no appreciation for my *own* good stuff. He wanted to sell my futon two-seater even after I explained it was the first piece of furniture I bought on my own . . . and I'd studied for final exams on this very couch for four years straight . . . and I actually owed my college education to the comfort of this benevolent couch.

He said it was "ugly." Obviously, one person's "ugly" is another person's "character."

After a few rounds, we finally came up with a mutually acceptable pile of stuff that would be sold come sun-up, but that was only half the battle.

Pricing is where things really got hairy. I hated to tell him that his garage sale assets had a net worth of about 75 cents. So we each priced our own things, went to bed, and waited for daybreak and the first customer.

We didn't have to wait long. Garage sale vultures didn't wait for daybreak; they circled their prey in the wee hours of the morning, waiting for the sun and the garage door to rise. Then they sprang from their cars and swooped up the drive.

These were not your average shoppers. They were the Green Berets of garage sales, picking off a bargain from blocks away. What's worse, they were also the Navy Seals of negotiating. We held strong during the first hour or so. There was no way we could accept $2 for a perfectly good electric can opener. No way. But as the morning wore on and the doughnuts ran out, we started to weaken.

"How much for your husband's neckties?"

"I'll take $1 for the entire box of them—if you get them out of here before he gets back from the bathroom," I said. Sold.

When my back was turned, Tom sold my bookcase for $5. A large, perfectly good piece of furniture. And he let it go for less than the cost of a meal at Arby's. It was his revenge for the pair of mammoth stereo speakers I "accidentally" sold for $30 when he really wanted $30 *apiece*.

Hmmm. After a few hours, we realized everything we didn't sell would have to be re-boxed—and brought back into the house. So, in the final hour, we slashed prices and agreed to throw in the card table if someone would just take the stuff away.

At noon, we gathered the sale scraps and hauled it to a charity drop-off. We used some of our proceeds to pay for lunch and then, satisfied, returned home for a long nap. We'd passed a marital milestone: our first garage sale.

Now, we need to agree how to redecorate our house. Sounds easy enough. . . .

Gwen Rockwood

Unbeknownst to Patty, Scott had registered them for wedding gifts at The Sportsman's Superstore.

The First Freeze

There is no joy in life like the joy of sharing.

Billy Graham

"I think we should. What do you think?"

"Maybe," I replied to my husband of less than four months. "Yes . . . no," I waffled in hesitation. "What do you think?"

Nervous giggles broke out as we paid our restaurant tab and debated about doing the unthinkable—jumping in to help a desperately understaffed diner in the midst of the Georgia Ice Storm of 2000.

It was Sunday morning and church was cancelled. We realized this only after braving the roads and marveling at how bright and clean our Atlanta suburb looked covered in ice. This was our first winter storm together, making the experience all the more heady.

Luke and I were caught up in "firsts" these days. We were in our first home, first year of marriage, and were discovering firsts about one another daily. He became acquainted with the laundry bin. I learned to buy new things at the grocery.

Our big joke surfaced each night as we got ready for bed. Marriage was like a slumber party because neither of us had to go home at the end of the night. We relished our newfound freedom as a married couple.

The late January ice storm took everyone by surprise. Even the meteorologists were caught off guard. We thought it was romantic—another first.

Since church was called off, our attention quickly turned to our growling stomachs. Luke and I went to find breakfast only to realize power was out everywhere. We happened upon a new place, noticing the neon "Open" sign was lit up. Luke eased our car into the 78 Diner; we were happy to be off the icy roads and out of the cold.

The renovated Denny's was practically empty. We found a booth and placed our order. Slowly the diner filled up to capacity. The wait staff, a team of brothers from Crete, scurried to keep up with the mob of customers.

That's when Luke posed the question, "Why don't we jump in and help?"

We bantered back and forth the pros and cons of pitching in. It is important to note neither one of us had ever waited tables.

As we finished paying the bill I got the nerve up to ask one of the brothers if we could assist. He handed us order booklets and scurried toward the kitchen while we looked at each other in disbelief and started to fill drink orders.

The diner became a bustling madhouse. The coffeepot was a bottomless pit and the cook (a Cretan cousin) was so overwhelmed by all the orders he was rendered nearly helpless.

When they found out we weren't real waiters, people refilled their own drinks; a teenage boy bussed tables; customers experienced in food services joined our sides. Before long an excited spirit filled the 78 Diner. We were all in this ice storm together.

At the height of the frenzy, the servers yelled for their breakfast platters. My order had been in for forty minutes and I found myself frying bacon beside the frazzled cook. Luke was having a hard time getting food to his tables. He felt sorry for the other servers and kept giving his customers' meals to them. Meanwhile no one in his section had food.

He asked if I could get their orders filled. I looked at him and thought only of the three orders I was about to place.

Then something inside me said, *What's his is yours. The two of you are one. If it's important to him it should be important to you.*

The reality sunk deep into my heart. For our marriage to thrive, I would have to begin putting Luke's needs on the same level of importance as my own. His request widened my heart and melted away the "single" mentality that said *my* desires took precedence. Another first.

I sighed and placed my order booklet in my front pocket. "Here, let me have your orders. You entertain all of our tables and make sure their drinks don't run out."

"Sounds great." I heard the relief in his voice. "I appreciate you."

I headed back into the kitchen to work on Luke's orders and check on the beleaguered cook. There was a lot of pancake and hash brown making to be done.

Hours later, with the crowds gone and the tables wiped clean, Luke and I exited the 78 Diner where a brilliant winter sun greeted us. *What an unexpected adventure,* I thought to myself. Not so much waiting tables, but learning to serve my new husband with an open and willing heart.

We held hands and smiled. The Georgia Ice Storm of 2000 and the lesson I learned about marriage would not soon be forgotten.

Paige M. Kolb

Dot-to-Dot

Live to learn and you will learn to live.

Portuguese Proverb

I fell head over heels in love with the perfect guy. My Prince Charming had no faults. Of course, it's easy for a girl of twelve to overlook imperfections. Three years later we started dating. We were young, carefree and totally oblivious to any problems that could arise in our relationship.

By age nineteen, we announced our engagement and set a wedding date. Ours was a fairy-tale romance and I looked forward to happily-ever-after.

Then we went to our pastor for premarital counseling. On a large piece of white paper, he drew a tiny black dot the size of a period at the end of a sentence.

"What do you see?" he asked.

"A spot," we answered without hesitation.

He smiled. "What else do you see?"

The two of us looked at each other in confusion. What else could there possibly be?

"You see only the spot," he said. "A tiny black dot I drew to represent all the troubles that could lie ahead in your marriage." Smiling again, the pastor pointed out what we obviously overlooked: the white space that made up the rest of the page.

"The good things are so obvious they can easily be ignored. Don't forget to look beyond the spots."

Our married life certainly hasn't been stress-free. There have been lots of tiny black dots. We've been laid off, changed jobs, moved six times, disagreed about money and housework, and—nine months and twenty-six days after our wedding—welcomed a daughter into our life.

But we look beyond to the white space. We have the love we shared as teenagers, countless blessings and three beautiful children. We really are living happily ever after!

Pamela Doerksen

Advice from the Groom's Dad

Try praising your wife, even if it does frighten her at first.

Billy Sunday

I have the most useless job in the world: father of the groom.

Our Stephen is getting married this weekend and, as father of the groom, I'm expected to do absolutely nothing.

Okay, I have to show up. But that's all. I have no duties. I don't have to hire a string quartet, arrange for flowers, select a modest but saucy little wine or walk down any aisle. I could nod off and no one would care. Or notice.

Well, not for me the role of nonparticipant, I want to get in my two cents' worth.

So, as my contribution to the wedding, I offer Stephen and his bride, Rhea, this advice on marriage:

Always eat a good breakfast. A good marriage requires lots of energy and you shouldn't start the day on an empty stomach.

Always put the other person first.

Never leave home without a kiss. It's nice. If you can work in a little pat, I'm all for that, too.

Have fun. If you don't make each other laugh, there is something wrong.

Accept early in marriage that there are some things you'll never agree on—the proper room temperature, station wagons, Capri pants, the three Stooges. Don't panic. This is normal.

Don't try to win every argument. Compromise with dignity. And no gloating.

Live within your means. Money management is a lot more important than you may think in marital bliss. Don't be afraid to do without. Things won't keep you together. When you look back, it isn't things you remember.

Surprises. You need lots of them. Just the other morning, I found a little poem left by my place at the table. That's why I think I have the finest life partner in the galaxy.

Don't sulk, whine or leave things in your pockets on washday.

Don't save your best smiles for strangers, people at the office, clients. Get your priorities straight.

Talk to each other. I'm a big believer in this.

Have a nice, big, cozy bed where you can start and end each day with a cuddle. If you're too busy to cuddle, you are probably suffering from a bad case of self-importance— fatal in a marriage.

Don't take each other for granted even if you're celebrating your golden anniversary.

Be faithful.

Don't figure romance is over once you're married. It's just started, if you play it right.

Have dinners at night with everyone around the table discussing the day's events. Don't have the TV on. Don't read the newspaper. Don't complain. It's time to lighten up and relax.

Serve whipped cream now and then. Whipped cream puts everybody in a good mood.

A little lace never hurt a marriage.

Have children. And when you have them, take care of them. Love them, enjoy them, spend time with them, say "no" to them, play with them, hug them. Children are probably the most important contribution you'll make to the world, so don't treat them like a hobby or leave them to strangers to raise.

Have a porch as soon as you can. And a couple of nice chairs. Sit out on summer evenings and watch sunsets. You don't always have to be on the go.

Be around when things go right, but also when they go wrong.

Listen, listen, listen. You'll be surprised what you learn.

No double standards.

Early in the morning, when you're still just half-awake, reach over and touch your partner to reassure yourself that he or she is there, and that things are all right. Tenderness is legal.

Gary Lautens
Reprinted from The Best of Gary Lautens

Time for a Tune-Up

In every house of marriage there's room for an interpreter.

Stanley Kunitz

I've lost quite a few points, enough for them to take away my license—my marriage license, that is. Communication is stalled. Sex drive is running on neutral. To be honest, most areas are at pretty low levels.

If I was my car, someone from Saturn would send me a "friendly tune up reminder," quite a few of them by now. They would have called, left messages, sent e-mails. But after ten years of marriage we have yet to receive an "important marriage reminder."

Not one call, one message, not even a mass-mailed postcard saying:

> *Dear Spouses,*
>
> *The marriage installed in your life could be due for its annual inspection, major tune up and cleaning. A properly maintained marriage operates more efficiently and lasts longer.*

Come to think of it, I don't know why they even bother giving out licenses for marriages. We didn't have to study. We didn't have to pass a test. There was no temporary permit allowing us to be married as long as we operated it in the presence of a qualified spouse and refrained from marriage after dark.

We just had to show up, spend a ton of money and throw a big party.

But I nearly forgot; we did take a marriage course. We spent a hundred bucks to sit in a school gym with thirty other couples and cram all of what they thought there is to know about marriage into one afternoon. Issues like financial planning, effective communication and getting-to-know-each-other exercises.

What a waste. What about the big issues like the proper way to squeeze toothpaste? (How was I to know I had been doing it wrong all my life?)

We needed help with the big questions. Not, "Do you want to have a baby?" We already talked about that. What about answers to things like, "Who pulls hair clogs from the bath drain—the spouse who cleans the tub or the spouse with the longest hair?" "Who changes the vacuum bag?" "Who cleans the fish tank?" (Thanks for nothing, guys, our fish died.)

They could have prevented many arguments by clearly stating that the first person in bed automatically claims all blanket rights. That doing the laundry includes putting it away. Ten years later, we still argue over the right way to load the dishwasher, butter toast and hang a roll of toilet paper. A little training would have gone a long way.

We weren't warned about the dangers of decorating together. And people wonder why divorce statistics are so high. If you want to educate people about making marriages work, don't belabor the miracles of two becoming one. Tell me what I can shove up his nose to stop him from snoring.

Yet, somehow—despite a lack of preparation, training and maintenance—our marriage still chugs along. Sure, it could use a tune up. It's had its dings and its fender benders. With two more passengers on board, my bumper's a little bigger (no comments, please).

But it runs. And it hasn't depreciated since we drove off the church lot those ten years past. In fact, it's worth even more.

It must be a classic.

Caroline Pignat

"I can't wait to get out of this
sweaty shirt so you can wash it!"

Reprinted by permission of Dan Rosandich.

Someday My Prince Will
—Bring Coffee

Listen to me, Mister. You're my knight in shining armor . . . don't you forget it.

Ethel Thayer to Norman Thayer
in *On Golden Pond*

The prince rode up on a white horse, in full costume complete with plumed hat.

He leaped from the horse and strode up to his future bride who waited for him in princess costume complete with tiara. He knelt before her on one knee and presented her with a diamond. The home video wobbled slightly as he asked, "Will you marry me?" Her tearful "yes" misted the eyes of every woman in the room.

For us, it was the high point of this week's couples meeting at our church. We all smiled dreamily at this intuitive young man who had rented costumes to make the day perfect for his future bride.

Meanwhile, a chorus of groans erupted from the men in the room, my husband among them. They turned to the "prince" and started ribbing him, unanimously agreeing that he was banned from their "guy movie nights."

The video reminded me how, back in our college days, my husband Don had been quite prince-like on occasion. When we were engaged, he and members of his service club stood under my dorm window and serenaded me on a crisp September evening. As the years passed, he definitely reverted to street clothes. But I don't mind. One thing I know for sure: the costume doesn't make the prince.

Don's faithfulness and devotion in the midst of day-to-day living keeps him my champion.

He comforted me through ten childless years, three miscarriages and two births, and then stepped in to help when postpartum depression overwhelmed me.

He mourned my father's death with me and helped me through that first painful Christmas three weeks later.

He held my hand at the news of my cancer, cried with me as we faced our uncertain future and nursed my scarred body after surgery.

He saw my round, bald scalp and lashless eyes after weeks of chemo, and did all he could to cheer me up.

He traded golf for Little League, steak for pizza and Schwarzenegger for Disney. He discreetly wiped away tears of pride when his kids performed and when caught, chuckled with embarrassment.

He spoke up when a waitress miscalculated in his favor. He gave a carton of milk and box of doughnuts to a homeless man in front of the grocery store.

Just last night I was working away at my desk when Don came in with a cup of coffee, black, one sugar, the way I like it. I smiled like a besotted newlywed and clutched his hand.

"Honey," I said, "you're wearing your prince costume again."

Deborah Thomas

A Husband for June Cleaver

*Twenty years from now you will be more disap-
pointed by the things that you didn't do than by
the ones you did do. So throw off the bowlines.
Sail away from the safe harbor. Catch the trade
winds in your sails. Explore. Dream. Discover.*

Mark Twain

My mother was the most conservative person I knew.
She was my dearest friend, but if there were ever conflicts
between mother and daughter it usually had to do with
her conservatism versus my free spirit. Once she was flab-
bergasted when she met me for lunch and I walked
through the lobby of the St. Louis Marriott wearing shorts.

"Honey, you should have long pants on inside of a
hotel," she whispered worriedly to me. "Mom, I don't
think anyone will faint over it," I teased.

She put June Cleaver to shame. When I was small, my
mother wore white gloves and a dress to her doctor's
appointments. Even at seventy-four, she was the epitome
of class and etiquette. So you can understand my surprise
by her phone call that morning.

"You're going where, Mom?"

"China Garden Buffet," she answered nonchalantly.

"You mean, a *date*?"

"Well, I think so, sweetie. Bill said he wanted to take me for Chinese and I told him I'd love to, but I insisted that we go Dutch, because since your dad died, I don't expect people to be taking care of me."

"Right."

"Well, he said no," she explained. "He said he was going to pay insisting that it was a *date*."

"A date?!" I shouted in shock.

"Well, that's what he said," she giggled.

I hadn't heard this kind of giddiness in my mother in twenty years.

My husband never understood why I worried about my mom after my dad died. "Honey, your mother went down the water slide at Water World. She's not an old lady, you know."

I knew that. But I still worried that being without my dad would destroy her unless I intervened. The responsibility of her widowhood weighed on me like a boulder that I couldn't lift off my shoulders. I was terrified that loneliness would eventually do her in.

"There's a condo development right near us. We could move her here to Colorado," I explained. "My grandmother started drinking when her husband died. I just can't leave her all alone."

The next morning my mom called to tell me about her date. Suddenly she had to go answer her ringing doorbell. I could hear her talking to someone, thanking them and laughing.

"Oh, sweetie, I just got the most beautiful bouquet of flowers."

"From who?"

"From Bill. He's right here."

"He came over this morning?" I couldn't believe my ears.

"Yes! He picked them for me on his walk."

The following week an envelope of photos arrived: pictures of Mom at the Botanical Garden and sitting hand-in-hand with Bill on a riverboat beneath the St. Louis Arch. Then came the last picture.

"Oh my God, she's sitting on a giant turtle!" I exclaimed.

"A turtle? Let me see," my husband said, grabbing the photo. "It's a statue. I guess they went to the children's zoo. She looks like a little girl."

"I know," I said rolling my eyes.

I realized that Bill was the opposite of my father who had been the company president and former ROTC sergeant. Bill had been a chaplain in the war and didn't think twice about joining his men by jumping out of an airplane behind enemy lines.

". . . to give them moral support," he said humbly.

He played the guitar, worked on houses for Habitat for Humanity and volunteered for six other organizations.

"We're going on a hike," my mom announced one day on the phone. "Bill needs my help because we're taking along four mentally retarded adults and we have to make sure they can stay on the trail."

I was so proud of her but I had to suppress my laughter. Was this really my mother doing all this?

Then she told me something that seemed to make the Earth move.

"Bill asked me to marry him and I said yes," she gushed. "We thought we'd have a small, private ceremony the day after Christmas so you kids could all be here."

I flew in a month before the wedding to help with the arrangements and to help mom find a dress.

"May I help you?" the middle-aged saleswoman asked.

"We need a wedding dress," I smiled.

"And will you be needing a mother-of-the-bride dress also?" she asked my mom.

"No, she *is* the bride," I said.

"Oh, how simply marvelous!"

My mother became the hit of Lord & Taylor. Every saleswoman over the age of sixty wanted to meet this septuagenarian who had beaten the odds and found true love again.

The day of her wedding, mom was getting dressed. "Look, new underwear!" she said holding up a pink and white striped bag.

"You went to Victoria's Secret, Mom?" I grabbed the bag laughing and pulled out the items.

"Well, I wanted something nice to get married in."

"Mom, I cannot believe that you, June Cleaver, actually walked into a Victoria's Secret."

"Oh don't be silly," she said placing the bag on her dresser. "It's just a pretty bra."

The wedding was perfect from the small ceremony in front of her pastor in the church vestibule, to the Mickey and Minnie Mouse atop their tiny wedding cake.

The next morning Mom and Bill came to see us with a few hours to kill before their flight. I noticed a bag in her hand.

"What's that?"

"Bob Evans," she laughed. "They have that all-you-can-eat breakfast bar and Bill loves their bacon."

"You went to Bob Evans' breakfast bar the morning after your wedding night?"

"Sure, why not?"

"They're very reasonable," Bill chimed in. "All you can eat for $5.99."

The next day she called from Disney World to tell me that they got on a shuttle bus full of cheerleaders from North Carolina who gave them a cheer on the bus when they found out she and Bill were newlyweds.

Then she went on to tell me that the wipers on the rental car kept squirting water and they had to drive it that way.

"We couldn't figure out how to turn it all off and it squirted the people next to us. I got the giggles so badly I almost wet my pants," she laughed.

"I wish my mother could have found a man," my friend Jody said as I showed her the picture of my mom and Bill hugging Mickey Mouse at Disney World.

"She could if she wanted to," I said without hesitation.

I realized that it's not a lack of good men out there. My mom had the only real ingredient necessary to become a bride. She knew how to do more than love. She also knew how to receive it.

Carla Riehl

Small Beds, Soft Hearts

*If you live to be a hundred, I want to live to be
a hundred minus one day, so I never have to live
without you.*

Winnie the Pooh

Preparing for a cross-country move, my wife and I had
big plans to ditch our queen-sized bed and buy a new
king-sized waterbed with dual heaters. Roomy and comfortable, exactly what we needed.

Or so I thought.

As hospital chaplain, I see a lot of people in bed. One
day, a nurse directed me to the room of an eighty-nine-
year-old man who had just died in her unit.

Filled with pictures and mementos, the room intentionally communicated to staff that this man was not to be
identified by number or diagnosis. He had a name, a life
and a family that loved him.

The bed swallowed the frame of this slight man enough
to allow his widow to perch on a small edge in the top corner of the mattress. She leaned into his stiff, sagging shoulder and held his hand while caressing his arm. His eyes
were closed and his mouth open.

As I sat and talked with the family, the widow told me she had shared a bed with this man for fifty-eight years. During all that time, the couple had used only a double—not a queen or king—just a double. Now she was wondering how cold the night would get without him.

"I just can't understand it," she said. "So many of our friends buy these big beds. They say they need the space. But the beds are so big, you lose each other."

Her amazement made her friends' beds sound like the Grand Canyon, not perhaps a simple, king-size waterbed with dual heaters.

She told me there was always enough room in their bed, because from the moment they slid in, both had their emotional compass set for a lifelong commitment. No matter what occurred during the day, they knew hard hearts are softened in small beds. In the center, they found each other's hand, and—so entwined—peaceful sleep came easily.

Now, in front of us that afternoon, a permanent peace had come as easily. Her husband had found his final rest, and, at her advanced age, she was likely to join him soon in a place where their souls would be permanently entwined.

As I looked at them, it occurred to me that while I had seen the pageantry of many formal weddings, it was rare to see the beauty I was witnessing here. This was the final fulfillment of vows taken by a couple that meant what they said when they promised "for better or for worse, 'til death do us part." The marriage that had begun with this vow had been fulfilled with the keeping of it.

Well, everything my wife and I own, from Tinker Toys to washing machines, is in a truck making its way down Interstate 5 toward Sacramento. And somewhere wedged between a dresser and a washing machine is an old queen-sized bed.

It will be our own nightly meeting place for years to come.

Norris Burkes

Until Death Do Us Part

Real love stories never have endings.

Richard Bach

Claire was ninety-three years old when I met her several years ago. I had recently gotten married and our conversation quickly turned to the wonders of love. Her face broke into an enormous smile and her eyes began to sparkle as she told me about her husband, Harold, now gone from this world.

"He was the perfect man and treated me like a queen," she told me, looking off in the distance, reliving a memory. "He's gone now, but that's all right. Part of life is accepting that it doesn't go on forever. And I'll be with him again, someday."

"I'm sorry he passed," I said, showing my respect and hoping I didn't bring back painful memories of his death. But Claire waved my sympathies away.

"Oh, it's been quite a while now. I definitely don't need anyone feeling sorry about it," she replied.

Her acceptance of her husband's death intrigued me. I've met many elderly people who live in a state of depression or anger because of the loss of a spouse. But not Claire.

"How long has it been?" I asked.

"Almost sixty years," she replied, her face still serene in memory.

"Sixty years? He must have been very young!" I said.

"Yes, yes he was. He was thirty-five. Had an accident at work. But it was quick, so he didn't suffer. We had been married five years, and we had two babies. It was a rough time, but I always knew he was with me, so I made it through."

"Did you ever remarry?" I couldn't imagine being widowed at thirty-three, with two small children.

"Oh, no! Why would I ever do that? I had perfection! There was no need to look for anything else."

I chose my words carefully. "Claire, I think it is incredible that you are so happy. I mean, five years? And you were left alone with two small children? A lot of women would be extremely bitter."

With the wisdom only a woman in her nineties can give, Claire took my hand and looked into my eyes. "Honey, how could I possibly be bitter? At one time in my life, I had something that women search their entire lives for, and many never find. True love. I would have been happy with a single day, but I had it for five entire years! How could I be anything but thankful?"

Claire is now with her perfect man again, and I'll never forget the smile she wore as she spoke of him on that day. It was the smile of a woman truly in love, love that survived death, love that survived decades.

I think of Claire's words often, and they make me appreciate that true love is a very precious gift. One that we all search for, but not all of us are fortunate enough to receive. Although I hope that I can spend sixty years with my husband, I have to accept that I will get "until death do us part." And whether that is for sixty years, or just one day, how can I be anything but thankful?

Kelly Gamble

The Trophy

Over the years, my grandparents' house became a tribute of their lives together. On the tranquil days I spent visiting them each summer, I would walk from room to room reading the plaques and decorations commemorating their wedding anniversaries—silver, gold and beyond.

I studied the pictures invariably showing my grandparents sitting side by side, smiling broadly, surrounded by their seven children. Styles of glasses and clothes changed, hair grew gray and thin, but the smiles never faded.

For sixty-seven years they worked on their memorial until my grandfather died at the age of ninety-one. Shortly after, unable to live in the house that held so many memories, my grandmother moved into a seniors' home.

Aunts shouldered the task of closing the house and dividing personal items among children and grandchildren. Everyone would have memories of the house and the people that had been so precious to us.

I received my portion of the mementos shortly after my new husband and I moved into our own house. A tablecloth and an apron reminded me of time spent in the kitchen and photographs conjured up thoughts of golden summer days.

But one item seemed a peculiar choice: a wall plate, rimmed with yellow roses, celebrating my grandparents' fiftieth wedding anniversary. I was at a loss; it belonged on my grandparents' wall, not mine. But to pack it away belittled its worth as a keepsake.

As I considered this, I began to think about the plate not as a familiar decoration but as a representation of a promise kept.

My grandparents had made a pledge and honored it— through births and deaths of children, through long days and nights apart when Granddad worked for the railroad . . . and through the growing interdependence of old age, surgeries, long recoveries, and one last illness. All those years, they kept a promise made to each other when they were young and had no idea what they would be facing.

The plate was . . . a trophy. A trophy won after fifty years of loving enough to stick with it.

I hung it on the wall of our bedroom in tribute to my grandparents—who did a remarkable thing in their unremarkable way—and as a goal for my husband and me.

Someday, we will earn the trophy for ourselves.

Daphne Dykeman

Love Everlasting

Love at first sight is easy to understand; it's when two people have been looking at each other for a lifetime that it becomes a miracle.

Amy Bloom

I have a friend who is falling in love.

She claims the sky is bluer, she's lost fifteen pounds and she looks like a cover girl. "I'm young again!" she shouts exuberantly.

As my friend raves on about her new love, I take a good look at my old one. My husband of almost twenty years, Scott, has gained fifteen pounds. His hairline is receding and his body shows the signs of working long hours and eating too many candy bars. Yet he can still give me a certain look across a restaurant table that makes me want to ask for the check and hurry home.

And then my friend asks, "What will make our love last?"

I run through all the obvious reasons: commitment, shared interests, unselfishness, physical attraction and communication. Yet there's more.

There is spontaneity. After slipping the rubber band off the rolled newspaper, Scott shot it playfully at me and started an all-out war. At the grocery store, we split the list and raced to see who could make it to the checkout first.

There are surprises. I came home to find a note on the front door—leading me to another note, then another, until I reached the walk-in closet where I found Scott holding a "pot of gold" (my cooking kettle) filled with the "treasure" of a gift package. In return, I've left notes on the mirror and presents under his pillow.

There is understanding. I understand why he must play basketball with the guys. He understands why, once a year, I must get away from the house, the kids—even him—to "play" with my sisters.

There is sharing. Household worries, parental burdens, even ideas—we share them all. Scott came home from a convention and presented me with a thick historical novel. Although he prefers thrillers and sci-fi, he read it on the plane because he wanted to be able to exchange ideas after I'd read it.

There is forgiveness. When I'm embarrassingly loud and crazy at parties, Scott forgives me. When he confesses losing some of our savings in the stock market, I give him a hug and say, "It's okay. It's only money."

There is sensitivity. Scott walked through the door with an it's-been-a-tough-day look. He wept as he described a stroke victim and her husband caressing her hand. How was he going to tell this man his wife would probably not recover? I shed a few tears myself . . . because my husband is still moved after years of hospital rooms and dying patients.

There is faith. One week I listened to the heartache of friends coping with cancer, divorce, aging parents and death. But I also noticed the boisterous blossoms of gladioli outside my window, the laughter of my son and the cheerful sight of a wedding party emerging from a neighbor's house. I described it all; Scott listened. And we helped each other acknowledge the cycles of life and joys that counter the sorrows. It was enough to keep us going.

Finally, there is knowing. I know Scott will throw his laundry just shy of the hamper every night, he'll be late to most appointments and he'll eat the last chocolate in the box. Scott knows I sleep with a pillow over my head, I'll lock us out of the house regularly and I'll eat the last chocolate if I find it first. I guess our love endures because it is comfortable.

So, no, my friend. With a lasting love, the sky is not bluer: It's just a familiar hue. And the two of us don't feel particularly young: we've experienced too much that has contributed to our growth and wisdom. It's taken a toll on our bodies, yet created our memories.

But, to my way of thinking, *that's* what makes love last.

Annette Paxman Bowen

Who Is Jack Canfield?

Jack Canfield is one of America's leading experts in the development of human potential and personal effectiveness. He is both a dynamic, entertaining speaker and a highly sought-after trainer. Jack has a wonderful ability to inform and inspire audiences toward increased levels of self-esteem and peak performance.

He is the author and narrator of several bestselling audio- and videocassette programs, including *Self-Esteem and Peak Performance, How to Build High Self-Esteem, Self-Esteem in the Classroom* and *Chicken Soup for the Soul—Live.* He is regularly seen on television shows such as *Good Morning America, 20/20* and *NBC Nightly News.* Jack has co-authored numerous books, including the *Chicken Soup for the Soul* series, *Dare to Win* and *The Aladdin Factor* (all with Mark Victor Hansen), *100 Ways to Build Self-Concept in the Classroom* (with Harold C. Wells), *Heart at Work* (with Jacqueline Miller) and *The Power of Focus* (with Les Hewitt and Mark Victor Hansen).

Jack is a regularly featured speaker for professional associations, school districts, government agencies, churches, hospitals, sales organizations and corporations. His clients have included the American Dental Association, the American Management Association, AT&T, Campbell's Soup, Clairol, Domino's Pizza, GE, ITT, Hartford Insurance, Johnson & Johnson, the Million Dollar Roundtable, NCR, New England Telephone, Re/Max, Scott Paper, TRW and Virgin Records. Jack also has been on the faculty of Income Builders International, a school for entrepreneurs.

Jack conducts an annual eight-day Training of Trainers program in the areas of self-esteem and peak performance. It attracts educators, counselors, parenting trainers, corporate trainers, professional speakers, ministers and others interested in developing their speaking and seminar-leading skills.

For further information about Jack's books, tapes and training programs, or to schedule him for a presentation, please contact:

Self-Esteem Seminars
P.O. Box 30880
Santa Barbara, CA 93130
phone: 805-563-2935 • fax: 805-563-2945
Web site: *www.jackcanfield.com*

Who Is Mark Victor Hansen?

In the area of human potential, no one is better known and more respected than Mark Victor Hansen. For more than thirty years, Mark has focused solely on helping people from all walks of life reshape their personal vision of what's possible. His powerful messages of possibility, opportunity and action have helped create startling and powerful change in thousands of organizations and millions of individuals worldwide.

He is a sought-after keynote speaker, bestselling author and marketing maven. Mark's credentials include a lifetime of entrepreneurial success, in addition to an extensive academic background. He is a prolific writer with many bestselling books such as *The One Minute Millionaire, The Power of Focus, The Aladdin Factor* and *Dare to Win,* in addition to the *Chicken Soup for the Soul* series. Mark has also made a profound influence through his extensive library of audio programs, video programs and enriching articles in the areas of big thinking, sales achievement, wealth building, publishing success, and personal and professional development.

Mark is also the founder of MEGA Book Marketing University and Building Your MEGA Speaking Empire. Both are annual conferences where Mark coaches and teaches new and aspiring authors, speakers and experts on building lucrative publishing and speaking careers.

His energy and exuberance travel still further through mediums such as television (*Oprah,* CNN and *The Today Show*), print (*Time, U.S. News & World Report, USA Today, New York Times* and *Entrepreneur*) and countless radio and newspaper interviews as he assures our planet's people that *"you can easily create the life you deserve."*

As a passionate philanthropist and humanitarian, he's been the recipient of numerous awards that honor his entrepreneurial spirit, philanthropic heart and business acumen, including the prestigious Horatio Alger Award for his extraordinary life achievements, which stand as a powerful example that the free enterprise system still offers opportunity to all.

Mark Victor Hansen is an enthusiastic crusader of what's possible and is *driven* to make the world a better place.

Mark Victor Hansen & Associates, Inc.
P.O. Box 7665 • Newport Beach, CA 92658
phone: 949-764-2640 • fax: 949-722-6912
FREE resources online at: *www.markvictorhansen.com*

Who Is Maria Nickless?

Maria Nickless is the Director of Marketing and Public Relations for Chicken Soup for the Soul Enterprises, Inc. With a background in marketing and event planning, she was initially invited to join the Chicken Soup team to launch *Chicken Soup for the Kid's Soul*, where she successfully orchestrated The Largest Book Signing Event in History, as recognized by *Guinness Book of World Records*. This, along with multiple other public relations campaigns, led to her current position where she oversees the marketing and public relations for all new *Chicken Soup* titles.

Prior to Chicken Soup for the Soul Enterprises, Inc., Maria worked in real-estate development, where she was involved in project management and corporate event programs for the retail division. Having a passion for event planning, over the years Maria has led community-driven charity events through her local church congregation. She is a member of Leadership Tomorrow, a nonprofit organization designed to empower citizens in their commitment to community service.

Maria is married to Ward Nickless, who inspired her to coauthor *Bride's Soul* after a fairy-tale engagement and honeymoon. Maria enjoyed creating their quarter-themed wedding and reception, which included a ride on a Ferris wheel with their wedding party and photographer.

Together with their children, Madison and Jack, they live in Southern California. Maria is also an avid photographer and enjoys antique shopping with her husband.

If you wish to contact Maria or *Chicken Soup for the Bride's Soul*, please e-mail her at *maria@chickensoupforthebridesoul.com* or visit *www.bridesoul.com*.

Who Is Gina Romanello?

Gina Romanello, a graduate of Arizona State University with a B.A. in journalism, was thrilled when given the opportunity to join the *Chicken Soup for the Kid's Soul* team. Her temporary position turned into six years of employment in their book-production department.

In her position as executive administrator to Patty Hansen and Irene Dunlap, she has played an integral part in the compiling and marketing of *Chicken Soup for the Kid's Soul, Chicken Soup for the Preteen Soul, Christmas Treasury for Kids, Chicken Soup for the Preteen Soul II* and *True,* a faith-based nonfiction book for teens authored by Irene Dunlap.

Gina helped build *PreteenPlanet.com,* a Web site founded by Patty Hansen for empowering preteens, and currently assists in its marketing and promotions.

Noticing many friends and family members endure the stress of planning a wedding, Gina, along with associate Maria Nickless, saw a need for *Bride's Soul,* a *Chicken Soup* title sure to comfort and enlighten a stressed-out bride-to-be planning her big day.

Gina loves living in Southern California with her dog Mattie, and enjoys an active lifestyle, the outdoors, traveling and spending time with her family and friends.

If you wish to contact Gina or *Chicken Soup for the Bride's Soul,* please e-mail her at *gina@chickensoupforthebridesoul.com* or visit *www.bridesoul.com.*

Contributors

Ariana Adams held positions as a CPA and as a recruiting manager before transitioning to a writing career in 2001. Ariana is a full-time business/marketing writer and aspires to become a mystery novel writer. She enjoys traveling, skiing and spending time with her husband and pets. She can be reached at *aadams@carolina.rr.com.*

Charlotte Adelsperger is an author and speaker from Overland Park, Kansas. She has written several inspirational storiess for more than ninety publications and compilations. Her story is dedicated to the memory of close friend Joan Miller who lived out her life with faith and compassion. Charlotte can be reached at *author04@aol.com.*

What a joy it is for **Donna Barstow** to draw and write cartoons! Her quirky drawings appear in over 200 publications, including *The New Yorker, The LA Times, Readers Digest, Harvard Business Review,* law publications, etc, and in many calendars, books and greeting cards, including other *Chicken Soup* books! Her own calendar, *What Do Women REALLY Want?* is in Barnes & Noble. Her favorite topics are relationships, computers, pets, and mayhem. You can see more of Donna's work at *www.reuben.org/dbarstow,* and please write to her at *dbarstow@hotmail.com.*

Elizabeth L. Blair lives with her husband Jeff in Arizona. With both ink and jet fuel in her blood, she works as a freelance writer and a flight attendant. Currently, she is working on her first book, tales of her humorous journeys in the airline industry. She can be reached at *elblair99@yahoo.com*

Ginger Boda contributes to various online publications, weaving faith, traditions and humor into her stories. She has penned her thoughts since she was a child, and writes from the heart. Ginger resides in California with her husband Mark, and three children: Jason, Danny and Alisha. She can be reached at *Rhymerbabe@aol.com.*

Barbara Loftus Boswell is a full-time mother of three and a part-time freelance writer. She volunteers at a crisis pregnancy center and works with the youth at her church. She is currently working to complete a devotional for busy housemoms. She can be reached at *Bx2Boswell@aol.com.*

Annette Paxman Bowen is the author of three books, plus multiple articles and short stories with worldwide distribution. She writes at her desk overlooking a gorgeous mountain lake in Washington state. She and her husband have celebrated over thirty years of marriage. They are parents of three grown sons.

Norris Burkes wrote this story while making the transition from military chaplaincy to civilian hospital chaplaincy. He also writes a syndicated column for Gannett News Service. E-mail him at *Norris@chaplainnorris.com* or visit his Web site at *www.chaplainnorris.com.*

Michele Wallace Campanelli is a national bestselling author. She's been published in more than thirty-one anthologies and has penned many novels, including *Keeper of the Shroud* and *Margarita*, published by Americana Books. Her personal editor is Fontaine Wallace. To contact Michele, go to: *www. michelecampanelli.com*.

Martha Campbell is a graduate of Washington University St. Louis School of Fine Arts, and a former writer/designer for *Hallmark Cards*.She has been a free-lance cartoonist and book illustrator since 1973.She can be reached at P.O. Box 2538, Harrison, AR, 72602, (870) 741-5323, or *marthaf@alltel.net*.

Bill Canty's cartoons have appeared in many national magazines, including the *Saturday Evening Post, Good Housekeeping, Better Homes & Gardens, Woman's World, National Review Medical Economics* and *Reader's Digest*. His syndicated feature, *All About Town (www.reuben.org/Canty)* appears in 30 newspapers.In 1983, Bill published a book of Cape Cod cartoons, "I Don't Care What It's Shaped Like . . ." and a limited amount of copies are still available on the Internet at *capecodtoday.com/pages/Books/*. Bill can be reached at P.O. Box 1053, So. Wellfleet, MA 02663, or by phone or fax 508-349-7549 and by e-mail, *wcanty@comcast.net*.

Theresa Chan is author of *The Creative Wedding Organizer and Planner*. Having planned the wedding of her dreams, Theresa leads interactive workshops inspiring couples to plan their own creative and personalized weddings. Owner of Fruition Sense, a keepsake company, Theresa lives in Toronto. She can be reached at *tcchan@fruitionsense.com*.

Eileen Chase is the mother of six children. She volunteers at the Texas Children's Hospital in Houston, as ombudsman for the Texas Department on Aging, and as a standardized patient for medical students at local colleges. She also paints, does needlework, enjoys singing and loves spending her husband's money.

Lorraine Cheeka is a thirty-one-year-old mother of three. She lives in central New Jersey with her daughters, Aprilynn, Evelyn and Madeline, and her husband Paul. Grandma lives nearby and remains a treasured part of all their lives.

Ann Cooke is still happily married to her darling, Marcus, and is now a survivor of breast cancer. Raising her daughter and son takes a lot of her time, but she still finds time for crocheting, patchwork and most crafts. She is also active in raising money for cancer research. She can be reached at *amazontiger2001 @yahoo.com.au*.

David Cooney's cartoons and illustrations have appeared in numerous *Chicken Soup for the Soul* books as well as magazines including *First for Women* and *Good Housekeeping*. David married his wonderful bride, Marcia, twelve years ago. They live with their two children, Sarah and Andrew, in the small Pennsylvania town of Mifflinburg. David's Website is *www.DavidCooney.com* and he can be reached at *david@davidcooney.com*.

Before embarking on her writing career, award-winning Canadian author **Valerie Coulman** spent ten years in the bridal industry as consultant and seamstress of bridal and formal wear. She currently lives with her groom of twelve years and their children in southern Oregon. See more at *www.valeriecoulman.com.*

Matthew Cummings received his Bachelor of Arts from Edinboro University in 2000. He is the coordinator of public relations for the Penn Hills School District in Pittsburgh. Emily teaches elementary reading in Pittsburgh. Matthew and Emily were married on October 25, 2003 and live in Pittsburgh.

Jenn Dlugos is a comedy writer and comedian living in New England. She is releasing a book entitled *Public Health Disturbance* in late 2003. She can be reached at *divinetrash@juno.com.*

Pamela Doerksen is happily married to her first crush, Conrad, and is a proud mom to Kiandra, Kezia and Kaden. In her spare time, she enjoys scrapbooking and cooking. Pamela prays that God will bless her children with lasting marriages, and that her own marriage can serve as an example to them.

Sandy Williams Driver and her husband, Tim, live in Albertville, Alabama, where both were born and raised. Their children are Josh (16), Jake (14) and Katie (12). Sandy is a homemaker and also writes a weekly parenting column for her local newspaper and freelances for several magazines.

Elaine G. Dumler, a presentation skills trainer, is also published in *Chicken Soup for the Nurse's Soul.* Her first book, *I'm Already Home—Keeping Your Family Close When You're on TDY,* helps military families lessen the impact of being separated. She enjoys quilting and traveling. She can be reached at *Elaine@ ElaineDumler.com.*

Daphne Dykeman studied English literature in college before becoming a high-school English teacher in Halifax, Nova Scotia. Now a full-time mother of two, she tries to find time to indulge in her love of books and of writing poetry.

T. Suzanne Eller is a speaker and author of three books. She is still in love with Richard after twenty-four years and three beautiful children. She can be reached at *tseller@daretobelieve.org* or *www.daretobelieve.org.*

Dr. Denise Enete is a licensed Christian psychotherapist. She loves to integrate Biblical principles with principles of good mental health. She is currently writing a book on *How to Study the Bible According to Your Personality.* She is happily married with four grown children. She can be reached at *DeniseEnete@aol.com*

Julie Firman is the mother of two daughters and one son. She has eight grandchildren and one great grandchild. She has retired from teaching and being a therapist. She and her daughters are the coauthors of *Chicken Soup for the Mother & Daughter Soul.* With her daughter Dorothy Firman, she has authored *Daughters and Mothers, Making It Work.* Visit her at *www.motherdaughterrelations.com.*

Peggy Purser Freeman is the author of *The Coldest Day in Texas* (TCU Press 1997); *Swept Back to a Texas Future,* a historical play (Hendrick-Long 1991) and numerous magazine articles. She currently teaches writing for children and presents the Student Writing Workshop to school districts across Texas. Visit her at *www.peggypurserfreeman.com.*

Carlienne A. Frisch has both a B.S. and M.S. degree, teaches college classes and has written more than twenty nonfiction children's books and numerous career profiles. She enjoys traveling; reading mysteries and historical novels; and decorating and furnishing dollhouses. She plans to write a young-adult novel.

Vicki and **David Frizzell**'s love story continues as they support each other's careers in Nashville, Tennessee. Vicki is a registered nurse, the clinical coordinator for an international healthcare-management company and a part-time emergency nurse. A retired orthopedic technician, David is following in his father Lefty's footsteps as a singer and songwriter. Visit them at *www.crockett frizzell.com.*

Kelly Gamble is the author of *The Dreamkeepers: Saving the Senoi,* a fantasy adventure for middle grade readers. She makes her home in Henderson, Nevada. Visit her at *www.thedreamkeepers.com.*

Nancy B. Gibbs is a weekly religion columnist, author of four books and a freelance writer. Nine of her stories have appeared in seven previous *Chicken Soup* books. She has been published in numerous books, devotional guides and magazines. Nancy is a pastor's wife, mother and grandmother. She can be reached at *Daiseydood@aol.com.*

Judith Givens resides in Florida and writes both fiction and nonfiction. She is a five-year veteran as fiction editor for "EWG Presents" and has written a weekly Winston Cup NASCAR column for *Woman Motorist* since 1999. She enjoys the beach, old rock 'n' roll and her beautiful grandchildren.

C. Capiz Greene is the owner of Greenelight Professional Development, Inc. based in Omaha, Nebraska. She provides keynotes, training sessions and meeting facilitation for organizations that want to create an environment where people can achieve and perform at their best. She can be reached at: *capizg@cox.net* or *www.capizgreene.com.*

Kathleen Happ received her Bachelor of Science in special education, with honors, from the Franciscan University of Steubenville in 1996. She is a member of the Catholic Writers Association. Kathleen lives in the Shenandoah Valley with her husband, Ron, and their two children.

Maryellen Heller lives in Connecticut with her husband Rob and their three children Kerry, Rob and Kathleen. She has worked as a reading specialist at Danbury High and is currently teaching special education at Somers High. Maryellen has a children's book with Richard C. Owens Publishers due to be published in fall 2004.

Lynette Baker Helms received her bachelor's degree in business administration from Nebraska Wesleyan University, and is now a special-events coordinator in St. Louis, Missouri. Lynette is energized by spending time with her husband and seventeen-month-old daughter, and has another baby on the way in January 2004.

Jeanne Hill has published two inspirational books and hundreds of articles and stories. Her award-winning fiction stories and nonfiction articles are often chosen for anthologies. She has been an inspirational speaker for state, regional and national groups. Jeanne is a contributing editor to *Guideposts* magazine.

Miriam Hill earned her Master of Educational Leadership degree. Her writing credits include: coauthor of *Fabulous Florida*, contributions published in *Reader's Digest*, articles published in *Grit Magazine, St. Petersburg Times*, and the Poynter Institute online. Her work was judged First Place for Inspirational Writing at the Southeast Writers Conference.

Raegan Holloway lives in southeastern Louisiana with her husband and two children. She writes short stories and is busy working on her first novel. She can be reached at *thollowa@charter.net*.

Holly Jensen Hughes grew up in Naperville, Illinois. She received a Bachelor of Arts degree in marketing from Valparaiso University in 1991. Holly is currently the director of marketing for a Chicago-based company that serves the education market. She resides in Plainfield, Illinois with her husband, Tim, and their children, Conor and Emma.

Shonna Milliken Humphrey is originally from northern Maine and after a long hiatus in Washington, D.C., has returned to the state with her musician husband and three kitties. She is still very much in love.

Michelle Isenhour is an Air Force wife and stay-at-home mother of two daughters. She is also a former award-winning Air Force journalist and an officer in the U. S. Coast Guard Auxiliary. She can be reached at *michelle_ isenhour@hotmail.com*.

Denise Jacoby is a legal secretary at a Manhattan law firm. She is a part-time student at the College of Staten Island where she is a January 2004 candidate for a Bachelor of Science in business management.

Barbara M. Johnson, the fifth of seven children, is a bankruptcy legal assistant. She loves life and enjoys the outdoors, hiking, kayaking, cross-country skiing, dancing and traveling. In her spare time, Barbara writes poetry. She self-published *Life Unfolds* and is also published in several poetry anthologies.

Sally Kelly-Engeman is a freelance writer who's had numerous articles and short stories published, and is currently writing an historical novel. In addition to reading, researching and writing, she enjoys ballroom dancing and traveling with her husband. She can be reached at *sallyfk@juno.com*.

Nora E. Kessel has been blissfully married to Thomas M. Kessel for nineteen years, and is the mother of three children: Stephen, (18), Johanna, (16) and Phillip (13). Nora left her nursing career to raise a family, and counts gardening, writing, making jewelry and reading among her hobbies. She loves to make people smile and insists on one good belly laugh a day. She has taught catechism for the last fifteen-plus years, is a lay counselor at Pregnancy Helpline, serves on the Hartland Consolidated Schools Board of Education, is a board member of Big Brothers Big Sisters of Livingston County, and also serves on the board of Livingston County Catholic Social Services. She feels blessed!

Jeannie Kim is a writer and editor in New York City. Her work has appeared in *Redbook, Shape, Modern Bride,* and many other magazines. She is the author of *The Whole You* (Scholastic), a series of self-discovery books for preteens.

Paige M. Kolb is a native Texan. In 1996 she joined CNN, first as a writer and eventually as an on-air correspondent for CNNRadio. She is now a mom, inspirational speaker and author. Her first book, *Reality Check,* was published in 2002 through PLACE Ministries. She can be reached at: *paigebr@aol.com.*

Debra Purdy Kong has published more than eighty short stories, essays and articles for publications in North America and England. She's also published a mystery novel called *Taxed to Death.* She lives in Canada's Pacific Northwest with her husband and two children.

Amanda Krug is an award-winning international author/writer and guest lecturer from Fishers, Indiana. Co-president/co-founder of The Jena Foundation, Inc., a nonprofit charitable organization, she also conducts writing workshops for children in local churches and schools. She and her husband, Michael, are the proud parents of four perfect-for-us children. She can be reached at 8883 Moll Drive, Fishers, IN 46038, *amanda@thejenafoundation.org* or *www.thejena foundation.org.*

Charlotte Lanham is a retired teacher and columnist. She resides in Duncanville, Texas with her husband, Ray. She is a contributor to *Chicken Soup for the Mother & Daughter Soul.* Charlotte can be reached at *charlotte.lanham@ sbcglobal.net.*

Cindy L. Lassalle is an elementary English teacher in Puerto Rico. She enjoys reading, playing with her dog, Sandy and working with children. She likes to write children's books. She can be reached at *angel_legend@hotmail.com.*

Gary Lautens, a popular Canadian humorist and columnist, was a writer at the *Toronto Star,* and was syndicated throughout Canada and briefly in the United States. His columns were also published in book form. Visit the Web site of his son, Stephen Lautens (the groom), who is also a writer: *www.lautens.com.*

Michelle Lawson resides in the Lower Mainland of British Columbia. Michelle enjoys spending time with her children, gardening, camping and writing. She has future plans of continuing to write short stories. She can be reached at *mskuro6692@shaw.ca.*

Veneta Leonard received her associate degree in business management in 1993. She currently resides in Northwest Indiana and enjoys spending time with her children and family. Her hobbies include playing bunco, bingo, cards and watching "SpongeBob" with her kids. She enjoys writing and hopes to have one of her books published one of these days.

Marie S. Lyle is an alumnas of St. John's College in Santa Fe, New Mexico, where she studied liberal arts. She lives in Michigan with her husband, baby and two dogs, where she works as a computer technician and writes science fiction.

Liza G. Maakestad met her husband in 1997 while they attended Syracuse University. Liza is a writer-illustrator and is currently working on her first children's book. You can see her work at *www.lgmaakestad.com*. She lives with her husband Tim in North Texas (fifteen minutes from Mom and Dad).

Steve Manchester, father of two sons, is the author of *The Unexpected Storm: The Gulf War Legacy, Jacob Evans* and *At the Stroke of Midnight,* as well as several books under the pseudonym Steven Herberts. Three of his screenplays have also been produced as films.

Michelle Marullo is a freelance writer who pursues her greatest passions as wife and mother. She is currently writing a book, *You Can Stop Chasing the Wind!*, a work describing how to avoid the daily obstacles that keep us from reaching God's purpose for our lives. She can be reached at *Mjmfreelance@ charter.net*.

Janet Matthews is a writer, editor, professional speaker and coauthor of the bestseller, *Chicken Soup for the Canadian Soul*. She is working on a book version of *The Navy's Baby* with Daniel Keenan, an amazing story appearing in *Chicken Soup for the Parent's Soul,* which she helped produce and edit. Janet can be reached at 905-881-8995, ext 28, or by e-mail at *janet@canadiansoul.com,* or *www.canadiansoul.com*

Carol Mell, raised in rural Oregon, earned a dance degree at Juilliard. She has lived in Navajoland and on the Arizona–Mexico border as a Spanish-speaking reporter. Now a columnist, feature writer and photographer for magazines and newspapers, as well as dance teacher and choreographer, she can be reached at *carolmell@msn.com*.

Patrick Mendoza is an internationally acclaimed storyteller, musician and author. Since 1976, he has performed over 18,000 performances all over the United States, Canada, the United Kingdom and the Fiji Islands. He is also a contributor to *Chicken Soup for the Volunteer's Soul*. He can be reached at *www.patmendoza.com*.

Greta Montgomery received her B.A. from Azusa Pacific University. She taught high-school English for seven years, and also coached volleyball and basketball. After getting married in 2002, she moved to Scotland, her husband's home, and is now a stay-at-home wife and mother. She can be reached at *garbohart@hotmail.com*.

Lad Moore enjoys several writing awards and more than 300 publishing credits in magazines and on the web. His collection, *Odie Dodie,* is available in literary paperback at all major booksellers. *Tailwind*, a forty-story set of short-story memoirs, was also released in 2003.

Edward Nickless, an Australian who moved to the United States in 1989, is the chief financial officer of an Orange County, California construction company. He is happily married to Maria Nickless, one of the coauthors of this book, and is very proud of the great job that she has done. In his spare time, he also enjoys writing humorous short stories on the quirks of daily life.

Thirty years after their wedding, **Adele Noetzelman** and her husband, Jim, live near Fort Collins, Colorado. They have three adult children (two married), a teenager still at home, and three grandchildren. Coauthor of a hospitality handbook, *A Cup of Cold Water*, Adele enjoys gardening, decorative painting and playing with horses.

Cathy L. Novakovich is employed as an administrative manager for an investment firm in Chicago. She has reduced her office hours to three days per week to allow more time for the things she loves most: her husband, her three daughters, her eight grandchildren and her passion for reading a good book.

Donald R. Novakovich told us the most important things in his life are his three children. He has two stepdaughters who stole his heart long ago, and have now made him "Papa" to eight grandchildren. And, if that wasn't enough, he and his wife have adopted yet another daughter to love!

Nicole Owens is an elementary educator and the mother of three energetic boys. Currently residing in Michigan, Nicole enjoys painting, hiking, camping and humorous attempts at gardening. She loves God, garage sales and double chocolate ice cream. She appreciates her husband's unwavering support of her writing career.

Amanda Parise-Peterson is a freelance writer and former newspaper reporter who lives in Minnesota with her husband, Jason. She has her B.A. in English writing and German from Concordia College. Amanda enjoys working with children, traveling, reading, photography and of course, dancing. She can be reached at *parise-peterson@excite.com*.

Mark Parisi's OFF THE MARK comic panel has been syndicated since 1987 and is distributed by United Media.Mark's humor also graces greeting cards, T-shirts, calendars, magazines (such as Billboard), newsletters and books. Lynn, is his wife/business partner and their daughter, Jenny, contributes with inspiration, (as do three cats).

Kathy Passero is an award-winning writer and essayist whose work has been published in a number of national magazines and newspapers. She is also the author of two nonfiction books. She lives in Manhattan with her husband and their baby daughter.

Mitali Perkins was born in Calcutta, India and grew up in the San Francisco Bay Area. She maintains a Web site called "The Fire Escape: Books For and

About Young Immigrants" (*www.mitaliperkins.com*) and is the author of two books, *Sunita!* (Little, Brown) and *Monsoon Summer* (Random House).

Penny Perrone is a freelance writer with a background in the mental health field and an M.S. in community health. She has completed an inspirational, healing-type manuscript for those overcoming overwhelming obstacles and is in the process of finding a publisher. She can be reached at *PennyPennedlt@worldnet.att.net.*

Pat Phillips enjoys writing inspirational and Christian stories based on her own personal experiences. She is happily married to Bob Phillips, her husband of twenty-eight years. Their two children and two grandchildren have become a great source in providing material for many of her stories.She can be reached at *patphillipselp@hotmail.com*

Kaylen Pierce is the mother of three wonderful daughters. She is also a grandmother of three, and greatly enjoys this new role. Her greatest passions are serving God and spending time with her family. She teaches a women's Bible study group, and would love to continue writing when she's not busy cuddling grandbabies.

Caroline Pignat met her husband, Tony, in eighth grade, and they've been together ever since. The Pignats claim the secret to their happy marriage is love, friendship and a lot of laughs. They live in Ottawa, Canada with their two kids, Liam and Marion. She can be reached at *pignat@magma.ca.*

Shad Purcell is a youth minister and guest speaker living in San Antonio Texas. He and his beautiful wife, April, enjoy hiking, running, reading and watching lots of movies together. He can be reached at *shadpurcell@juno.com.*

Carol McAdoo Rehme, an inspirational freelance writer, is an experienced Mother of the Bride: She married off two daughters in two years. Now, she feathers her empty nest with writing and editing for *Chicken Soup for the Soul* and directing Vintage Voices, Inc., a nonprofit agency that provides programs in eldercare facilities. She can be reached at *carol@rehme.com* or *www.rehme.com.*

Carla Riehl is a *Chicken Soup* contributing author and motivational speaker who tours nationally speaking on "Calm Confident and Assertive for Women". She won three Clios (advertising's Oscar) and an Emmy for singing TV and radio commercials. Her latest book is entitled *52 MIRACLES: A Year of Truly Miraculous Stories of Ordinary People.*

Kimberly Ripley lives with her husband, five children and faithful dog, Philly, in New Hampshire. The author of five books, her *Freelancing Later in Life* has received numerous awards and is now facilitated as a writing workshop throughout many states. Visit Kim's site at *www.kimberlyripley.writergazette.com.*

Gwen Rockwood received her Bachelor of Arts with honors from the University of Arkansas in 1995. She writes a humor column called "The Rockwood Files" for several newspapers in Arkansas and Missouri. She is currently working on a compilation book of her columns. She can be reached at *rockwood@cox-internet.com*.

Leigh P. Rogers is a writer residing in California. She has been published in *Spies, Wives, Nudges from God* and has other stories pending publication. She was raised all over the world as the daughter of a CIA agent, and is currently working on a manuscript about her experiences abroad.

Cartoonist **Dan Rosandich** has been published for over 25 years I hundreds of publications ranging from *Barron's* to *Reader's Digest.*He also specializes in creating custom artwork for any professional commercial endeavor.Reach Dan at: 906-482-6234 or *danscartoons@msn.com* and visit his extensive portfolio & online catalog at *DANSCARTOONS.COM*.

Kris Hamm Ross is a fifth-grade teacher at Grace School in Houston, Texas. Her memoirs have appeared in the *Houston Chronicle, San Antonio Express-News, Chicken Soup for the Teacher's Soul* and *Chicken Soup for the Grandparent's Soul.* She can be reached at *klross@pdq.net*.

Bob Schochet is an award-winning cartoonist.Bob started out as a graphic design artist in advertising.But, he discovered his true passion when he painted "cartoons" on the day room walls while in the army.He works out of his home in the Hudson Valley and draws 40 cartoons a week.His career spans 36 years with over 80,000 cartoons to his credit.His cartoons appear in many venues, including *TV Guide, Saturday Review, Good Housekeeping, Wall Street Journal* and the *National Enquirer*.

Lucy Akard Seay, a popular Christian conference speaker and author, is founder of Biblical Etiquette Ministries, an organization dedicated to teaching believers how to use the Bible as an etiquette book in everyday family and social situations. She enjoys reading, cooking and entertaining friends. She can be reached at *BiblicalEtiquette@juno.com*.

Kathy Shaskan ditched a successful career as a marketing executive to pursue her interest in humor writing and cartooning.(This fact alone prompted her friends to burst out laughing.)Her work has since appeared in many publications and she has two children's books in development with the Dutton Press division of Penguin Putnam Publishing

Lisa Solomon is a freelance writer based in Washington. She graduated from CSU with a B.A. in sociology. Lisa has worked as a professional ballerina in Nevada, an activist and employee for pro-choice organizations in Arizona, and now writes while accompanying her husband on his job assignments around the world.

Carrie St. Michel is a contributing editor at *Good Housekeeping* magazine and a frequent contributor to numerous other national publications. Previously a syndicated columnist at *The Los Angeles Times*, she can be reached at *cstmichel1@cs.com*.

Kelly Stevens-Hartley married her true love, David, on April 21, 2001. She has a B.A. in history, and works as an early childhood educator in Windsor, Ontario. Kelly is grateful to her parents, sister Keri, friends and the Frugal Brides (*www.frugalbride.com*), who continue to offer their unconditional love and support.

Carol M. Sturgulewski is a lifelong Alaskan. A newspaper and magazine writer and editor for more than twenty-five years, she is also coauthor of *Chicken Soup for the Gardener's Soul* and *Kodiak: Alaska's Emerald Isle*. She and her husband of twenty years live in Anchorage with their three sons.

Patty Swyden Sullivan is a freelance writer living in Kansas. She is blessed with the legacy of love shared by her parents, Victor and Vivian Swyden, and the loving support of a husband who encourages her to follow her dreams.

Sylvia Suriano is a songwriter, composer and pianist from Toronto. She enjoys teaching music to young children, and aspires to fulfill her creative spirit by writing in many different genres. She can be reached at *sylc@rogers.com*.

Annmarie B. Tait lives in Conshohocken, Pennsylvania with her husband, Joe, and Sammy the "Wonder Yorkie." The youngest of five children, Annmarie has written numerous stories recalling the fond memories of her Irish Catholic childhood. *Snow Cloud* is the second to be published in the *Chicken Soup* series.

Deborah Thomas is the youth services coordinator for a parks and recreation program, and is also a freelance writer of inspirational women's and children's fiction. She has been happily married for twenty-seven years.

Renata Waldrop received her degree in English from the University of Tennessee in 1998. She currently divides her time between writing pursuits, spiritual teaching and caring for her husband and son. She can be reached at *writeontime@peoplepc.com*.

Rachel Wallace-Oberle has an education in radio/television broadcasting as well as journalism/print. She is a freelance writer who has written for numerous publications. She also co-hosts a Sunday morning radio program and loves long walks, classical music and canaries. She can be reached at *rachel w-o@rogers.com*.

Denise N. Wheatley received her Bachelor of Arts from the University of Illinois in 1996. Her first novel, *I Wish I Never Met U*, will be published in the summer of 2004. When she is not writing, Denise enjoys movies, tennis and spending time with family and friends.

David R. Wilkins is a director at a medical device manufacturer in northern California, but would love to be a full-time writer. He earned his B.A. in management at St Mary's College, is a father of two and a husband of twenty-eight years. He's written a nonfiction book (looking for a publisher) and is currently writing a novel. He can be reached at *bestseller2005@yahoo.com*.

Keith A. Wooden is an author, pastor, communicator, freelance writer and mostly a story teller. He is a husband of one, and a father/stepfather to four. He finds ample illustration in his own living room.

Nicolle Woodward lives in Bennington, Vermont. She is an office worker whose hobbies are writing, reading, photography, painting and counted cross stitch. This is Nicolle's second story published in the *Chicken Soup* series, the first appearing in *Chicken Soup for the Gardener's Soul*.

Mike Zeballos has an A.A. degree in electronics engineering. He currently does Web-design work in Los Angeles. Mike enjoys cycling, hiking and reading.

Permissions

We would like to acknowledge the many publishers and individuals who granted us permission to reprint the cited material. (Note: The stories that were penned anonymously, that are in the public domain or that were written by Jack Canfield, Mark Victor Hansen, Maria Nickless or Gina Romanello are not included in this listing.)

Foreword reprinted by permission of Beverly Clark. ©2003 Beverly Clark.

Twenty-Six Years—An Unfolding Romance. Reprinted by permission of Kris Hamm Ross. ©2001 Kris Hamm Ross.

My Love Is Like a Red, Red Marker. Reprinted by permission of Carrie St. Michel. ©2000 Carrie St. Michel. Appeared in *Good Housekeeping;* Issue: *Light Housekeeping;* April 2000, p. 214.

A Second Chance. Reprinted by permission of Ariana Adams. ©2003 Ariana Adams.

Roses Not Required. Reprinted by permission of Rachel Wallace-Oberle. ©2003 Rachel Wallace-Oberle.

A Change of Heart. Reprinted by permission of Denise Jacoby. ©2003 Denise Jacoby.

Dancing in the Aisles. Reprinted by permission of Amanda Jane Krug. ©2000 Amanda Jane Krug.

The Porsche Factor. Reprinted by permission of Mitali Perkins. ©2000 Mitali Perkins.

Treasure Hunt. Reprinted by permission of Steven Manchester. ©2002 Steven Manchester.

The Last Quarter. Reprinted by permission of Edward Nickless. ©2002 Edward Nickless.

The Changing Tide and *The Best One.* Reprinted by permission of Michelle Marullo. ©2003 Michelle Marullo.

Until Death. . . . Reprinted by permission of Barbara Boswell. ©2000 Barbara Boswell.

Storybook Proposal. Reprinted by permission of Matthew Cummings. ©2002 Matthew Cummings.

Love Is in the Air. Reprinted by permission of Lynette Helms. ©2003 Lynette Helms.

Hidden Treasures. Reprinted by permission of Michelle Isenhour. ©2002 Michelle Isenhour.

A Trail of Love. Reprinted by permission of Shad Purcell. ©1997 Shad Purcell.

Lawson.

Coming Full Circle. Reprinted by permission of Denise N. Wheatley. ©2003 Denise N. Wheatley.

Built on Love. Reprinted by permission of Miriam Hill. ©2002 Miriam Hill.

Raining Love. Reprinted by permission of Kelly Stevens-Hartley. ©2003 Kelly Stevens-Hartley.

A Tale of Two Fathers. Reprinted by permission of Kimberly Ripley. ©2002 Kimberly Ripley.

The Unconditional Step. Reprinted by permission of Donald R. Novakovich. ©2002 Donald R. Novakovich.

Bedtime Fears and *Golden Slippers.* Reprinted by permission of Charlotte Lanham. ©1998 Charlotte Lanham.

Going Home. Reprinted by permission of Liza G. Maakestad. ©2003 Liza G. Maakestad.

Angie's Wedding Day. Reprinted by permission of Judith Givens. ©1999 Judith Givens.

The Music Played On. Reprinted by permission of Nancy B. Gibbs. ©2000 Nancy B. Gibbs.

This Is Our Dance. Reprinted by permission of Amanda Parise-Peterson. ©2003 Amanda Parise-Peterson.

The Unlikely Best Man. Reprinted by permission of Jennifer M. Dlugos. ©2003 Jennifer M. Dlugos.

Given Away. Reprinted by permission of Renata Waldrop. ©2003 Renata Waldrop.

That's Entertainment! Reprinted by permission of Maryellen Heller. ©2003 Maryellen Heller.

House to Home. Reprinted by permission of Michael Zeballos. ©2002 Michael Zeballos.

Princess Bride. Reprinted by permission of Veneta Leonard. ©2002 Veneta Leonard.

Te Amo, Te Quiero, Cariña. Reprinted by permission of Patrick Mendoza. ©2000 Patrick Mendoza.

In the End. Reprinted by permission of Barbara M. Johnson. ©2002 Barbara M. Johnson.

A Second Chance at Remembering. By Becky Knutson, as told to Jeannie Kim. Copyright ©2002 Jeannie Kim. Originally published in *Redbook,* June 2002.

Chicken Soup for the Soul®

Improving Your Life Every Day

Real people sharing real stories—for nineteen years. Now, Chicken Soup for the Soul has gone beyond the bookstore to become a world leader in life improvement. Through books, movies, DVDs, online resources and other partnerships, we bring hope, courage, inspiration and love to hundreds of millions of people around the world. Chicken Soup for the Soul's writers and readers belong to a one-of-a-kind global community, sharing advice, support, guidance, comfort, and knowledge.

Chicken Soup for the Soul stories have been translated into more than 40 languages and can be found in more than one hundred countries. Every day, millions of people experience a Chicken Soup for the Soul story in a book, magazine, newspaper or online. As we share our life experiences through these stories, we offer hope, comfort and inspiration to one another. The stories travel from person to person, and from country to country, helping to improve lives everywhere.